A Medic's Guide to
Essential Legal Matters

D1422218

A Medic's Guide to Essential Legal Matters

EDITED BY

Jane Sturgess MBBS MRCP FRCA PgDipMEd
Consultant Anaesthetist,
Associate Lecturer,
West Suffolk Hospital, UK

Derek Duane MB BCh, BAO, FRCA, MSc(NS), MPhil
Consultant Neuroanaesthetist,
Cambridge University Hospitals NHS Foundation Trust, UK

Rebekah Ley LLB (Hons), MSc
Assistant Director Medico-Legal Department,
Cambridge University Hospitals NHS Foundation Trust, UK

OXFORD
UNIVERSITY PRESS

OXFORD
UNIVERSITY PRESS

Great Clarendon Street, Oxford, OX2 6DP,
United Kingdom

Oxford University Press is a department of the University of Oxford.
It furthers the University's objective of excellence in research, scholarship,
and education by publishing worldwide. Oxford is a registered trade mark of
Oxford University Press in the UK and in certain other countries

© Oxford University Press 2019

The moral rights of the authors have been asserted

First Edition published in 2019

Impression: 1

Published in the United States of America by Oxford University Press
198 Madison Avenue, New York, NY 10016, United States of America

British Library Cataloguing in Publication Data

Data available

CIP data is on file at the Library of Congress

ISBN 978–0–19–874985–1

Printed in Great Britain by
Bell & Bain Ltd., Glasgow

Foreword

'Support a lawyer—send your child to Medical School!' So runs a bumper sticker that was spotted by a colleague during a trip to the US some years ago. The relationship between law and medicine (or, more generally, between law and healthcare) can sometimes be antagonistic. But law is not just there to catch healthcare professionals out or to call them to account. At a minimum, law offers rules that seek to guide people's behaviour. The rules perform a variety of functions, including setting out rights, entitlements and obligations, laying down conditions, and facilitating relationships.

Of course, how the law does all this, and the terms in which it seeks to do so, can be bewildering. One striking law word, which I encountered while undertaking research as a postgraduate student, is 'logonomocentrism'. This rhythmic mouthful refers to attempts to depict law as a coherent, unified, and rational body of rules; a jigsaw puzzle, all the pieces of which are present and slot neatly together.

So much for the theory (or that theory, at least). Many legal scholars would agree that law *should* aspire to the values implied in logonomocentrism; after all, if law is to have any purchase in the real world, by serving to guide people's behaviour, then it should be consistent and grounded in reason. But the real world also shows us that law is much more complex and fragmented than this; it can indeed be puzzling, as the pieces of law's puzzle are sometimes missing or misplaced and even the all-important edges can be hard to locate.

As it is a branch of law, medical law can also be puzzling. The very label used to describe this branch of law is contested, with some preferring 'healthcare' (or even just 'health') law to capture the range of people and practices involved. Some of the complexity might be attributed to the origins of this branch of law, whatever we might call it, since it has grown from and fused together such other branches of law as public law, civil law, family law, and criminal law. How, then, can non-lawyers—such as doctors or medical students—hope to grasp what it is that the legal puzzle requires of them?

Enter this book. It is to the great credit of the editors and authors of this volume that they have managed to capture and convey, as the title suggests, so many of the 'essentials' of medical law. There are chapters here covering everyday elements of medical practice, such as consent, confidentiality, and caring for older and dying patients, as well as more specialized areas, such as organ transplantation (although you will have to look elsewhere, for example, for guidance about reproduction and termination of pregnancy).

The authors introduce the reader to important pieces of the medicolegal jigsaw as it is currently configured, and in so doing they take in such contemporary topics as confidentiality in the social media age, as well as major topics not often covered in books of this sort, such as the role of the coroner, and insurance, NHS complaints, and financial compensation for those harmed during treatment. Although it is the nature of both law and medicine that some areas will have moved on by the time you are holding this book, keep an eye out for future developments in professional regulation and in relation to the withdrawal of clinically assisted nutrition and hydration from patients with prolonged disorders of consciousness, for example.

The writing is clear and concise throughout. Although there is nothing so bewildering as 'logonomocentrism', there is a useful glossary and an opening chapter that helpfully walks the reader through the intricacies of the legal system. Contradictions, complexities, and subtleties are not overlooked: for example, there is coverage of the numerous laws concerning confidentiality, the confusing element of 'causation' in informed consent cases, and the tensions around organ donation.

The volume manages these complexities elegantly and is invigoratingly practical, which is unsurprising given the diverse expertise of the contributors, who include academics and a range of (health and legal) practitioners. Good advice abounds. Some will hopefully be obvious (such as avoiding the crimes referred to on p. 46 !), but every chapter has something useful to convey, via summaries of key points, 'pearls and pitfalls', illustrative scenarios, flow diagrams, suggested sources of advice and support, and (online) MCQs to check your understanding.

There is much here that will be of value to a range of healthcare professionals, as well as to patients and their families. The title nevertheless suggests that you, the reader, will be a 'medic'. Assuming that is the case, perhaps we can re-write that bumper sticker: 'Support a medic—get this book!'

Richard Huxtable
Professor of Medical Ethics and Law
Director, Centre for Ethics in Medicine,
Medical School, University of Bristol

Preface

All those involved in any aspect of delivering healthcare to patients, those in nursing or medical careers, students or professional clinicians, those involved in many of the allied medical services, and all health-related administrative staff, have a duty to familiarize themselves with legal matters concerning their work practices. The law is ever-changing to accommodate and guide the public's needs and expectations. New legislation and updates to old statutes has intensified the complexity of how and why the law is applied to the healthcare arena, making the need to maintain currency in this subject a challenging endeavour.

This book has evolved from the simple intention on the part of the authors to provide all healthcare practitioners with an up-to-date essential working knowledge of legal principles they can apply to their everyday clinical practice. Thirteen chapters cover pertinent areas of medical law from the structure of the legal system, consent, confidentiality, negligence, child health, elderly care, mental health, end-of-life care, and organ donation to current legal practices in relation to medical regulation, prescribing, healthcare management, and the workings of the Coroner's Court.

There has been a concerted effort to present the information in a straightforward bullet point fashion. Chapters begin with details of the contents and a summary of all the important legal concepts that are contained within the chapter. Important case law, relevant statutes, newer legislation, and professional guidance are highlighted, along with their online access addresses. Each section of a chapter is followed by a key points box, which can act as an aide-memoire as well as allowing for quick revision of a particular legal topic, while the text will provide those less familiar with a more detailed explanation. Case scenarios are provided in some chapters to make some difficult legal concepts easier to comprehend. All chapters conclude with a pearls and pitfalls section, reflecting the expertise and experience of the authors, many of whom are practising legal practitioners in the field of medical law in various public and private institutions. A short list of suggested further reading is provided to enable the reader to supplement and further explore their topic of interest.

The law is in a constant state of evolution and, like any resource, some of the information contained within this book will inevitably undergo change to reflect current legal trends. Most legal practitioners would also acknowledge that the law can often appear imprecise and convoluted to the uninitiated and thus this book cannot substitute for professional legal advice, which is sometimes necessary to bring clarity to complicated and involved legal issues. However, a starting point can be created when accessing this book for the essential medicolegal knowledge related to a particular matter with the hope that it can guide the reader in making consistent legal and ethical decisions when caring for patients.

We are indebted to our chapter authors who, despite busy clinical and legal practices, collaborated with us, but any errors remain our responsibility. We are also grateful to staff at the Oxford University Press for their guidance and encouragement and, finally, to our immediate professional colleagues, families, and friends for their unstinting support.

Jane Sturgess
Derek Duane
Rebekah Ley

Contents

Abbreviations

ADRT	advance decision to refuse treatment
A&E	accident and emergency
CAF	common assessment framework
CANH	clinically assisted nutrition and hydration
CCG	clinical commissioning group
CDF	Cancer Drugs Fund
CDOP	child death overview panels
CGA	comprehensive geriatric assessment
CHM	Commission on Human Medicines
CJEU	Court of Justice of the European Union
CMCHA	Corporate Manslaughter and Corporate Homicide Act
COD	cause of death
COPD	chronic obstructive pulmonary disease
CPR	cardiopulmonary resuscitation
CQC	Care Quality Commission
CRG	Clinical Reference Group
DBD	donation after brainstem death
DCD	donation after circulatory death
DH	Department of Health
DNACPR	Do Not Attempt Cardiopulmonary Resuscitation
DoLS	deprivation of liberty safeguards
DPP	Director of Public Prosecutions
DVLA	Driver and Vehicle Licensing Agency
ECHR	European Convention on Human Rights
ECtHR	European Court of Human Rights
EEA	European Economic Area
EMA	European Medicines Agency
FDA	Food and Drug Administration
GMC	General Medical Council
GMP	good manufacturing practice
GP	general practitioner
HMP	homeopathic medicinal products
HPSS	Health and Personal Social Services
HRA	Human Rights Act 1998
HSE	Health and Safety Executive
HT	human tissue
HTA	Human Tissue Authority
HTAct	Human Tissue Act
ICU	intensive care unit
IFr	individual funding request
IOP	Interim Orders Panel
IOT	Interim Orders Tribunal
IP	intellectual property
JCIO	Judicial Complaints Investigation Office
LPA	lasting power of attorney
MCA	Mental Capacity Act
MCCD	medical certificate as to the cause of death
MDDUS	Medical and Dental Defence Union of Scotland
MDT	multidisciplinary team
MDU	Medical Defence Union
MHA	Mental Health Act
MHRA	Medicines and Healthcare Products Regulatory Agency
MOD	Ministry of Defence
MoU	memorandum of understanding
MPS	Medical Protection Society
MPTS	Medical Practitioners Tribunal Service
MSC	Medical Schools Council
NCAA	National Clinical Assessment Authority

NCAS	National Clinical Assessment Service	**OPG**	Office of the Public Guardian
NHP	national homeopathic products	**PBSC**	peripheral blood stem cells
NHS	National Health Service	**PFD**	prevent further death
NHSBT	NHS Blood and Transplant	**QALYs**	quality-adjusted life years
NICE	National Institute for Health and Care Excellence	**SAB**	Safeguarding Adult Board
NMW	national minimum wage	**SAP**	single assessment process
NSPCC	National Society for the Prevention of Cruelty to Children	**SMC**	Scottish Medicines Consortium
ODR	organ donor register	**SPC**	summary of product characteristics
OPCS	Office of Population Censuses and Surveys	**TCM**	traditional Chinese medicine
		UKLKSS	UK Living Kidney Sharing Scheme
		WHO	World Health Organization

Contributors

Richard Biram, MBBS BSc FRCP, Consultant Geriatrician, Cambridge University Hospital NHS Foundation Trust, UK

Victoria Butler-Cole, Barrister, 39 Essex Chambers, 81 Chancery Lane, London, UK

Belinda Cheney, BA, LLB (Hons), LLM, Tribunal Judge, Assistant Coroner Cambridgeshire and Northampton, Director Medico Legal Training Ltd, UK

Anna Curley, MB BCh BAO MA MD MRCPI LLB DCH, Director of Neonatal Intensive Care Unit and consultant neonatologist, National Maternity Hospital, Ireland

Sarah Elliston, Senior Lecturer, School of Law, University of Glasgow, UK

Elizabeth Fistein, Department of Public Health and Primary Care, School of Clinical Medicine, University of Cambridge, UK

Zoë Fritz, MBBS (Hons) PhD MRCP, Department of Acute Medicine, Cambridge University Hospitals NHS Foundation Trust, UK

Martin Goddard, BA MB BCh FRCS FRCPath, Consultant Histopathologist, Royal Papworth Hospital, Papworth Everard, Cambridge, UK

Natalie Hayes, BSc (Hons) MB ChB (Hons) MD MFFLM GDL, Medico-Legal and Regulatory Consultant, Covalon Technologies Ltd, Mississauga, Canada

Anthony Holland, Cambridge Intellectual and Developmental Disabilities Research Group, Department of Psychiatry, University of Cambridge, Cambridge and Peterborough Foundation NHS Trust, UK

Annabel Lee, BA (Oxon), LLM, Barrister, 39 Essex Chambers, 81 Chancery Lane, London, UK

Nigel Spencer Ley, MA, Barrister, Farrar's Building, Temple, London, UK

Rebekah Ley, LLB (Hons), MSc, Assistant Director Medico-Legal Department, Cambridge University Hospitals NHS Foundation Trust, UK

David de Monteverde-Robb, BSc(Hons) DipPharmPract MSc(ClinRes) MRPharmS(IP) ADA, Lead Pharmacist for Perioperative Services and Pharmacy Research, Cambridge University Hospitals NHS Foundation Trust, UK

David S. Morris, Former HM Coroner for Cambridgeshire, Bedfordshire and Luton, UK

Roddy O' Donnell, MBBS, MA, PhD, MRCP, FRCPCH, FFICM, Associate Specialty Director in Ethics and Law, School of Clinical Medicine, University of Cambridge, UK

Keith Rigg, MB BS FRCS MD, Consultant Surgeon, Nottingham University Hospitals NHS Trust, UK

William R. Roche, MD, MSc, FRCPath, SFFMLM, Emeritus Professor, University of Southampton, Hon. Consultant Pathologist, University Hospitals Southampton, Chair, Wessex Clinical Senate, NHS England, UK

Vikram Sachdeva, QC, BCL, BM BCh, MA, Barrister, 39 Essex Chambers, 81 Chancery Lane, London, UK

Jane Sturgess, MBBS MRCP FRCA PgDipMEd, Consultant Anaesthetist, Associate Lecturer, West Suffolk Hospital, UK

Cathy Walsh, Consultant Psychiatrist, Cambridge and Peterborough NHS Foundation Trust, Cambridge, UK

Digital media accompanying the book

Individual purchasers of this book are entitled to free personal access to accompanying digital media in the online edition. Please refer to the access token card for instructions on token redemption and access.

These online ancillary materials, where available, are noted with iconography throughout the book.

✔ Multiple choice questions

The corresponding media can be found on *Oxford Medicine Online* at: www.oxfordmedicine.com/

If you are interested in access to the complete online edition, please consult with your librarian.

CHAPTER 1

The English Legal System

Vikram Sachdeva, Victoria Butler-Cole, and Annabel Lee

CONTENTS

CHAPTER SUMMARY

Criminal and Civil Law

This can be broadly divided into civil and criminal law. *Criminal law* is enforced by the state and sanctions are imposed for breaching the criminal law. *Civil law* may extend to any law that is not criminal law and generally governs the relationship between private individuals. It includes contracts, torts, and property law.

Primary Sources of Law

There are two primary sources of law: statute and common law. Statutes are Acts of Parliament. The common law is case law decided by judges, which sets precedents to be followed by lower courts in subsequent cases.

Courts of England and Wales

The main courts of England and Wales are:

(1) Magistrates' Court

(2) County Court

(3) Crown Court

(4) High Court

(5) Court of Appeal

(6) Supreme Court.

There are also specialist courts, including the Court of Protection and Coroner's Court.

Legal Sanctions and Remedies

There are a variety of legal sanctions and remedies available depending on the type of case. In criminal cases, the courts can sanction a guilty party by imposing a prison sentence or a fine. In civil cases, the most common remedy is financial compensation. The courts can also make declarations.

Expert Witnesses

Medical practitioners are often asked to give evidence in court for a variety of purposes. Expert witnesses should comply with their professional duty of candour at all times and be honest and trustworthy when giving evidence to courts or tribunals. Most evidence from medical practitioners is written and a general guide to writing an expert report is set out in the following section.

1.1 Criminal and Civil Law

1.1.1 Criminal Law

The practical application of the law can be broadly divided into civil and criminal law. Criminal law is imposed and enforced by the state by means of:

1. A criminal prosecution (taken by the Criminal Prosecution Service).
2. A criminal trial (if heard in the Crown Court, this is likely to involve a jury).
3. A sentence is passed by a judge.

Civil law involves private individuals suing other legal persons (e.g. other private individuals, a public authority, or a company) in the County or High Court, before a judge, who will decide both liability and the quantum of any damages payable. There are other types of proceedings, such as care proceedings in family law, which contain some of the public interest elements in criminal proceedings, but which, for the purposes of classification, remain civil proceedings.

A criminal offence is an act that is forbidden by the criminal law and carries with it a punishment for breaching the law, which may include loss of liberty. It is made up of two distinct elements:

1. The *actus reus*.
2. The *mens rea*.

Every crime can be analysed in terms of these two constituent parts. The *actus reus* refers to the physical act of the crime. The *mens rea* is the mental state of mind. For example, a person is guilty of the criminal offence of murder if he or she causes the death of a victim (the *actus reus*) with an intention to cause death or grievous bodily harm (the *mens rea*). The state seeks to enforce the criminal law by prosecuting and punishing offenders. Criminal cases are prosecuted by the state in the name of the Crown and are reported in the form of Regina v Dr X (abbreviated to R v Dr X).

1.1.2 Civil Law

In contrast, the civil law concerns the relationship between private individuals. For example, contract law, tort law, and property law are all part of the civil law. The purpose of the civil law is to enforce civil legal rights and obligations between individuals. The state does not generally interfere in civil law cases in which a claimant sues (or 'brings an action against') a defendant. Most litigation involving doctors concerns actions for clinical negligence, and contains allegations that the treatment provided to an individual fell below the standard expected of a responsible body of medical opinion. This is part of the civil law of tort. The law relating to claims for clinical negligence is considered in more detail in Chapter 4.

It is important to bear in mind that one set of factual circumstances may give rise to civil or criminal liability or both or neither. It may also give rise to disciplinary proceedings. If a doctor provides a treatment without explaining all of the risks that a reasonable patient would wish to know, it may constitute a lack of informed consent and the doctor may be liable in civil law for the *tort of battery* (the application of force without consent). If the doctor fails to provide relevant information in a more fundamental way, such as failing to explain the nature or purpose of the proceedings, he or she may be liable in criminal law for the *crime of battery*. In either case the General Medical Council (GMC) may wish to bring proceedings for breach of the rules of professional conduct.

KEY POINTS—CRIMINAL AND CIVIL LAW

- Criminal law is enforced by a criminal prosecution, trial, and sentence by a judge.
- Civil law involves private individuals, County or High Courts with liability, and damages decided by a judge.
- The *actus reus* refers to the physical act of the criminal offence.
- The *mens rea* is the mental state of the criminal perpetrator.
- Most litigation involving doctors concerns actions for clinical negligence.
- Inadequate or absent consent can attract a liability for the tort or crime of battery.

1.2 Statutes and Common Law

1.2.1 Statutes

There are two primary sources of law in our domestic legal system: statutes and common law. Statutes are contained in written Acts of Parliament (also referred to as 'primary legislation'). There is a parliamentary process that needs to be followed before a Bill becomes an Act of Parliament. It involves five distinct stages in each House of Parliament: first reading, second reading, committee stage, report stage, and third reading. There may then be a stage of consideration of amendments. A Bill becomes an Act of Parliament when it is given Royal Assent. This is the normal process by which an Act of Parliament is made, but there are exceptions.

The legislation underpinning healthcare is very complex. Significant statutes include:

- The Health and Social Care Act 2012, which makes provisions for clinical commissioning groups and regulation of health services.
- The National Health Service Act 2006, which contains a legal obligation on the Secretary of State to promote health services.
- The Mental Capacity Act 2005, which applies to people in England and Wales who cannot make decisions for themselves.
- The Mental Health Act 1983, which covers the reception, care, and treatment of mentally disordered persons.

1.2.2 Common Law

Common law is law that is created by judges when deciding cases. Decided cases create precedents that are generally followed in subsequent cases under a doctrine called *stare decisis*. The doctrine refers to the general order within the legal hierarchy where decisions of a higher court are binding on a lower court in the hierarchy. If a precedent was set by a court of equal or higher status to the court deciding the new case, then the judge should follow the rule set in the earlier case.

KEY POINTS—STATUTES AND COMMON LAW

- Statutes are contained in written Acts of Parliament.
- Before a Bill becomes an Act of Parliament it goes through five stages.

- These stages are first reading, second reading, committee stage, report stage, and third reading.
- There is a lot of legislation underpinning healthcare in the UK.
- Common law is made by judges when deciding cases, thereby creating precedents.
- Decisions of a higher court are binding on a lower court.

1.3 Rights and Obligations

1.3.1 Duty of Candour

All healthcare professionals have a duty of candour, which is a professional responsibility to be open and honest with patients when things go wrong. This means that a healthcare professional must tell the patient when something has gone wrong, apologize to the patient, and offer an appropriate remedy. The healthcare professional must also support and encourage colleagues to be open and honest and to report concerns where appropriate. The professional duty of candour is explained in more detail in the GMC's guidance, entitled 'Openness and honesty when things go wrong: the professional duty of candour'.

1.3.2 Expert Witness Obligations

When giving evidence as an expert, the rules governing procedure in court make clear that the duty of an expert is to assist the court and this overrides any party providing instructions or paying the expert's fees. It is important that an expert witness is truthful as to the facts, honest in their opening and comprehensive in their coverage to the relevant matters. This means that an expert witness is under an obligation to give a true opinion, even if this may sometimes run counter to the interests of his client. An expert witness should also be mindful of any potential conflicts of interests and has a responsibility to draw this to the attention of the court and the parties if necessary. The corollary of all of this is that the court can rely on expert evidence as independent, objective, and unbiased.

The GMC has published helpful guidance on 'Acting as a witness in legal proceedings' (2013). In particular, it draws attention to the following key points:

- You must be familiar with guidelines and developments that affect your work.
- You must keep up to date with, and follow, the law, GMC guidance, and other regulations relevant to your work.
- You must recognize and work within the limits of your competence.
- You must be honest and trustworthy when giving evidence to courts or tribunals.
- You must take reasonable steps to check the information.
- You must not deliberately leave out relevant information.
- You must cooperate with formal inquiries and complaints procedures.
- You must respect confidentiality.
- You must make clear the limits of your competence and knowledge when giving evidence or acting as a witness.

KEY POINTS—RIGHTS AND OBLIGATIONS

- All healthcare professionals have a professional duty of candour.
- Doctors have a responsibility to be open and honest with patients when things go wrong.
- The duty of an expert witness is to assist the court.
- An expert witness is under an obligation to give a true opinion, which overrides any party providing instructions or paying fees.
- GMC has guidance—Acting as a witness in legal proceedings (2013).

1.4 Burden and Standard of Proof

1.4.1 Burden of Proof

The burden of proof identifies who bears the burden of proving the claim. In general, the person making an allegation must prove his or her claim. Thus, in criminal cases the burden lies with the prosecution, who must prove the case against the defendant to succeed. This means that there is no burden of proof on the defendant to prove his innocence, but the prosecution must prove every element of the crime. In civil cases, the burden of proof lies with the claimant. In very rare cases, the burden of proof may be reversed in relation to certain elements of a claim.

1.4.2 Standard of Proof in Criminal Cases

The burden of proof should not be confused with the standard of proof. The standard of proof refers to the level of proof required to succeed in the claim. In criminal cases, the standard of proof is 'beyond all reasonable doubt'. This means that the prosecution must prove their case 'beyond all reasonable doubt'. The standard of proof in criminal cases is a high one, but the phrase 'beyond all reasonable doubt' does not mean 'beyond a shadow of a doubt' or as a matter of absolute certainty. It has been described as being the same as being 'satisfied so that you are sure'.

1.4.3 Standard of Proof in Civil Cases

In contrast, the standard of proof in civil cases is the lower standard of 'the balance of probabilities'. This means that the facts to be proved must be shown to have been more likely than not to have occurred; in other words, more than 50% likely. In a civil case, the burden of proof is on the claimant to prove his or her case 'on the balance of probabilities'. The difference in standard of proof between criminal and civil cases raises the real possibility of someone being able to succeed in a civil claim, although there may be insufficient evidence for a criminal prosecution.

KEY POINTS—BURDEN AND STANDARD OF PROOF

- The person making the allegation must prove their claim.
- In criminal cases, the prosecution must prove a case against the defendant.
- In civil cases, the burden of proof lies with the claimant.
- Standard of proof in criminal cases is 'beyond all reasonable doubt'.
- Standard of proof in civil cases is 'the balance of probabilities'.
- Insufficient evidence for a criminal prosecution may still lead to a successful civil claim.

1.5 The Courts

The court structure in England and Wales is labyrinthine in complexity, but has some basic features which are simple.

1.5.1 Criminal—Magistrates' and Crown Courts

Criminal cases are normally heard in the Magistrates' Court or Crown Court. Most minor criminal offences are dealt with in the Magistrates' Court, but more serious criminal cases are transferred to the Crown Court. Cases in the Crown Court are normally heard by a judge sitting with a jury. The

Crown Court can sometimes hear appeals from the Magistrates' Court. Appeals from the Crown Court generally go to the Court of Appeal (Criminal Division).

1.5.2 Civil—County and High Courts

Civil cases generally start in the County Court (for low-value cases) or the High Court (for high-value or complex cases). Clinical negligence cases, being civil law cases, are normally decided by the County Court, with only a small proportion being heard by the High Court (where the value and/or complexity of the claim is exceptional). Appeals from final decisions of the County Court or of the High Court generally go to the Court of Appeal (Civil Division).

1.5.3 Courts of Appeal

Appeals from the Court of Appeal, in civil and criminal cases, go to the Supreme Court, which is the court of final appeal in domestic law. It only hears cases of general public importance. Appeals to the Supreme Court require permission either from the Court of Appeal or (more usually) from the Supreme Court itself to proceed.

1.5.4 European Courts

Outside of the UK, there are two European courts that have had a profound influence on domestic law. There are two different European courts, which are often confused.

1.5.4.1 Court of Justice of the European Union

One of these courts is the Court of Justice of the European Union (CJEU), which sits in Luxemburg, and the other is the European Court of Human Rights (ECtHR), which sits in Strasbourg, France. The CJEU is an institution of the European Union (EU), which decides cases relating to EU law.

1.5.4.2 The European Court of Human Rights

The ECtHR is an international court, which rules on cases alleging violations of the European Convention on Human Rights (ECHR). The UK has international obligations to adhere to the ECHR, and can be sued in the ECtHR in Strasbourg. The Human Rights Act 1998 (HRA) requires domestic courts to 'take into account' Strasbourg decisions, but they are not bound to apply them regardless of the domestic court's view of their correctness. By contrast, EU law cases may be directly effective in English law.

1.5.5 Specialist Courts and Tribunals

Within this general structure, there are a number of specialist courts in this country, which medical practitioners may encounter from time to time.

1.5.5.1 Court of Protection

The Court of Protection is a specialist court that was set up as a result of the Mental Capacity Act 2005. It deals with cases involving adults who lack capacity to make a particular decision. In such cases, the Court of Protection has the power to make a decision on behalf of the incapacitated person in relation to their welfare, including giving or refusing consent to medical treatment. Where a patient lacks capacity to consent to medical treatment, and there is a dispute about whether it is in the patient's best interests to receive that treatment, then an application should be made to the Court of Protection. there is currently some uncertainty over whether it is necessary to make an application where there is agreement between the patient's family and the clinicians as to the patient's best interests. This is being considered by the Supreme Court: see *NHS Trust v Mr Y* [2017] EWHC 2866 (AB). For more information about the Mental Capacity Act, see Chapter 2.

1.5.5.2 Coroner's Court

Medical practitioners may also be required to attend the Coroner's Court. The duty of a coroner is to investigate certain deaths, mainly where the coroner has reason to suspect that the deceased died a violent or unnatural death, or the cause of death is unknown, or the deceased died while in custody or otherwise in state detention. The purpose of a coroner's investigation is to ascertain who the deceased was, and how, when, and where the deceased came by his or her death. A coroner may sit alone or, in limited circumstances, with a jury. Doctors may be required to give evidence about a post-mortem examination or any medical conditions that the deceased may have been suffering from prior to his or her death. This is considered in more detail in Chapter 5.

1.5.5.3 Tribunals System

Parallel to the courts system is the tribunals system. The First-tier Tribunal (Mental Health) is part of the tribunals system. It is an independent judicial body that reviews the cases of patients detained under the Mental Health Act 1983. The tribunal normally sits with three members: a judge, a doctor, and a mental health expert. For more information about mental health cases, see Chapter 10 on Mental Health Law.

KEY POINTS—THE COURTS

- Criminal cases are heard in the Magistrates' Court or Crown Court.
- Civil cases are heard in the County or High Courts.
- Appeals from civil and criminal cases go to the relevant division of the Court of Appeals.
- Appeals from the Appeals Court are heard in the Supreme Court.
- European Courts include the CJEU (Brussels) and the ECHR (Strasbourg).
- The Court of Protection is a specialist court that was set up as a result of the Mental Capacity Act.
- The Coroner's Court hears cases of unnatural or unknown cause of death.
- A tribunal is an independent judicial body that reviews cases of patients detained under the Mental Health Act.

1.6 Legal Sanctions and Remedies

1.6.1 Criminal Cases

The law provides for a range of sanctions and remedies that are available depending upon the type of case. In criminal cases, the judge may sentence a guilty party to a term of imprisonment, a fine, or community service.

1.6.2 Civil Cases

In civil claims, including claims for clinical negligence, the most common remedy is damages, i.e. financial compensation paid to the claimant for the injury and its consequences. The intention behind financial compensation is to put the claimant in the position he or she would have been in if the legal wrong had not occurred.

Two basic types of damages are routinely awarded in clinical negligence cases. The first is general damages awarded for pain, suffering, and loss of amenity attributable to the injury. The financial value of these losses is difficult to quantify and there is a combination of general guidelines and case law to help estimate the appropriate amount in a particular case. The awards are calculated according to the Judicial Studies Board Guidelines, which set a range from which awards for a particular injury are selected. The Guidelines are regularly updated and case law is used so that individuals with similar injuries receive similar levels of compensation.

The second type of damages is special damages, which are actual losses attributable to the negligently caused injury specific to the individual. This includes past losses, such as reduced earnings, equipment costs, and travel costs, and future losses.

1.6.3 Declaratory Relief

The courts may also provide declaratory relief in the form of a declaration. For example, the court can make declarations as to whether a proposed course of conduct is lawful, and, where the case concerns an incapacitated patient, can also give or refuse consent on behalf of the patient. However, bare declarations in the Court of Protection regarding best interests are probably best avoided as this practice was discouraged by the Court of Appeal in *Re MN* [2015] EWCA Civ 411.

1.6.4 General Medical Council Sanctions

There is also a broader regulatory regime that governs the medical profession itself. The GMC regulates medical practitioners in the UK and has power to impose various sanctions, including suspension and striking off the medical register. This is considered in more detail in Chapter 11 on Regulatory Procedures.

KEY POINTS—LEGAL SANCTIONS AND REMEDIES

- Sanctions for criminal cases include imprisonment, a fine, or community service.
- Civil cases are usually awarded damages, i.e. financial compensation.
- General damages are awarded for pain, suffering, and loss of amenity.
- Special damages are awarded for reduced earnings, equipment, and future losses.
- The Court of Protection can make declarations on behalf of patients.
- The GMC has the legal right to impose sanctions on doctors.

1.7 Preparing Reports and Giving Evidence

Doctors may be called upon in legal proceedings to give evidence as a witness, which will be used to inform the judge's decision. Evidence from doctors is mostly given in writing in the form of reports, but sometimes doctors are required to attend court to give oral evidence and answer questions. How a report should be written will depend on its purpose. A doctor may be required to give factual evidence relating to facts that are within his or her own knowledge; for example, a doctor may be requested to set out a patient's history. In other cases, a doctor may be asked to give an expert opinion using his or her technical knowledge and understanding. For example, a doctor may be asked to give an opinion on a patient's future prognosis, which will require the doctor to exercise his or professional judgement or he or she may be asked to give his or her opinion on a hypothetical situation.

The contents of the report will depend upon the purpose for which it is being used. As a general guide, an expert report should, at the very least, set out:

- The expert's background and qualifications.
- A record of what the expert has been asked to do; in other words, the substance of his or her instructions.
- A description of the patient and factual background as are within his or her own knowledge (where the information is obtained from others, it should say so; and, if facts are disputed, it may be necessary to analyse the situation on the basis of the alternative versions of the facts).
- An explanation of the range of medical opinions and the reason(s) for the opinion held.
- References to any literature on which the expert has relied upon to formulate his or her opinion.
- A conclusion with supporting references where appropriate.

- A statement confirming that the expert understands his or her overriding duty to the court (if in court proceedings, under Part 35 of the Civil Procedure Rules).

This guide can be modified according to the circumstances and specific purpose for which the report is to be used.

KEY POINTS—PREPARING REPORTS AND GIVING EVIDENCE

- A doctor's evidence for court is usually written in the form of a report.
- A doctor may be required to attend court to give evidence.
- In a report, factual evidence or expert opinion can be sought.
- The contents of a report will usually follow a set protocol.

1.8 Further Reading

- Coroners and Justice Act 2009. Access via www.legislation.gov.uk
- General Medical Council. (2013). *Acting as a Witness in Legal Proceedings*. www.gmc-uk.org
- General Medical Council. (2015). *Openness and Honesty When Things Go Wrong: The Professional Duty of Candour*. www.gmc-uk.org
- Human Rights Act 1998. Access via www.legislation.gov.uk
- Judicial College. (2015). *Guidelines for the Assessment for General Damages in Personal Injuries*, 13th edn. Oxford: Oxford University Press.
- Mental Capacity Act 2005. Access via www.legislation.gov.uk
- Mental Health Act 1983. Access via www.legislation.gov.uk
- Part 35—*Experts and Assessors*. www.justice.gov.uk

1.9 Multiple Choice Questions

✅ Interactive multiple choice questions to test your knowledge on this chapter can be found in the Online appendix at www.oxfordmedicine.com/essentiallegalmatters.

Consent to Treatment

Sarah Elliston

CHAPTER SUMMARY

Legally Valid Consent

At common law, everyone has the right not to suffer a violation of bodily integrity without consent. A legally valid consent to treatment requires that the patient has legal capacity, the decision is voluntary, and that the patient understands the nature and purpose of the act.

Civil Wrong or Criminal Offence

Failure to obtain a legally valid consent is a civil wrong (a trespass to the person: battery) and it may even be a criminal offence.

Verbal or Signed Consent

Consent may be given verbally and there is generally no legal requirement for consent to be documented in writing or signed. A signed consent form is only evidence of consent and can be displaced by other evidence; for example, that the patient did not in fact understand or lacked capacity.

Adequate Explanation

Indications that a patient has agreed to treatment by their conduct should not be relied on as consent unless an adequate explanation of the nature and purpose of the procedure has been given and understood.

Refusal of Treatment

An adult patient who has capacity to consent to treatment is equally entitled to withhold consent. This applies even if it would result in the death of the patient or endanger a viable fetus. The decision does not have to be regarded as rational by others and the patient does not have to give a reason.

Understanding and Capacity

Despite the generality of the right to give and withhold consent without giving reasons, there may be a need to make reasonable enquiries to ensure that the patient has understood and has capacity to make the decision.

Incapacity

People aged 16 and over must be presumed to be competent unless they meet the requirements for lack of capacity under the Mental Capacity Act (MCA) 2005. They may then be treated in their best interests, but there are a number of conditions that must be met in considering this issue. Cases involving serious medical treatments must be brought before the Court of Protection.

Emergencies

In addition to treatment under the MCA 2005 there are limited exceptions to the need for a legally valid consent to treatment, such as an emergency where the patient temporarily lacks capacity and the consequences of failure to treat would be severe.

Sufficient Information

Consent must be informed and patients have a right to sufficient information in terms they can understand to make their decisions.

Material Risk

Information must be provided about all material risks. A material risk is one to which a reasonable person in the patient's position would be likely to attach significance, or the doctor is or should reasonably be aware that the particular patient would be likely to attach significance to it. Failure to provide adequate information may lead to a negligence claim.

Withholding Information

In exceptional cases withholding information may be justified if disclosure would cause severe harm to the patient. Patients also have the right to refuse information.

Lawful Treatment

Consent may only be given to lawful treatment and a patient cannot insist on treatment that is against appropriate clinical judgement.

IMPORTANT CASE LAW

2000–2015

- Montgomery v Lanarkshire Health Board [2015] 2 WLR 768, [2015] UKSC 11 (UK Sup Ct)
- Connolly v Croydon Health Services NHS Trust [2015] All ER (D) 157 (QB), [2015] EWHC 1339 (QB)
- Birch v UCL Hospital NHS Foundation Trust (2008) 104 BMLR 168, [2008] EWHC 2237 (QB)
- R (Burke) v General Medical Council [2006] QB 273, [2005] EWCA Civ 1003 (CA)
- Chester v Afshar [2005] 1 AC 134, [2004] UKHL 41 (HL)
- B (adult refusal of medical treatment) [2002] 2 All ER 449, [2002] EWHC Fam 429

1995–1999

- Pearce v United Bristol Healthcare NHS Trust (1999) 48 BMLR 118 (CA)
- St George's NHS Trust v S (Guidelines) [1999] Fam 26 (CA)

1990–1994

- R v Brown [1994] 1 AC 212 (HL)
- Airedale NHS Trust v Bland [1993] AC 789 (HL)
- T (adult refusal of medical treatment) [1993] Fam 95 (CA)
- F v West Berkshire Health Authority [1990] 2 AC 1 (HL)

1985–1989

- Sidaway v Board of Governors of the Bethlem Royal Hospital [1985] AC 871 (HL)
- Freeman v Home Office (No 2) [1984] QB 524 (CA)

Prior to 1985

- Chatterton v Gerson [1981] QB 432 (QB)
- Bolam v Friern Hospital Management Committee [1957] 1 WLR 582 (QB)
- Barnett v Chelsea and Kensington Hospital Management Committee [1969] 1 QB 428 (QB)

RELEVANT STATUTES AND LEGISLATION

- Mental Health Act 2007
- Mental Capacity Act 2005
- Human Rights Act 1998
- Female Circumcision Act 1985
- Public Health (Control of Disease) Act 1984
- Mental Health Act 1983
- European Convention on Human Rights and Fundamental Freedoms 1950

  Access via www.legislation.gov.uk

PROFESSIONAL GUIDANCE

- British Medical Association. (2008). *Mental Capacity Toolkit*. www.bma.org.uk
- British Medical Association. (2009). *Consent Toolkit*. www.bma.org.uk
- Court of Protection. *Practice Direction 9E: Applications Relating to Serious Medical Treatment*. www.judiciary.gov.uk
- Department of Health. (2009). *Reference Guide to Consent for Examination and Treatment*, 2nd edn. London: Department of Health. www.dh.gov.uk
- General Medical Council. (2008). *Consent: Patients and Doctors Making Decisions Together*. www.gmc-uk.org
- General Medical Council. (2013). *Good Medical Practice* www.gmc-uk.org
- Mental Capacity Act 2005: *Code of Practice* (2007, Chapters 1–9 and 15). www.gov.uk

2.1 Introduction

The need to obtain valid consent is a fundamental principle of medical ethics and medical law. In requiring that consent be given before treatment the law recognizes the individual's right to autonomy, which includes protection of bodily integrity and freedom of choice. Failing to obtain a legally valid consent before providing treatment may have consequences in both criminal law and civil law. It may, in addition, raise human rights issues.

Any treatment given to a patient without his or her consent—indeed, any touching of a patient—could result in the practitioner being sued by the patient or even lead to prosecution in sufficiently serious cases. It may also be a disciplinary matter for the General

Medical Council (GMC) or employers. There are special considerations where a person temporarily or permanently lacks capacity to consent to treatment. Consent also requires one to be sufficiently informed, and failure to provide adequate information can result in a negligence claim.

This chapter considers general principles of consent to treatment. Additional issues arise in the treatment of children and in treatment for mental illness or disorder, and these are considered in the relevant chapters. In general, the law as stated pertains to England and Wales. While many approaches are the same in Scotland and Northern Ireland there are some important differences and separate statutory provisions apply; these are not dealt with here.

2.2 Legally Valid Consent

2.2.1 The Requirement for Consent

At common law, everyone has the right not to suffer a violation of bodily integrity without consent. A legally valid consent to treatment requires that the patient has capacity, that the decision is voluntary, and that the patient understands the nature and purpose of the act (F v West Berkshire Health Authority [1990] 2 AC 1 (HL)). Giving treatment to a competent adult patient without consent would be a civil wrong: the tort of battery, which is a trespass to the person. This would be the case regardless of an objectively beneficial outcome of the treatment, since the action is concerned with physical intervention that was not consented to rather than the outcome of the intervention.

Some violations of bodily integrity may be a criminal offence, such as assault causing actual or grievous bodily harm. In addition, consent cannot provide a defence to a treatment or procedure that is unlawful or contrary to public policy (R v Brown [1994] 1 AC 212 (HL)). Treatment without consent may also raise human rights issues under the European Convention on Human Rights (ECHR) 1950 and the Human Rights Act 1998, including: Article 3 (prohibiting torture and cruel and inhuman treatment), Article 5 (deprivation of liberty), Article 8 (privacy), and Article 9 (freedom of conscience and religion).

2.2.2 Conditions for a Legally Valid Consent

2.2.2.1 Competence

The age of majority in England and Wales is 18, but different ages may be set for various matters. All people aged 16 or above are presumed to be competent to consent to medical treatment (MCA 2005). People under the age of 16 may be able to legally give or withhold consent to treatment, under case law and statute. However, the treatment decisions of those under the age of 18 may in some cases be overridden by parents or the courts in their best interests. This is discussed in Chapter 9 on Child Health Law. For this reason, this chapter considers adults as those aged 18 or older unless specifically stated otherwise.

2.2.2.2 Voluntariness

The patient must have a free choice whether to accept or decline treatment. The consent of people in an institutional setting may need to be considered with particular care (Freeman v Home Office (No 2) [1984] QB 524). Although Freeman concerned a prisoner, this may also apply to people in long-term residential or nursing care. Practitioners must also ensure that relatives or people in other significant relationships are not putting undue pressure on the patient to agree to what they believe to be the right decision, for whatever reason (T (adult refusal of medical treatment) [1993] Fam 95 (CA)).

2.2.2.3 Understanding of the Nature and Purpose of the Act

Patients must be informed in broad terms of the nature and purpose of the treatment or other procedures (Chatterton v Gerson [1981] QB 432). Failure to provide adequate information about risks and alternatives does not in itself make a consent invalid but it may give rise to an action in negligence.

KEY POINTS—LEGALLY VALID CONSENT

- The absence of consent is a civil wrong and may attract a tort of battery.
- In some circumstances, an action without consent maybe a criminal offence if it leads to bodily harm.
- Treatment without consent is a breach of human rights.
- In general, you must be 16 years old to give a legally valid consent.
- Patients must have capacity, give their decision voluntarily and without undue influence, and they must understand the nature and purpose of what is proposed.

2.3 Forms of Consent

Consent may be given verbally and there is generally no legal requirement for consent to be documented in writing or signed, although there are some rare statutory requirements; for example, fertility treatment under the Human Fertilisation and Embryology Acts 1990 and 2008. Documenting consent for more serious interventions is recommended but it is important to remember that written consent, at least in respect of NHS treatment, is not a contract and in all cases a signed consent form is only evidence of what was agreed. If there is other evidence that the patient did not understand, for example, because of language difficulties or the effects of illness or treatment, then the consent may not be regarded as valid.

The conduct of the patient, such as proffering an arm for a blood sample to be taken, is sometimes referred to as implied consent. However, great caution should be exercised in relying on conduct as evidence of consent unless an adequate explanation has been given to the patient beforehand of the nature and purpose of the procedure, since the patient must understand this before they can consent to it.

KEY POINTS—FORMS OF CONSENT

- In general, there is no legal requirement for consent to be documented in writing or signed.
- Documenting consent for more serious interventions is recommended.
- A signed consent form is only evidence of what was agreed and is not a contract in relation to National Health Service (NHS) treatment.
- Caution should be exercised in relying on conduct as evidence of implied consent.
- An adequate explanation should be given, explaining the nature and purpose of the procedure.

2.4 Refusal of Treatment

An adult patient who has capacity to consent to treatment is equally entitled to withhold consent. This applies even if this would result in the death of the patient or endanger a viable fetus (B (adult refusal of medical treatment) [2002] 2 All ER 449, [2002] EWHC Fam 429, St George's NHS Trust v S (Guidelines) [1999] Fam 26 (CA)). Different rules may apply to treatment for mental illness or disorder under mental health legislation or where the patient is under 18, and there are some statutory exceptions that allow for compulsory examination and detention.

The decision does not have to be regarded as rational by others and the patient does not have to give a reason for it. That the decision is contrary to what is to be expected of the vast majority of adults is only relevant if there are other reasons for doubting the patient's capacity to decide (T (adult refusal of medical treatment) [1993] Fam 95 (CA), Montgomery v Lanarkshire Health Board [2015] 2 WLR 768, [2015] UKSC 11 (UK Sup Ct)). However, a practitioner may only be able to assess whether the patient has properly understood the proposed treatment and the implications of withholding consent by exploring the reasons for the choice, as it may be that a decision was made on the basis of misunderstanding or inadequate recall of information.

There may also be doubts about capacity and in such circumstances doctors must make a careful assessment of the patient's mental state and ensure that the treatment refusal is not due to factors such as temporary feelings of depression or poor pain management. Decisions to withhold consent are challenged with much greater frequency than decisions to proceed with it, although this misunderstands the purpose of seeking consent, which is to enable the patient to exercise choice, not to ensure that treatment is given. It may be that the patient wants the treatment to cease, but his or her relatives ask the medical staff to continue with the treatment. Here the doctor's primary responsibility is to the patient, whose wishes should be respected, even where they conflict with the wishes of relatives.

A competent refusal of treatment made in contemplation of a possible future need for such treatment continues to be applicable if the patient loses capacity provided that it is sufficiently clear and was intended to apply in the circumstances (Airedale NHS Trust v Bland [1993] AC 789). Although this principle was established at common law, it has now been enshrined in statute in the MCA 2005. There are formal requirements before an advance decision refusing life-saving treatment would be regarded as legally valid.

KEY POINTS—REFUSAL OF TREATMENT

- An adult with capacity is entitled to refuse treatment even if death is the outcome.
- The decision does not have to be regarded as rational by others and the patient does not have to give a reason for their refusal.
- In general, advance decisions to refuse treatment are valid provided they are clear and apply in the circumstances.
- There are formal requirements before an advance decision refusing life-saving treatment would be regarded as legally valid.

2.5 Adults Who Lack Capacity

At common law, no one (including the court) can give consent on an adult's behalf even where the patient lacks capacity. However, at common law it was held that doctors could lawfully give treatment if it was in the best interests of the patient either to save the patient's life, to ensure improvement, or prevent deterioration in their physical or mental health (F v West Berkshire Health Authority [1990] 2 AC 1 (HL); Airedale NHS Trust v Bland [1993] AC 789 (HL)). This general principle was enacted and expanded upon in the MCA 2005.

2.5.1 The Mental Capacity Act 2005—General Principles

The MCA 2005 is not confined to decisions about medical treatment but covers all decisions in connection with a person who lacks capacity. Most of the statute applies to everyone 16 years of age or over in England and Wales. There is some overlap here with the powers of courts and parents to make decisions for those aged between 16 and 18. There is also a Code of Practice, which provides more detailed guidance and examples. Practitioners are under a legal duty to have regard to the Code of Practice and it can be referred to in civil or criminal proceedings. For example, in considering whether a practitioner has acted in the best interests of the patient, the court can treat the failure to comply with the Code as evidence. Decisions concerning the MCA 2005 are heard by a specialist court: the Court of Protection. The Act is underpinned by five key principles.

Principle 1: A presumption of capacity—every adult has the right to make his or her own decisions and must be assumed to have capacity to do so unless it is proved otherwise.

Principle 2: Individuals must be supported to make their own decisions—a person must be given all practicable help to make their own decisions. Even if lack of capacity is established, it is still important that the person is involved as far as possible in making decisions.

Principle 3: The right to make unwise decisions—people have the right to make decisions that others might regard as unwise or irrational.

Principle 4: Best interests—anything done for or on behalf of a person who lacks capacity must be done in their best interests.

Principle 5: Least restrictive option—someone making a decision or acting on behalf of a person who lacks capacity must consider whether it is possible to decide or act in a way that would interfere less with the person's rights and freedoms of action, or whether there is a need to make a decision or act at all. Any intervention should be weighed up in the particular circumstances of the case.

KEY POINTS—ADULTS WHO LACK CAPACITY—MENTAL CAPACITY ACT

- The MCA applies to those 16 years of age or over.
- There should always be a presumption of capacity.
- Every effort must be made to involve patients in decisions about their treatment.
- No one can give consent on behalf of an adult patient.
- Doctors can treat incapacitated patients in their best interests.
- When acting on behalf of a person who lacks capacity the least restrictive options must be taken.

2.5.2 Establishing Lack of Capacity

A person lacks capacity if his or her mind is impaired or disturbed in some way, and this means that the person is unable to make the decision in question at that time. Incapacity may be considered to be permanent, such as brain damage, or temporary, such as loss of consciousness or intoxication. It may also be as a result of a mental health condition or severe learning disabilities. However, it is important to remember that the presumption is that everyone over the age of 16 has capacity and it would need to be established that the person lacks capacity for treatment to be provided without their consent. It is also important to note that capacity is to be judged in relation to the specific decision and that a person may have capacity to make some decisions but not others. A decision must not be made that a person lacks capacity based upon age, appearance, medical condition, or diagnosis or behaviour alone.

A person is unable to make a decision if they cannot meet any one of these criteria:

- understand information about the decision
- remember that information
- use that information to make a decision
- communicate their decision by talking, using sign language, or by any other means.

Suitable support and assistance must be provided to seek to enable a person to fulfil these criteria. The Act places a duty on the decision-maker to consult other people listed in the Act, where practical and appropriate. An assessment must be made whether it is more likely than not that the person lacks capacity. Practitioners must be able to demonstrate reasonable belief in, and objective grounds for, their conclusions, so documentation of relevant matters is advisable.

KEY POINTS—ADULTS WHO LACK CAPACITY—ESTABLISHING LACK OF CAPACITY

- A lack of capacity can be temporary or permanent.
- It is judged in relation to a specific question for which the patient may have capacity.
- It is not based solely on age, appearance, diagnosis, or behaviour.
- A patient lacks capacity if he or she fails to understand and remember information, fails to use information in his or her decision, and fails to communicate his or her decision by some means.
- Practitioners must be able to demonstrate reasonable belief in, and objective grounds for, their conclusions about a patient's capacity, so documentation is advisable.

2.5.3 Treating Adults with Incapacity

A person must take reasonable steps to establish whether the person lacks capacity. If, having done so, he or she reasonably believes both that the person lacks capacity and that it is in his or her best interests to receive care or treatment, then legal liability is not incurred for providing it. This covers actions that would otherwise result in a civil wrong or crime concerning protection of the person's rights against violation of bodily integrity. This provision is not limited to healthcare practitioners, but includes any person providing care or treatment in the best interests of the patient.

Restraint is only permitted if the person using it reasonably believes it is necessary to prevent harm to the incapacitated person and if the restraint used is proportionate to the likelihood and seriousness of the harm. The MCA 2005 was amended by the Mental Health Act 2007 to introduce safeguards on deprivation of liberty. If a person cannot be treated under this Act, it may be necessary to consider whether treatment can be provided under mental health legislation. However, using this legislation as an alternative is not possible if the patient's mental condition does not justify detention in hospital or where the patient needs treatment only for a physical illness or disability.

2.5.4 Other Decision-Makers

Under the MCA 2005, people over the age of 18 with mental capacity may register a document granting a lasting power of attorney (LPA), which appoints other people to make health and welfare decisions for them if they lose capacity. Attorneys must exercise their powers in the best interests of the individual. If there is no welfare attorney, a court may appoint a deputy to make decisions if this is in the adult's best interests. Court-appointed deputies cannot make a decision to refuse consent to life-saving medical treatment. The Office of the Public Guardian deals with the registration of LPAs and deputies, supervises court-appointed deputies, and provides information to help the Court of Protection make decisions.

2.5.5 Determining Best Interests

Section 4 of the MCA 2005 sets out a non-exhaustive checklist of factors that must be considered in deciding what is in a person's best interests. This includes the person's past and present wishes and feelings, beliefs, and values. However, there is a distinction between expressing treatment preferences and an advance decision to refuse treatment. If valid and applicable, an advance decision refusing treatment must be complied with, but there is no obligation to provide treatment that is clinically unnecessary or inappropriate. In addition, family members and people involved in caring for the person lacking capacity should be consulted, if it is practical and appropriate to do so. Welfare attorneys and court-appointed deputies must make the decisions on any issues about which they have been appointed. Ultimate responsibility for determining best interests lies with the decision-maker, subject to the Court of Protection.

2.5.6 Advance Decisions to Refuse Treatment

Under Sections 24–26 of the MCA 2005 a person of 18 years or over with mental capacity can make a decision to refuse future treatment if a need for treatment arises when they lack capacity. Practitioners must consider whether an advance decision was validly made and intended to apply in the circumstances that have arisen. There are no particular formalities about the format of an advance decision and it can be written or verbal, unless it deals with life-sustaining treatment. An advance decision to refuse treatment is not valid in respect of life-sustaining treatment unless the decision is in writing, signed, and witnessed. In addition, there must be an express statement to the effect that the decision stands 'even if life is at risk'. Even if an advance decision does not meet statutory requirements it should be considered as part of the best interests assessment.

2.5.7 The Court of Protection and Serious Medical Treatment

The Court of Protection has issued practice directions concerning serious medical treatment of people who lack capacity, which should be brought to the court. All cases involving decisions about the proposed withholding or withdrawal of artificial nutrition and hydration from a person in a permanent vegetative state or a minimally conscious state, involving organ or bone marrow donation, and all cases involving non-therapeutic sterilization of a person are regarded as serious medical treatment. Other examples of serious medical treatment include certain terminations of pregnancy, treatment for the purpose of donation to another, where force would be required to administer treatment, experimental or innovative treatment, and cases involving an ethical dilemma in an untested area. However, other matters of concern or dispute may also be referred to the court.

KEY POINTS—ADULTS WHO LACK CAPACITY

- Treatment must always be in a patient's best interests.
- Checklist for best interests assessment is extensive.
- Advance decisions allow patients to refuse treatment.
- There is no obligation to provide unnecessary treatment.
- Deprivation of liberty is unlawful so restraint is used only to prevent harm to a patient.
- Lasting power of attorney covers health and welfare issues.
- The Court of Protection must decide on serious medical matters for patients who lack capacity.

2.6 Exceptions to Obtaining Consent

There are limited exceptions to the need for consent, such as emergency medical treatment of an unconscious patient. A practitioner is lawfully entitled, and is likely to be bound, to carry out treatment necessary to safeguard the life and health of a patient in his or her care, acting in the patient's best interests (Connolly v Croydon Health Services NHS Trust [2015] All ER (D) 157

(QB), [2015] EWHC 1339 (QB)). However, this is subject to a valid advance decision refusing such treatment. Only reasonable steps need be taken to discover whether an advance decision exists.

Other examples include additional procedures that become necessary during surgery. If it is not reasonably possible to seek consent or to postpone these procedures until the patient can be asked for his or her consent they may be undertaken, but this must be limited to interventions that are immediately necessary to prevent serious harm to the patient (Connolly v Croydon Health Services NHS Trust [2015] All ER (D) 157 (QB), [2015] EWHC 1339 (QB)).

The Mental Health Acts (1983 and 2007) permit people with some mental health conditions to be detained in a hospital or psychiatric clinic and appropriate treatment to be given without their consent if this is considered necessary to protect them or others. This includes treatment of physical health problems only to the extent that such treatment is part of, or ancillary to, treatment for mental disorder, such as treating self-inflicted wounds as a result of mental disorder.

Measures to protect public health authorize the medical examination of a person who is suspected of having specified infectious diseases and their detention in hospital to prevent spread of the disease. However, compulsory examination or detention may only take place with the authority of an order obtained in accordance with the Public Health (Control of Disease) Act 1984. This does not authorize treatment without consent. There are also some other exceptions to the requirement for consent to medical examination apart from this.

KEY POINTS—EXCEPTIONS TO OBTAINING CONSENT

- For medical emergencies, life-saving interventions are permitted.
- During surgery if needed to prevent serious harm.
- Under some provisions of the Mental Health Act.
- Under some provisions of the Public Health Act.

2.7 Information Disclosure (Negligence)

A patient may give a legally valid consent to treatment because he or she understands the broad nature and purpose of it. However, patients may still claim that the information they were given was not sufficient to enable them to have come to a proper decision in balancing the risks, benefits, and alternatives to treatment. Where patients suffer an injury as a result of medical treatment they may claim that, if they had been properly informed, they would not have consented to the treatment, and so would have avoided the injury. This legal action is based on negligence. In other words, it is alleged that the practitioner failed in his or her duty of care to the patient, in this case by not providing sufficient information. However, it differs from claims based on negligence in diagnosis or treatment, although in some cases such a claim may also be made as a separate breach of the doctor's duty of care. Where a negligence claim is based on insufficient information disclosure, the medical treatment may have been carried out to an acceptable standard, but all treatments carry some degree of risk and it is for the patient to decide whether or not to accept those risks.

The general principles of establishing a negligence claim are discussed in Chapter 4, but, in brief, a negligence claim requires the patient to establish on the balance of probabilities that he or she was owed a duty of care; that the duty was breached (the doctor fell below the appropriate standard of care and was negligent); and that the breach of duty caused harm to the patient. It is generally not difficult to establish that the patient was owed a duty of care since it is intrinsic in the doctor/patient relationship. However, establishing what the appropriate standard of care is and that this caused harm are more complex in information disclosure cases.

2.7.1 Development of the Standard of Care in Information Disclosure

One of the leading cases in this area has been Sidaway v Board of Governors of the Bethlem Royal Hospital [1985] AC 871 (HL), but this case was complicated by the fact that the judges took different approaches to what information should be disclosed. The majority adopted the Bolam test (Bolam v Friern Hospital Management Committee [1957] 1 WLR 582 (QB)) and so applied a professional standard, although some modified it to require that significant risks should be disclosed. An example of a significant risk was described as a 10% chance of a serious consequence, such as a stroke. It was said that this kind of risk should be disclosed even if medical evidence suggested it was acceptable not to do so. Only one judge, Lord Scarman, adopted a different test from Bolam and which is generally known as a prudent (or reasonable) patient standard. This standard required that all material risks be disclosed to the patient. A risk would be 'material' if a court was satisfied that a reasonable person in the patient's position would be likely to attach significance to the risk.

Subsequent cases initially appeared to favour the direct application of the Bolam test to information disclosure as just another aspect of the doctor's professional judgement, but later cases began to depart from that. For example, in Pearce v United Bristol Healthcare NHS Trust (1999) 48 BMLR 118 (CA) it was said that, if there was a significant risk that would affect the judgement of a reasonable patient, then in the normal course it is the responsibility of a doctor to inform the patient of that significant risk, if the information is needed so that the patient can determine for himself or herself as to what course he or she should adopt. In this case it was recognized that, in terms of significance of risk, it was not possible to talk in precise percentages. The decision of the Court of Appeal in Pearce and the dissenting opinion of Lord Scarman in Sidaway have been approved by the UK Supreme Court in the important case of Montgomery v Lanarkshire Health Board [2015] 2 WLR 768, [2015] UKSC 11 (UK Sup Ct).

This case concerned a baby born with severe disabilities as a result of shoulder dystocia during vaginal delivery. The mother was diabetic and at risk of a carrying a larger baby. She claimed that, although she had expressed her concern to the doctor whether she could safely deliver the baby vaginally, the doctor had failed to inform her about the 9–10% risk of severe damages from shoulder dystocia and that she had not been offered a Caesarean section, which would have prevented the damage to the baby. The case reached the UK Supreme Court, which upheld her claim. In doing so it held that:

> The doctor is under a duty to take reasonable care to ensure that the patient is aware of any material risks involved in any recommended treatment, and of any reasonable alternative or variant treatments.

The test of materiality is whether, in the circumstances of the particular case, a reasonable person in the patient's position would be likely to attach significance to the risk, or the doctor is, or should reasonably be aware that, the particular patient would be likely to attach significance to it.

The assessment of whether a risk is material cannot be reduced to percentages. The significance of a given risk is likely to reflect a variety of factors. The assessment is therefore fact-sensitive, and sensitive also to the characteristics of the patient.

The doctor's advisory role involves dialogue, which will only be performed effectively if the information is comprehensible.

A doctor is not obliged to discuss the risks inherent in treatment with a person who makes it clear that he or she would prefer not to discuss the matter.

The therapeutic exception, whereby information as to a risk may be withheld if the doctor reasonably considers that its disclosure would be seriously detrimental to the patient's health, is very limited and must not be abused.

2.7.2 The Effect of Montgomery on the Standard of Care

The decision has confirmed the move away from reliance on medical evidence to establish what the patient should have been told, save in respect of establishing what the medical risks were and what alternatives were available. The need to advise about alternative treatments that had been considered necessary in Birch v University College London Hospital NHS Foundation Trust (2008) 104 BMLR 168, [2008] EWHC 2237 (QB) was also upheld in Montgomery. It is therefore essential that the practitioner provides information that would be necessary and relevant to a reasonable patient, but must also go further and tailor information to meet the specific needs of the individual patient. In doing so the law has endorsed an approach that was already part of professional guidance (for example, in GMC, Good Medical Practice (2013)). Factors that will need to be considered include the magnitude of the risk, the nature of the risk, the effect that its occurrence would have upon the life of the patient, the importance to the patient of the benefits sought to be achieved by the treatment, the alternatives available, and the risks involved in those alternatives. The patient's questions must be answered truthfully and fully.

The doctor must take reasonable steps to ensure that the patient understands the information provided: simply providing technical information that the patient cannot reasonably be expected to grasp is not sufficient. While the court did not address this, it seems to follow that the level of comprehensibility of written materials and the language in which they are provided to the patient may also need to be considered. However, information about risks need not be given to a person who makes it clear that he or she does not want it.

Withholding information as to risk on the grounds that it would be seriously detrimental to the patient's health is a limited exception to the general principle. It does not allow the doctor to prevent the patient from making an informed choice on the grounds that the doctor considers that a patient will make a decision that is contrary to the patient's best interests.

2.7.3 Causation

In negligence cases it is also necessary to establish that the breach of duty caused the harm alleged both as a matter of fact and as a matter of law. The legal requirement in information disclosure cases has traditionally been that the patient has to establish the he or she would not have gone ahead with this treatment at any point, and therefore would not have been exposed to its inherent risks (Barnett v Chelsea and Kensington Hospital Management Committee [1969] 1 QB 428 (QB)). However, the Court of Appeal in Chester v Afshar [2005] 1 AC 134, [2004] UKHL 41 (HL) modified this to give greater protection to the patient's right to be informed about risks before consenting to treatment. The patient in this case did not claim that she would never have consented to the treatment but that she would have taken time to consider other options, so would not have had the surgery on the day that she did. Her claim succeeded, so it is now no longer necessary for a patient to establish that he or she would never have consented to the same treatment in the future. There are logical difficulties in this since, unless postponing the operation would have affected the level of risk in some way, the exposure to an inherent risk materializing would be the same whenever it was performed. Nevertheless, this test appears to have been accepted and this reinforces the need to provide adequate information to patients.

There are also issues raised concerning whether patients may make a claim that they would have withheld consent, acting with the benefit of hindsight. A variety of approaches has been adopted to this. Some courts have taken the view that this is simply a matter of the credibility of the patient, others have held that the decision of the patient should be looked at in terms of what the reasonable patient would have decided if properly informed. It appears from the approach in more recent cases that a test that combines both these approaches is finding most favour so that the court will examine what the reasonable patient would have decided but consider whether there were special factors relating to the individual that would have led him or her to make a different decision.

KEY POINTS—INFORMATION DISCLOSURE

- Inadequate information can result in a negligence claim.
- The Bolam test of professional judgement no longer applies.
- Patients must be made aware of any material risks of procedures.
- Material risk is any that a reasonable patient would find significant.
- Information supplied must be understandable to a reasonable patient.
- Information must meet the specific needs of the patient.
- Information on alternative procedures must be given.
- Doctors are not obliged to provide detailed information if the patient declines.
- Use of therapeutic privilege to withhold information is not to be abused.
- In proving causation, the court will examine what a reasonable patient would have decided and any special factors that would have led him or her to make a different decision.

2.8 Limits to Consent

Consent may only be given to lawful treatment (R v Brown [1994] 1 AC 212 (HL)). It is therefore not a defence to actions which are unlawful at common law, such as voluntary euthanasia or in statute, such as the Female Circumcision Act 1985. A right to give informed consent to treatment is also not a right to insist on a particular treatment (R (Burke) v General Medical Council [2006] QB 273, [2005] EWCA Civ 1003 (CA)). Doctors are under no legal or ethical obligation to agree to a patient's request for treatment if they consider the treatment is not in the patient's best interests.

KEY POINTS—LIMITS TO CONSENT

- Consent may only be given to lawful treatment and not that which is considered unlawful.
- Patients have no rights to insist on particular treatments.
- Doctors can refuse treatments if not in a patient's best interests.

2.9 Pearls and Pitfalls

2.9.1 Pearls

- Consent is based on respect for the individual.
- For those who lack legal capacity, a decision on best interests still depends on:
  - a careful evaluation of the individual;
  - his or her wishes and values.
- Documenting the basis for decisions:
  - is good practice;
  - helpful as evidence;
  - establishes the practitioner met the required legal standards.

2.9.2 Pitfalls

- Do not make assumptions about:
  - a patient's capacity to consent;
  - what information should be disclosed;
  - what is in his or her best interests.

2.10 Further Reading

- Mason J.K., Laurie, G.T. (2010). *Law and Medical Ethics*, 9th edn. Oxford: Oxford University Press.

2.11 Multiple Choice Questions

Interactive multiple choice questions to test your knowledge on this chapter can be found in the Online appendix at www.oxfordmedicine.com/essentiallegalmatters.

CHAPTER 3

Confidentiality and Release of Medical Information

Rebekah Ley and Natalie Hayes

CONTENTS

CHAPTER SUMMARY

Keep Medical Information Confidential

Keeping medical information confidential is a fundamental principle that underpins medical care and treatment. If patients cannot be certain that information given to doctors will be kept confidential, there is a risk that medical advice and assistance might not be sought.

The Law and Confidential Medical Information

How confidential medical information is managed and when it is released is governed not just by statute, but also by aspects of common law, including tort and contract law. Doctors' professional and ethical obligations in terms of confidentiality must also be considered.

Sharing Confidential Information

There are certain circumstances in which it is permitted to share confidential information.

IMPORTANT CASE LAW

- W v Edgell [1990] Ch 359, [1990] 1 All ER 835
- Gillick v West Norfolk and Wisbech Health Authority [1984] QB 581, [1984] 1 All ER 365; on appeal [1986] AC 112m [1985] 1 All ER 533, CA; revsd [1986] AC 112, [1985] 3 All ER 402, HL
- Campbell v MGN (HL) [2004] UKHL 22; [2004] 2 AC 457; [2004] 2 WLR 1232; [2004] EMLR 247

RELEVANT STATUTES AND LEGISLATION

- Data Protection Act 1998
- Access to Health Records Act 1990
- European Convention on Human Rights
- Human Rights Act 1998
- Freedom of Information Act
- Mental Capacity Act 2005

PROFESSIONAL GUIDANCE

- General Medical Council. (2007). *0–18 Years: Guidance for All Doctors*.
- General Medical Council. (2009). *Confidentiality*.
- General Medical Council. (2012). *Protecting Children and Young People; The Responsibilities of All Doctors*.

All can be accessed at www.gmc-uk.org

3.1 Introduction

> Whatever, in connection with my professional practice, or not in connect with it, I see or hear in the life of men, which ought not be spoken abroad, I will not divulge, as reckoning that all such should be kept secret.
>
> **Hippocratic Oath**

CASE STUDY 1

You are a junior doctor working a busy night shift in a Critical Care Unit. It is midnight and a patient has just been transferred from A&E; he has been involved in a fight and is intubated and ventilated. His identity is unknown. At 02:00 two individuals arrive on the Unit and say they are police officers; they have ID badges but are not in uniform. They say that they are investigating your patient's attempted murder and have detained someone in custody. They say that they urgently need a copy of the patient's medical records for a court hearing and need them immediately. What do you do?

The duty of confidentiality that a doctor owes to a patient is probably as old as the practice of medicine and is essential for trust between doctors and their patients. However, it is not an absolute duty and there are instances when a doctor is entitled, and in certain circumstances obliged, to disclose confidential information without patient consent to do so. This chapter is concerned with doctor–patient confidentiality and when medical information can reasonably be released. We do not cover the Freedom of Information Act, which is concerned with the release of information held by public bodies, including National Health Service (NHS) Trusts. Confidentiality is covered by a mixture of UK statute, common law, tort law, and the European Convention on Human Rights. It is also a core component of the professional guidance given to doctors by the profession's regulatory body, the General Medical Council (GMC), to which all doctors registered with it are expected to adhere.

The Data Protection Directive (Article 2) defines personal data as 'any information relating to an identified or identifiable natural person; an identifiable person is one who can be identified, directly or indirectly, in particular by reference to an identification number or one or more factors specific to physical, physiological, mental, economic, culture or social identity'. The law recognizes two types of data: personal and anonymous. For the purpose of this chapter, we are looking at the first type; sensitive personal data.

KEY POINTS—INTRODUCTION

- The duty of confidentiality is not absolute.
- Under certain circumstances a doctor is obliged to disclose confidential information without a patient's consent.
- Legally, confidentiality is covered by multiple laws and statutes.
- Confidentiality is a core component of GMC professional guidance.

3.2 Personal Data and Disclosures Required by Law

There is no bar on releasing information about a patient to a third party if the patient consents to the disclosure and additional information about another individual is not also inadvertently disclosed. As such, patient consent should always be sought wherever practically possible, but there are some instances when a patient is unable to give consent (including the scenario as discussed, for example). Furthermore, there are also circumstances when the disclosure of medical information is actually required by law, irrespective of whether the patient has consented to the disclosure or not. The number of Acts that provide for access to personal information about patients is large and they cover a wide range of purposes, from the investigation of NHS fraud to motor vehicle driving licensing and counter terrorism investigations (Box 3.1).

The statutes listed can oblige organizations holding information about an individual to release it in some circumstances. However, any such request must specifically set out details of the information that is sought and the parts of the statute relied upon in making the request.

When considering statutory requests for personal information about a patient, doctors must be mindful of their ethical and professional obligations, set out by the GMC in its key document on confidentiality, entitled 'Confidentiality' (2017). This requires doctors to satisfy themselves that the disclosure sought is indeed required by law or can be justified in the public interest (paragraph 18)

Box 3.1 List of Acts Governing Access to Patient's Personal Information

- Criminal Appeal Act 1995
- Terrorism Prevention and Investigation Measures Act 2011
- Health and Social Care Act 2008
- Health and Social Care (Community Health and Standards) Act 2003
- Regulation of Care (Scotland) Act 2001
- Health and Personal Social Services (Quality, Improvement and Regulation) (Northern Ireland) Order 2003
- Public Health (Control of Disease) Act 1984
- Road Traffic Act 1988
- NHS Act 2006 and NHS (Wales) Act 2006
- Medical Act 1983

and that, whenever practicable, the patient should be informed of the disclosure even if their consent is not required unless this would undermine the purpose of the disclosure, such as in the case of a criminal investigation, for example (paragraph 19). You should always seek further information from the person requesting the information and/or independent legal advice if you are unsure of the legal basis for a request for information about a patient without their consent (legal annex, paragraph 3).

Specific guidance is available for some of the circumstances outlined, such as disclosing information to the Driver and Vehicle Licensing Agency (DVLA), complying with Court Orders, notification of communicable diseases, reporting of gunshot and knife wounds to the police, and disclosure to public bodies such as Mental Health Tribunals, the Care Quality Commission, and the healthcare regulatory bodies. You should consult the relevant guidance as well as your defence organization and senior colleagues when faced with a request for patient information in these settings, and you should consider each case on an individual basis.

KEY POINTS—PERSONAL DATA AND DISCLOSURES REQUIRED BY LAW

- Confidential information can be released if a patient gives consent.
- A patient's consent should always be sought wherever possible.
- Disclosure of medical information is sometimes required by law irrespective of consent—a statutory request.
- If consent is not required patients should still be informed of disclosure.
- Information can only be released if required by law or justified in the public interest.
- Always seek advice and consult relevant guidance before disclosure.

3.3 Individuals' Access to Data

Individuals have a right to request access to confidential clinical information held about them. It therefore follows that documentation in medical records should be capable of being read by a patient without causing offence or unnecessary upset. In addition, it is important that any third party information contained in the requested records (such as relatives' comments or contact details that may have been noted) is removed before disclosure to avoid an inadvertent breach of confidentiality in respect of the third party(s).

All healthcare providers should provide information to patients explaining how their personal information is held and confirming that information will be shared with other clinicians and/or the wider clinical team as necessary for the provision of health care for the patient. However, if a patient expressly states that he or she does not want information to be shared with anyone else, including the healthcare team, this request must be respected. If the decision not to share information with other health professionals could put the patient at risk, this should be explained carefully to the patient and the discussion documented fully in the clinical records.

KEY POINTS—INDIVIDUALS' ACCESS TO DATA

- All patients have a right to access their clinical information.
- Content of clinical notes should avoid offensive or personal remarks.
- Third party information contained within notes cannot be disclosed.
- Patients should be informed of how their personal information is shared.
- A patient's decision not to share information must be respected and the consequences explained and documented.

3.4 Disclosure in the Public Interest

As discussed earlier in the chapter, there is clear benefit to society in a doctor's duty of confidentiality to patients in that it encourages the public to seek medical advice and treatment. However, there are also circumstances in which the benefit of keeping information about an individual confidential is outweighed by a public interest in disclosing it, even in the absence of patient consent to do so, or, exceptionally, withholding of that consent.

These situations may arise when the information disclosure is required to protect the patient or to protect others, and are generally considered to be those wherein a failure to disclose the information would expose the patient or others to the risk of death or serious harm (see paragraphs 36–39 and 51–56 of 'Confidentiality' (2009) GMC). The GMC gives examples of such situations in its guidance and these include those in which disclosure is required to assist in the prevention, detection, or prosecution of a serious crime such as murder, rape, or child abuse.

Doctors who are asked to disclose information in this type of situation, or who are told information that leads them to be concerned for the safety of the patient or others, should still seek the patient's consent if possible. If this is not practicable or consent is refused, and you feel that the risk created by not disclosing the information creates a risk so severe that it outweighs the patient's interest in confidentiality, you should disclose the information promptly to an appropriate person and, if possible, inform the patient of your decision to do so (paragraph 55, 'Confidentiality' (2009) GMC). When dealing with such situations, it is helpful to seek the advice of trusted colleagues, or your local Caldicott Guardian, for example, and you should carefully document your decisions and reasons for them.

In terms of the common law position concerning public interest and breach of confidence, there are two leading cases: X v Y [1988] 2 All ER 648 and W v Edgell [1990] 1 All ER 835.

X v Y concerned a newspaper that obtained information from a health authority employee concerning two general practitioners (GPs) who were HIV-positive. The newspaper argued that it was in the public interest to know about the HIV status of the doctors. However, the court supported an injunction preventing publication of the names of the GPs on the grounds that the risks of individuals with HIV not seeking treatment that would be created if information was published was greater than the public interest in publishing it.

In W v Edgell, the court upheld the breach of confidence alleged by patient W by his/her psychiatrist. The psychiatrist had examined W to prepare a report for a mental health review tribunal to consider W's transfer from a secure hospital to a secure unit and then a parole board hearing for W's possible release from a secure hospital. W had been convicted of the manslaughter of five people and wounding of others. Dr Edgell's report concluded that W remained a danger to the public and his application to the mental health review tribunal was withdrawn. W's solicitors did not send a copy of Dr Edgell's report to the hospital where he was detained but Dr Edgell did. An action for breach of confidence was brought by W. The Court of Appeal held that in this particular case, the duty of confidentiality owed by Dr Edgell to W must be balanced against the risk to the public that preserving it would create. They confirmed that Dr Edgell owed his patient a duty of confidentiality but that the duty was not absolute and his actions to disclose confidential information about W were correct in the circumstances.

We mentioned earlier that common law principles underpin the concept of confidentiality, but the European Convention Articles 8 (right to privacy) and Article 10 (right to freedom of expression) also have a role to play. The case of Campbell v Mirror Group Newspapers [2004] UKHL 22 concerned the publication of photographs covertly taken of the model Naomi Campbell leaving a Narcotics Anonymous meeting. Ms Campbell was initially awarded damages of £3500, but this decision was subsequently overturned by the Court of Appeal, which found that disclosure of Ms Campbell's attendance at the meeting was in the public interest. The House of Lords subsequently evaluated the tension between Articles 8 and 10 and found that Ms Campbell's Article 8 rights (to privacy) took precedence over the press freedom and public interest arguments made under Article 10.

KEY POINTS—DISCLOSURE IN THE PUBLIC INTEREST

- Confidential information can be disclosed in the public interest.
- The public interest often relates to the risk of death or serious harm.
- Disclosure is required to assist in the prevention, detection, or prosecution of a serious crime such as murder, rape, or child abuse.
- Patients should be informed of non-consensual disclosure and advice sought from your local Caldicott Guardian.
- Decisions for non-consensual disclosure should be documented with appropriate reasons.
- Rights to privacy (Article 8) and rights to freedom of expression (Article 10) are often in contention.

3.5 Patients Who Lack Capacity

For adult patients who lack capacity to consent, it is important to note that no one is able to provide consent on their behalf, and that family members and friends have no special status in such situations. However, their opinions can be helpful in making a decision to disclose information or not. The GMC expects that doctors will continue to make the care of the patient their first concern, respect his or her privacy and dignity, and encourage the patient to be involved as far as possible in decisions about disclosure of their information even if they are not able to consent or otherwise to this (paragraph 59, 'Confidentiality' (2009) GMC).

In terms of legal requirements, The Mental Capacity Act 2005 Section 4(7) requires doctors to consult appropriate persons if possible, and these may include individuals whom the patient asks to be involved, or those who have legal authority to make decisions on the patient's behalf, or who have been legally appointed to represent them. As such, if a patient has created a lasting power of attorney (LPA) that covers personal welfare, you must take into account the views of the individual(s) who have been given the legal authority to make decisions on behalf of the patient. Similarly, if the Court of Protection has appointed a deputy in respect of the patient, that person should be consulted in relation to any intended disclosure of the patient's information. If you are concerned that the patient may be subject to neglect or abuse or is otherwise vulnerable and unable to consent to disclosure of information in this context, you should promptly contact the relevant responsible person in your organization or local authority if you feel that disclosure of information is in the best interests of the patient or is necessary to protect others from serious harm (for more information, see paragraph 63, 'Confidentiality' (2009) GMC).

KEY POINTS—PATIENTS WHO LACK CAPACITY

- No one can give consent to disclose information for incapacitated patients.
- Family and friends can add to opinions in a best interests determination.
- Persons appointed by a LPA should be consulted.
- Deputies of the Court of Protection should also be consulted.
- Vulnerable patients will need representation.

3.6 Children

In respect of children and young people, the same duty of confidentiality applies as to adult patients. However, for children who are too young to consent to disclosure of information about them, consent is usually sought from those with parental responsibility (see also Chapter 9).

When assessing a child's capacity to provide consent, it is important to note that children will attain the necessary maturity and level of understanding at different times, and this may in some cases be before they reach the age of 16. By 16, children are deemed to be able to provide consent but before this an individual assessment should be made in each case.

The important case in respect of children and consent is Gillick v West Norfolk and Wisbech Area Health Authority [1986] AC 112. The case concerned guidance prepared by the Department of Health concerning family planning discussions with children without the consent of their parents. Mrs Gillick sought a declaration that the guidance was unlawful. The case was eventually heard in the House of Lords, which held that a child under the age of 16 who understood the advice being given and could not be persuaded to inform her parents should be given that advice without her parent's knowledge if the clinician considered it was in the patient's best interests to give it. This also applies to the provision of investigations or treatment, although it is essential that children are encouraged to involve parents or guardians if possible, and that the responsible clinician is satisfied that the child understands the nature of the investigation or treatment (or disclosure) and the consequences of it, or of refusing it. The GMC provides useful guidance in paragraphs 24–29 and 43–52 of its key document, '0–18 Years: Guidance for All Doctors' (2007).

As with adult patients, if a child or young person under 18 does not consent to disclosure of information about him or her, there are some circumstances in which the information should still be disclosed and these are primarily when there is a public interest in disclosure that overrides the individual's confidentiality; when the child does not have the necessary understanding or maturity to make a decision about disclosure and that disclosure is felt to be in their best interests; and when the disclosure is required by law; for more information see paragraph 46, '0–18 Years: Guidance for All Doctors' (2007).

In situations where child abuse or neglect are suspected, there is a presumption of disclosure rather than withholding information based on the principle that a child protection concern may only become apparent when several people involved in the child's life share their individual concerns. You must still be able to justify any disclosure you make as being in the interests of the patient or others, and you should limit the amount of information you disclose to the minimum needed. However, you must also be able to justify a decision not to share a concern you have about a child and, in such cases, it is advisable to take advice from senior colleagues, local child protection leads, and professional or medical defence organizations; for more information see paragraphs 56–63, '0–18 Years: Guidance for All Doctors' (2007).

If a child patient does not have capacity to consent, it should generally be sought from his or her parents, guardian, or whomever has parental responsibility for the child. For young people aged between 16 and17 and who lack capacity, the legal basis for consent differs between the four countries in the UK. In England, Wales, and Northern Ireland, the young person's parents can consent to treatment and investigations if they are in his or her best interests, and, in England and Wales, treatment that is in the patient's best interests can be given even in the absence of parental consent. However, the opinions of the parents or guardians may be helpful in determining what those best interests are (Mental Capacity Act 2005; Mental Capacity Act Code of Practice). In Northern Ireland, emergency treatment can be given to the young person in his or her best interests without parental consent if the parents cannot be contacted, but, for anything other than this or for significant treatments, a Court Order may be required and so legal advice should be sought. In Scotland, treatment can be provided to safeguard or promote the patient's health and, for these purposes, a 16- or 17-year-old is considered as an adult (Adults with Incapacity (Scotland) Act 2000).

KEY POINTS—CHILDREN

- For children, the same duty of confidentiality applies as for adult patients.
- By 16 years children are deemed to be able to provide consent.
- Prior to 16 years, an individual assessment should be made in each case for the level of understanding.
- Disclosure based on statutory requirements and best interests also apply to children.
- In situations where child abuse or neglect are suspected, there is a presumption of disclosure.
- Those with parental responsibility can give consent for incapacitated children.

3.7 Confidentiality and Death

3.7.1 Coronial Investigations

A doctor's duty of confidentiality to his or her patient continues after the patient's death and, as such, if prior to death the patient had asked for information to be kept confidential after he or she has died, this should generally be respected (paragraph 70, 'Confidentiality' (2009) GMC). However, more often, the patient will not have left any such instructions and you may be asked to disclose confidential information after their death, to their relatives or other healthcare professionals in the context of responding to a complaint or in a report to the coroner, for example.

When considering requests for information in the absence of any known wishes of the patient, you should consider whether disclosing this information is likely to cause distress to, or benefit, the patient's family, why the information has been requested, and whether the information sought is already public knowledge. You should consider whether disclosure of the information would also inadvertently disclose information about a third party (paragraph 70, 'Confidentiality' (2009) GMC). It is also advisable to notify the executor of the patient's estate if he or she had made a will (or the personal representative if not) of the request and ask him or her to confirm that he or she does not have any objections to the disclosure. It is important to note, though, that you are not obliged to comply with any requests made by the executor or personal representative not to disclose the information unless the reason given is compelling. It may be helpful to seek independent legal advice and the opinions of trusted senior colleagues in such cases.

CASE STUDY 2

Active care has been withdrawn from a patient in the critical care unit following discussion with her husband. Having agreed with this decision, the patient's husband and son say their goodbyes and leave the unit. The patient is transferred to a side room for dignity and end-of-life care. Her brothers later arrive and remain with her until her death. They subsequently send a letter of complaint to the hospital concerning the attitude of the nurses and the cleanliness of the ward. There is nothing in the medical records that indicates what the patient would have wanted in terms of information disclosure after her death and so the complaints manager contacts the complainants and explains that she would like to inform the patient's husband that a complaint has been made and confirm that she would like to be able to include information about the patient's care in her response so that it is as detailed and informative as possible. The patient's brothers ask that their brother-in-law is not contacted by the hospital about this as they do not want to upset him but they do expect a written response to their concerns. What should the complaints manager do?

Here, it would be helpful for the complaints manager to point out to the brothers that not involving the patient's husband in the complaints response may potentially cause more harm at a later date if he subsequently became aware of it. She should also summarize the ethical obligations on the medical staff in terms of disclosing information about a deceased patient and explain that they must evaluate whether disclosing information to address the complaint is likely to be of benefit or detriment to the family as a whole, and to the patient's husband. It may be possible to respond to the complaint without disclosing any information about the patient and this could be explored if the complainants insist that the patient's husband is not contacted.

The legal position in respect of the release of information concerning a deceased individual is given in the Access to Health Records Act 1990. The Act stipulates that disclosure can be made to the patient's personal representative, executor, or administrator of the patient's estate, or anyone who might have a claim on the estate. What constitutes a 'claim' on the patient's estate has generated some debate amongst legal advisers; perhaps in this case, the complainants have a claim on the patient's estate by virtue of being her brothers and this would enable them to request information about her under this Act. However, the arguments around this are complex and it may therefore be helpful to seek independent legal advice if faced with such situations.

Doctors are obliged to assist coroners, procurator fiscals, and equivalent officers with inquests and official investigations concerning a patient's death, and this will usually require the writing of a medical report (see Chapter 5). It is important to ensure that any third party information contained in the patient records is not inadvertently disclosed and guidance can be sought from the coroner's office or medical defence organizations concerning the amount of information that is required and the amount if disclosure that is justifiable.

KEY POINTS—CONFIDENTIALITY AND DEATH

- A doctor's duty of confidentiality to their patients continues after death.
- The balance between distress or benefit to the patient's family must be weighed in information disclosure after death.
- No information on a third party can be disclosed in a doctor's report.
- The executor of the patient's estate should be informed of any disclosure.
- Responding to an executor's request for information disclosure is not mandatory.
- Doctors are obliged to assist in coronial investigations and disclose justifiable information.

3.8 Recording Patients (Audio and Visual)

The recording of patients either with an audio recording, photographs, or video should only be done with the consent of the patient and this includes, but is not restricted to:

- Images of internal organs or structures
- Images of pathology slides
- Laparoscopic and endoscopic images
- Recordings of organ functions
- Ultrasound images/X-rays.

When seeking patients' consent to record them or their clinical images, you should explain the purpose of any recording, any secondary uses that may take place, and how the recording will be kept and stored, and for how long. Even if the patient has consented to the recording, you should stop recording immediately if you are asked to do so or the patient changes his or her mind. Recordings should be handled and stored in the same way as formal clinical records.

Covert recordings of patients should only be undertaken where there is no other means of obtaining the information required and in situations where the risk to the patient or others in not recording the information outweighs patient confidentiality. Such a situation may arise when the recording is required for the investigation or prosecution of a serious crime, or to protect the patient or another person from serious harm, i.e. suspected child abuse. The legal position in respect of such recordings is extremely complex and outwith the scope of this chapter. If you are faced with such a request, you should take prompt advice from your senior colleagues, local Caldicott guardian, and your defence organization before proceeding.

Many NHS organizations have been slow to respond to the increasing use of mobile telephones by patients to record conversations with clinicians and to photograph or video them. It would be expected that a patient or relative would seek permission from the consulting clinician before recording and any recording should take place away from other patients and clinical areas to avoid unintentionally capturing confidential information about someone else. If a patient or relative indicates that they have covertly recorded a consultation with you and intend to share it through a social media platform, you can explain that a recording taken without permission should not be passed on to a third party.

Sometimes there are legitimate reasons for recording conversations in a healthcare setting and if you think a patient or relative is recording something you are entitled to ask them if they are. If they indicate that they are and you are not comfortable with this, you may explain this. If the patient continues to record without your permission, this may cause you to feel uncomfortable and you should explain that, by doing so, they are undermining the trust that needs to exist between you for you to continue to provide medical care for them. It is worth exploring why the recording is being made and if you can offer the information in another format with which you feel more comfortable; if the patient is recording the consultation to act as an aide-memoire later, for example, he or she might benefit from you providing a copy of your letter to the GP instead. The GMC has published specific guidance in this area, in its document 'Making and Using Visual and Audio Recordings of Patients' (April 2011), which is available on its website.

KEY POINTS—RECORDING PATIENTS (AUDIO AND VISUAL)

- Consent is needed for any patient recording modality.
- Purpose of recording, storage method/length of timem and sharing are important topics for consent discussions.
- Covert recording is a complex legal issue and needs further advice.
- Patients should seek permission to record consultations.
- Recording other patients and confidential information inadvertently is not permitted.
- Sharing recorded information without permission is unlawful.

3.9 Storing Information and Email

All sensitive patient information should be stored securely and the GMC guidance and Data Protection Act has set out helpful principles to guide organizations. It is important to note that the Information Commissioner can impose heavy financial penalties on organizations that lose data or otherwise cause distress to individuals through their handling of personal data loss. The penalties imposed can be as large as £500,000, and individuals may also have separate claims for damages so the financial consequences of failure to act appropriately can be substantial.

Patients are increasingly using email to contact clinicians and healthcare providers, and it is important to note that email exchanges with patients form part of the patient's medical records in the same way that other forms of written correspondence do. It goes without saying that complex matters or symptoms should not be dealt with by email, and you should familiarize yourself with your organization's advice and guidance on the use of email in the clinical setting, and suitable levels of encryption and security.

In terms of communicating with colleagues, the nhs.net email system is a secure way to exchange information within the NHS, but if you are in doubt about its use or the use of other email systems, it is advisable to seek advice from the information governance lead at your organization. Following the rise of email as a means of almost instantaneous communication, the use of facsimile messaging is becoming less frequent, and the fact that simple mistakes such as misdialling can lead to confidential information being sent to and received by an unintended recipient make it less suitable for communicating confidential information about patients. Fax numbers should always be carefully checked and verified before transmission takes place and it is wise to follow up with a telephone call to check that the information has been received by the intended recipient. Many organizations now use 'safe haven' faxes to avoid potential breaches of confidentiality, and it is advisable to use these in preference to other machines with a more general purposes if they are available.

KEY POINTS—STORING INFORMATION AND EMAIL

- Sensitive patient information should be stored securely.
- The Data Protection Act sets out guidance principles.
- Failure to protect patients' data can lead to hefty fines.
- Emails form part of a patient's medical records but should not be used for complex clinical matters.
- Secure and encrypted networks are required for email systems.
- If fax communications are used a follow-up call is prudent to confirm receipt of information.

3.10 Social Media

The public nature of social media means that extra care should be taken when using such platforms to avoid unintentionally disclosing confidential information about patients or, indeed, colleagues. It is inevitable that the use of social media is likely to continue to increase and may offer new ways of working with patients and their carers. However, the risk of inadvertent confidentiality breaches means that these avenues of communication should be approached with caution. Guidance from NHS Employers entitled 'New to the NHS? Your Guide to Using Social Media in the NHS' offers a helpful reminder that the standard of 'behaviour' expected on social media is the same as is expected generally of doctors by the profession's regulatory body, the GMC. The GMC's own guidance on this topic advises that, if you are using social media that is accessible to the general public in the context of your clinical role, you should make this clear and also use your full name (Paragraph 17, 'Doctors' Use of Social Media' (2013), GMC; www.gmc-uk.org).

The rationale behind this is that writing as a clinician confers weight upon the opinions that you may be expressing, and these may be relied upon by the audience reading them. As such, you should think carefully before writing anything that maybe interpreted as clinical advice and you must be especially careful to ensure that you do not reveal information about a patient that may make him or her identifiable. It goes without saying that photographs should not be taken of patients for personal use on services such as Instagram and Facebook.

The nature of social media occasionally means that social and professional boundaries can become unclear. There may be instances where a patient contacts you about their care or professional matters through your private profile. If this type of contact occurs you should indicate that you cannot mix social and professional relationships and, where appropriate, direct them to your professional profile (paragraph 11, 'Doctors' Use of Social Media' (2013), GMC; www. gmc-uk.org). If the inappropriate contact continues, you should seek support from senior trusted colleagues, your organization's legal team, and your professional body or defence union. Social media providers are in a position of moderation and if you are concerned about abusive material or comments made then you should feed back directly to the provider concerned.

KEY POINTS—SOCIAL MEDIA

- Using social media may risk unintentional disclosure of confidential information about patients or colleagues.
- Avoid using social media for clinical purposes if it is accessible to the general public.
- What your write on social media may be interpreted as clinical advice.
- Patient contact through social media to your private profile is inadvisable.
- Patients doing so should be discouraged and/or directed to your professional profile.

3.11 Remedies

Whilst a patient can apply to court for an injunction to prevent disclosure, this can only happen if they know about it before the disclosure is made. Most issues arise when the breach has already occurred and the patient feels that they have been harmed in some way or inconvenienced as a result.

If the breach has already occurred, damages can be awarded by a court if the patient chooses to bring a civil claim against the person or organization responsible for the breach. However, such action is costly and, in reality, this is not often seen.

What is more likely and more significant for individual clinicians is the possibility of a complaint. If not handled correctly, complaints alleging a breach of patient confidentiality can quickly escalate and come to the attention of the relevant ombudsman (these differ in name across the four jurisdictions in the UK). The possible outcomes are numerous, but include being asked to offer an apology, recommendations for a change to practice, and being asked to make a payment to the patient. In addition, a serious breach of patient confidentiality could result in a disciplinary investigation by your employer, or even by the GMC, the result of which could restrict your ability to practise in the UK.

Confidentiality underpins the relationship of trust between doctor and patient and should be guarded carefully. The consequences of breaching it without permission can be dire for both parties. As such, any decision to disclose information without the consent of the patient must be justified and, in doing so, it is sensible to discuss such cases with senior colleagues carefully and take advice from local Caldicott guardians and your defence organizations whenever they arise.

KEY POINTS—REMEDIES

- Court injunctions to prevent disclosure are uncommon in medicine.
- Civil claims can be brought for a breach of confidentiality.
- A significant breach in patient confidentiality often results in a complaint.
- Fines and disciplinary proceedings by the GMC are possible consequences for breaches of confidentiality.

3.12 Pearls and Pitfalls

3.12.1 Pearls

- Find out who, within the organization you work for, is responsible for releasing information so that requests can be appropriately redirected.
- The Data Protection Act is not a barrier to release of information.
- To the uninitiated, it is difficult legislation to digest but the appendices are worth a look.
- No one should ever object if you need to seek guidance from a colleague or need to confirm the identity of an individual.
- Always refer to another appropriate individual if you cannot assist personally with matters on information disclosure.

3.12.2 Pitfalls

- Do not assume that it is automatically necessary to comply with a request from police or social care.
- There are certain instances in which information release is not automatic and a Court Order must be obtained by the police and/or social care to override the doctor's duty of confidentiality to the patient.
- Some statutes do compel disclosure in certain circumstances.
- If in doubt, seek advice first, either from your organization's legal department or your professional organization or defence body.
- Do not assume that information release to next of kin is always acceptable.
- Do not assume that information can always be shared with another health care provider.

3.13 Further Reading

- Brazier, M., Cave, E. (2011). *Medicine, Patients and the Law*. London: Penguin Books.
- Cowley, R. (1994). *Access to Health Records and Reports: A Practical Guide*. Oxford: Radcliffe Medical Press.
- Fortin, J. (2009). *Children's Rights and the Developing Law*. New York: Cambridge University Press.
- Foster, C., Peacock, N. (2000). *Clinical Confidentiality*. Sudbury: Monitor Press.
- Laurie, G.T., Harmon, S.H.E., Porter, G. (2016). *Mason and McCall Smith's Law and Medical Ethics*. Oxford: Oxford University Press.

3.14 Multiple Choice Questions

✓ Interactive multiple choice questions to test your knowledge on this chapter can be found in the Online appendix at www.oxfordmedicine.com/essentiallegalmatters.

CHAPTER 4

Medical Negligence and Complaints

Nigel Spencer Ley and Jane Sturgess

CONTENTS

CHAPTER SUMMARY

Negligence

Not all poor outcomes result from negligent care and not all complaints result from poor outcomes.

To claim for personal injury, a breach of duty that results in harm must be proven within a time limit.

Negligence claims can be difficult to prove, but claims involving inadequate consent are more likely to succeed.

Legal Tests

The 'Bolam' test can no longer be used to defend matters of inadequate consent.

The 'Bolitho' test may override the Bolam test if the course of medical management is considered illogical.

Information that a reasonable person would require is now the legal standard in cases where informed consent is in dispute.

Indemnity

National Health Service (NHS) indemnity provides legal cover for hospital doctors where they are caring for NHS patients but private insurance is required to cover non-NHS patients.

NHS indemnity does not cover general practitioners (GPs). Claims in primary care are often brought against the clinician rather than the NHS.

Criminality

Gross negligence is considered a crime punishable in criminal law. A jury determines if treatment is 'grossly negligent'.

The crime of manslaughter with a possible custodial sentence is a possible outcome of a verdict of gross negligence.

Charges of corporate manslaughter can be brought against NHS organizations if their activities/processes cause a patient's death by breach of duty.

Product Liability

Manufacturers bear liability under the Consumer Protection Act for harm caused by faulty equipment or drugs.

The hospital or organization will be liable for incorrect use or storage of a product.

Complaints and Resolution

Complaints can be made directly to the hospital, GPs practice, commissioning group, or General Medical Council.

Patients who are unhappy with the resolution of their complaint can refer the matter to the Health Service Ombudsman.

IMPORTANT CASE LAW

- Bolam v Friern Hospital Management Committee [1957] 1 WLR 582
- Bolitho v City & Hackney Health Authority [1998] AC 232
- Pearce v United Bristol Healthcare NHS Trust [1999] PIQR P53
- Chester v Afshar [2005] 1 AC 134
- Montgomery v Lanarkshire Health Board [2015] 2 WLR 768
- Hotson v East Berkshire Health Authority [1987] AC 750
- Bailey v MOD [2009] 1 WLR 1052
- R v Cornish and Maidstone and Tunbridge Wells NHS Trust [2016]

RELEVANT STATUTES AND LEGISLATION

- Civil Liability (Contribution) Act 1978
- Corporate Manslaughter and Corporate Homicide Act 2007
- Consumer Protection Act 1987

PROFESSIONAL GUIDANCE

- Judicial College. (2015). *Guidelines for the Assessment of General Damages in Personal Injury Cases*, 13th edn. Oxford: Oxford University Press.

4.1 Introduction

Medicine is not a perfect science and doctors are not infallible. Throughout any medical career there will be cases of poor outcomes. Sometimes the treatment may not work, sometimes the patient will be made worse, and sometimes a patient may die. The cause of a poor outcome may simply be the nature of the condition from which the patient is suffering. However, in some cases the cause may be mistakes by the treating clinicians. The purpose of this chapter is to consider the legal consequences of such mistakes.

4.2 Civil Liability

In English law where someone suffers an injury (physical or psychiatric) as a result of another person's negligence, the injured person can bring a claim for compensation both for the injury itself and for any consequent financial loss. To succeed in a claim for personal injury, the claimant must prove: (a) that the defendant is in breach of duty (i.e. has acted negligently or in breach of a statute); and (b) that the claimant's injury was caused by that breach. The general rule is that claims for personal injury must be brought within 3 years of the date of injury, or the claimant's date of knowledge of the injury. However, this can be extended in certain circumstances. These principles apply as much in the context of medical treatment as in any other context (road accident claim, employers' liability claims, etc.). However, a number of special rules apply to clinicians.

4.2.1 Breach of Duty

The classic test of whether a clinician has acted negligently was set out in the case of Bolam v Friern Hospital Management Committee [1957] 1 WLR 582. A doctor is 'not guilty of negligence if he has acted in accordance with a practice accepted as proper by a responsible body of medical men skilled in that particular art'. In practical terms, this means that, even if a majority of doctors would not defend the clinician's decision (to give a particular treatment, or to withhold a particular treatment, or to perform a procedure using a particular method, etc.), provided that some responsible doctors would have made the same decision, the clinician is not guilty of negligence.

There are two important caveats to this test.

In 1997 (in the case of Bolitho v City & Hackney Health Authority [1998] AC 232) the House of Lords held that, in 'rare cases', if it had been demonstrated that the professional opinion defending the doctor's action was incapable of withstanding logical analysis, the action could be regarded as negligent. The court was not obliged to hold that a doctor was not liable for negligent treatment or diagnosis simply because evidence had been called from medical experts who genuinely believed that the doctor's actions conformed with accepted medical practice. The reference in Bolam to a 'responsible body of medical men' meant that the court had to satisfy itself that the medical experts could point to a logical basis for the opinion they were supporting. This does not simply mean that the expert witness called for the defendant doctor has to be able to justify his views logically, but that the practice being defended must also be logically defensible. So, for example, assume that there are two surgical procedures for treating a particular condition, procedure A and procedure B. The literature has clearly shown that procedure B is much safer and more reliable than procedure A. Despite this, many doctors still use procedure A as it was the one which they were taught. A patient suffers injury as a result of undergoing procedure A. Under the Bolam test the doctor is not guilty of negligence as a responsible body would defend it. Applying the Bolitho test, however, the court might find that there was no logical basis for using procedure A and therefore the doctor was negligent.

The second exception involves consent. The Bolam test does not apply to consent cases. Doctors are under a duty to take reasonable care to ensure that patients are aware of any material risks involved in any recommended treatment, and of any reasonable alternative treatments. The test of materiality is whether, in the circumstances, a reasonable person in the patient's position would be likely to attach significance to the risk, or the doctor was or should reasonably be aware that the particular patient would be likely to attach significance to it. Precisely what risks the patient should be warned of depend on the chance of the adverse event occurring and how serious the consequences of the event would be. Thus it may not be negligent to fail to warn of a 20% risk of a headache following a particular procedure, but it would almost certainly be negligent to fail to warn of a 1% risk of death or blindness following the procedure.

In assessing negligence, the experience and specialism of a doctor may be relevant. So, for example, a GP is not expected to have same the knowledge of heart conditions as a consultant cardiologist. Equally, a first-year trainee doctor is not expected to have the same knowledge as his supervising consultant. The medical world is now full of guidelines and protocols, issued by the National Institute of Health and Care Excellence (NICE), by the Royal Colleges, by the GMC, by many hospitals, and by a host of other bodies. Failure to follow a guideline or protocol is not automatically negligent. However, where you are aware of a guideline or protocol and decide not to follow it, it would be wise to document your reasons for departing from it. Another practical way to protect oneself against an allegation of negligence is to seek a second opinion from a colleague, or discuss the patient's case at a multidisciplinary team (MDT) meeting.

KEY POINTS—CIVIL LIABILITY (BREACH OF DUTY)

- A claimant must prove breach of duty and causation to succeed in a claim.
- A breach of duty must satisfy the Bolam and Bolitho tests.
- The Bolam test does not apply to consent but the test of materiality does.
- In negligence cases, the experience and specialism of a doctor may be relevant.
- Failure to follow a guideline is not automatically negligent but should be capable of a logical defence.
- Seeking a second opinion and MDT case discussions help mitigate against negligence.

4.2.2 Causation

To succeed in a claim for damages, it is not enough for the patient to prove that the treating doctor has acted negligently; the patient must also prove that he or she has suffered some harm as a result of the negligence. For example, if a doctor accidentally prescribes the wrong dose of a drug, but this has no effect on the claimant's treatment, there can be no claim for damages. Perhaps more surprisingly, if a poor outcome was more likely than not to occur, even if the treating doctor's negligent actions have increased the risk of the poor outcome, the doctor is not liable. Imagine a patient who has suffered a serious leg injury. Even with appropriate treatment there is a 60% chance that amputation is required. The treating doctor provides negligent treatment, and an amputation becomes inevitable. The treating doctor is not liable for the amputation. The claimant must prove on the balance of probabilities (i.e. more likely than not) that, as a result of the doctor's action, or omission, he has suffered:

- a physical injury; and/or
- an additional period of pain and suffering; and/or
- a worse outcome than would have been the case with appropriate treatment; and/or
- a psychiatric injury.

It can sometimes be very difficult to say whether the patient's poor outcome or death was caused by his or her underlying condition or by negligent medical treatment. In a case where it is impossible to say whether or not the injury would have occurred but for the negligent act, it is sufficient for the claimant to prove that the contribution of the negligent cause was more than negligible.

The law is slightly different in respect of claims involving lack of consent. Consider a case where the claimant suffers a poor outcome following treatment (which was competently undertaken), and is able to prove that he or she was not given the appropriate warnings prior to consenting to the treatment. If the claimant would have agreed to the treatment despite being given the appropriate warnings, then he or she has no claim. If the patient would have refused the treatment had he or she been given the appropriate warnings, then the claim will succeed. However, the claim will also succeed if he or she would not have agreed to the treatment at the time of consent had appropriate warnings been given, even if the patient accepts that he or she might have agreed to it at a later time (perhaps after having obtained a second opinion).

If the patient suffers a psychiatric injury as a result of a physical injury (or poor outcome) or because of fear that he or she might suffer a physical injury, then the normal rules apply. However, if the claimant suffers a psychiatric injury as a result of the death or injury of someone else then special rules apply. To recover damages, the claimant must prove:

- Close ties of love and affection with the primary victim (usually a marital or parental relationship is required).
- The psychiatric injury occurred as a result of a sudden and unexpected shock to the claimant's nervous system.
- The claimant was either personally present at the scene of the incident/injury or was in the immediate vicinity and witnessed the aftermath.
- The psychiatric injury was caused by witnessing the death of, extreme danger to, or injury and discomfort suffered by the primary victim.

4.2.3 Contributory Negligence

Where a claimant's own negligent actions contribute either to the occurrence of an accident, or to the extent of injuries suffered as a result of an accident for which he or she is not to blame, the damages may be reduced to reflect his or her own culpability. So, for example, a pedestrian who steps out in front of a speeding car or a passenger in a car who suffers worse injuries because he was not wearing a seatbelt will have their damages reduced for contributory negligence. In theory, the same principle applies to claims for clinical negligence. In practice it is very rare for allegations of contributory negligence to be made against patients. However, in a case where the patient's outcome has been made worse by a failure, for example, to take his medication, to cooperate with medical treatment, or to attend medical appointments, it is certainly arguable that damages should be reduced.

KEY POINTS—CIVIL LIABILITY (CAUSATION AND CONTRIBUTORY NEGLIGENCE)

- A patient must prove that he or she has suffered some harm as a result of negligence (causation).
- Harm can be a physical/psychiatric injury, pain and suffering, or a worse outcome.
- The standard of proof for the claimant is on the 'balance of probabilities'.
- A claim will succeed if a patient would not have accepted treatment had he or she been properly warned of the consequences.
- A claim for psychiatric injury as a result of death or injury of someone else may also be pursued.
- Awarded damages may be reduced as a result of a patient's contribution to the injury (contributory negligence).

4.3 Damages and Costs

If a claimant establishes liability, he or she will be entitled to damages. Such damages are not intended to punish the defendant, rather to compensate claimants for their loss. So far as possible the damages are intended to place claimants back into the same position that they would have been in had they not been injured. Damages in all personal injury claims fall into several main categories.

4.3.1 Damages for Pain, Suffering, and Loss of Amenity

This is compensation for the injury itself rather than financial losses. The precise award depends on many factors, including the claimant's age, the severity of the ongoing symptoms, and the effect on his or her lifestyle. The Judicial College (the body that trains judges) published detailed guidelines on the appropriate level of such damages. These are principally aimed at injuries suffered in accidents and therefore can be hard to apply to clinical negligence claims. Here are some examples of suggested awards:

- minor injury from which recovery is made within a few days: up to £600;
- simple leg fractures from which a complete recovery is made: up to £7,990;
- below-knee amputation of one leg: £85,910 to £116,620;
- paraplegia: £192,090 to £249,270;
- total blindness: £235,630.

4.3.2 Special Damages

This is the financial loss that the claimant has suffered up to the date of trial. It will include loss of earnings (this will be based on the claimant's earnings net of tax, as damages are not subject to tax), the cost of any care or domestic assistance which the claimant has required as a result of the injury (including assistance provided gratuitously by his family), the cost of medical treatment if sourced privately (note: an injured claimant can claim the cost of private medical treatment even when he is entitled to free NHS treatment), and out-of-pocket expenses such as travel costs to medical appointments, prescriptions, etc.

4.3.3 Future Loss

This is the financial loss that the claimant will suffer in the future as a result of the injury. It may include ongoing full or partial loss of earnings, loss of promotion prospects, the cost of employing carers, the cost of moving to new accommodation (where this is needed as a result of the injury), and ongoing medical treatment. In serious cases, future loss will be the largest part of the claim. Traditionally, awards of a single lump sum covering the rest of the claimant's life are made. However, it is now possible for the court to order annual payments covering certain aspects of the claimant's ongoing needs (e.g. to cover the cost of employing carers). Where there is a risk of a future deterioration in the claimant's condition, it is possible for him or her to seek an order for provisional damages. If such an order is made, the claimant can return to court for additional damages in the event that the deterioration occurs.

Pending the resolution of the claim, it is possible for the claimant to seek an interim payment on account of damages. Interim payments are only made where the hospital admits liability, or liability has been proved at a preliminary trial. Once the claim is resolved, successful claimants can also add their legal costs of pursuing the claim. In cases where claimants have died, the estate can claim the damages discussed in respect of the period prior to death, and the family can claim damages for loss of financial dependency (together with funeral expenses and in some cases an award for bereavement, which is currently fixed by statute at £12,980).

KEY POINTS—DAMAGES AND COSTS

- Damages are not intended to punish the defendant but to compensate the claimant for his loss.
- Damages for pain and suffering depend on the claimant's age, the severity of the ongoing symptoms, and the effect on lifestyle.

- Special damages are awarded for financial losses (earnings, domestic assistance, medical treatment, travel, etc.).
- Future losses are those that the claimant will suffer in the future as a result of the injury—often the largest part of the claim.
- Additional damages can be sought for future deterioration.

4.4 Indemnity Insurance

Three categories of clinicians need to be considered, NHS employees undertaking NHS work, clinicians employed in the private sector, and everyone else.

4.4.1 NHS Employees

NHS employees who are acting in the course of their employment will be covered by NHS indemnity. This means that if someone wants to bring a claim for clinical negligence in respect of something they have done, the claim will be brought against their NHS employer rather than against them personally. The claim will be handled by the NHS, and (perhaps most importantly) any legal costs or damages will be paid by the NHS. In England, such claims are handled by NHS Resolution (in conjunction with the employer). There are equivalent organizations in Scotland, Wales, and Northern Ireland.

There are a few grey areas:

- Doctors undertaking waiting list initiative work in NHS hospitals for which they bill the NHS privately—NHS indemnity will apply.
- Doctors undertaking waiting list initiative work in private hospitals for which they bill the NHS privately—NHS indemnity will usually apply.
- Doctors undertaking clinical trials on NHS patients in NHS hospitals—NHS indemnity will usually apply even if the research is funded by a non-NHS body.

NHS indemnity does not apply to:

- Private work undertaken by the doctor.
- Some clinical trials.
- Work for voluntary or charitable bodies.
- Work overseas.

It follows that, if you are a clinician working solely as an employee within the NHS, there is no need for you to organize your own insurance. Despite this, most employed doctors choose to have limited cover with one of the medical defence unions. If no private work is undertaken the cost is relatively low. The advantage for the doctor is that if he or she ever needs legal advice this can be obtained for free. Notwithstanding NHS indemnity, there are many situations where doctors may wish to have their own legal representation; for example, in the event of a complaint about them to the GMC, if disciplinary action is taken against them by their employers, or (exceptionally) at an inquest.

4.4.2 Employees in the Private Sector

Clinicians working in private hospitals or clinics will either be employees or independent contractors (i.e. not on the payroll but submitting invoices either to the hospital or the patient for their work). Most doctors working in the private sector work as independent contractors (i.e. not employees); however, some clinicians (e.g. nurses, physiotherapists, etc.) are employed by the hospital or clinic. Such employees are in the same position as NHS employees. In the event of a claim arising from their negligence in the performance of their duties, their employer will be vicariously liable for the claim. In the circumstances the claim will again be brought against the hospital or clinic, rather than against the clinician personally. The hospital's insurers will deal with the claim and be responsible for any legal costs or damages. So again, there is no need for such an employee to have their own insurance.

4.4.3 Everyone Else

This category includes:

- Hospital doctors undertaking private work.
- Most GPs, including locum GPs, and salaried GPs employed by a practice (note: there are a few GPs who are NHS employees; however, this is quite unusual).
- Anyone undertaking medical work on a self-employed basis.

In the event of a claim arising from the negligence of a person in this category the claim will be brought personally against the clinician (and also possibly against his or her partners if he or she is working in a partnership, as is the case with many GPs). Such clinicians need to have adequate professional indemnity insurance. Indeed, undertaking clinical work without appropriate insurance will be regarded as professional misconduct and could lead to being struck off the register.

Such insurance may be very costly, and may influence the decision as to whether or not to undertake a particular area of private work. Most doctors obtain such insurance through a medical defence organization. These are mutual non-profit-making organizations, owned by their members. They all provide members with 24-hour access to advice and assistance on medicolegal issues arising from clinical practice which fall outside the scope of NHS indemnity. There are three medical defence organizations; the Medical Defence Union (MDU), the Medical Protection Society (MPS), and the Medical and Dental Defence Union of Scotland (MDDUS). The precise benefits of membership of each organization differ.

KEY POINTS—INDEMNITY INSURANCE

- NHS employees acting in the course of their employment are covered by NHS indemnity.
- NHS Resolution handles all claims in England.
- NHS indemnity does not apply to private work, some clinical trials, charitable, or overseas work.
- Self-employed practitioners and GPs must have professional indemnity insurance.
- Performing clinical work without appropriate insurance is regarded as professional misconduct.

4.5 Criminal Liability

We are not concerned here with what may be termed deliberate criminal acts (e.g. stealing money or equipment from the NHS, punching a patient in the face, setting fire to the hospital, etc.). Rather, the question is whether a doctor simply undertaking medical treatment, with no intention to cause harm, can be criminally liable for his or her conduct? The answer is yes, but only in exceptional circumstances. If a patient dies as a result of medical treatment that was 'grossly negligent' the doctor may be found guilty of manslaughter. This is an offence that carries a maximum sentence of life imprisonment. In R v Adomako (1994) 3 All ER 79, the House of Lords set out the requirements for this offence:

- A duty of care must be owed to the deceased (note: where a clinician is appointed to take charge of a patient they owe the patient a duty of care; however, simply being a doctor or nurse in a hospital will not necessarily mean there is a duty of care to a specific patient).
- There must be a breach of that duty of care, which causes (or significantly contributes to) the death of the victim.
- The breach should be characterized as gross negligence, and therefore a crime.

It is the last of these requirements that causes the most difficulty. Sadly, many patients die each year as a result or inadequate or negligent medical treatment. The question is, how bad does that treatment need to be before it can be characterized as 'grossly negligent'? Ultimately this is a matter for a jury to decide. The conduct must go beyond simple carelessness and be regarded as reprehensible. However, there is no clear test, and it is hoped that juries will simply know it when they see it. The following are some illustrative cases.

4.5.1 Cases of Criminal Liability

4.5.1.1 R v Prentice & Sullman

Doctors Prentice & Sullman were junior doctors at Peterborough Hospital. Malcolm Savage was a 16-year-old patient who was suffering from leukaemia. He attended the hospital for injections of cytotoxic drugs. Once a month he required intravenous injections of vincristine and every other month he required intrathecal (i.e. into the spine) injections of methotrexate. In February 1990 he attended for both drugs to be administered. Dr Sullman was a house officer. He had undertaken a lumbar puncture only once previously, and it had been unsuccessful. Dr Prentice was a pre-registration house officer. He had never previously undertaken a lumbar puncture. Notwithstanding this lack of experience Dr Prentice was instructed to administer the drugs under Dr Sullman's supervision. Dr Sullman handed Dr Prentice a syringe of vincristine without checking what the syringe contained. Dr Prentice injected the vincristine into Malcolm's spine, with fatal results. Both doctors were convicted by a jury of gross negligence manslaughter, and sentenced to 9 months' imprisonment suspended for 12 months. The convictions were quashed on appeal, largely on the grounds of their inexperience.

4.5.1.2 R v Adomako

A patient undergoing an operation died after his anaesthetist, Dr Adomako, failed to check that the oxygen supply remained connected to his endotracheal tube during retinal surgery, or to react to the consequent cessation of movements of breathing, or to the cessation of the ventilator's indicators of oxygen delivery. Dr Adomako was an experienced doctor in his 40s, but not a consultant. Expert witnesses described his care as 'abysmal' and concluded that he had shown a gross dereliction of duty. He was convicted of gross negligence manslaughter and sentenced to 6 months' imprisonment suspended for 1 year. His conviction was upheld on appeal.

4.5.1.3 R v Misra & Strivastava

In June 2000 Sean Phillips underwent surgery to repair his patella tendon at Southampton General Hospital. Unfortunately, he became infected with *Staphylococcus aureus*. The condition was untreated. There was a gradual build-up of poison within his body, which culminated in toxic shock syndrome from which he died on June 27. Drs Misra and Strivastava were senior house officers involved in Mr Phillips' postoperative care during the period beginning on the evening of June 23 until the afternoon of June 25. Despite the fact that Mr Phillips was obviously very unwell during this period neither doctor took any steps to arrange investigations or treatment. Each was convicted of gross negligence manslaughter and sentenced to 18 months' imprisonment suspended for 2 years. Their appeals were dismissed.

4.5.1.4 R v Sellu

Mr David Sellu was a 66-year-old general surgeon. One of his patients developed abdominal symptoms after routine orthopaedic surgery. Mr Sellu did not make the careful assessment of the patient on the following morning that was required. He failed to operate until 40 hours later, and did not go and see his patient. The patient, Mr Hughes, later died. Mr Sellu was convicted of manslaughter and sentenced to 2½ years' imprisonment. The sentence was not suspended.

4.5.1.5 R v Amaro & Bawa-Garba

Jack Adcock, aged 6, who had Down's syndrome and a heart condition, was admitted to Leicester Royal Infirmary with vomiting and diarrhoea. Amaro, an agency nurse, failed to monitor Jack's condition as he deteriorated. Bawa-Garba, a doctor, stopped providing cardiopulmonary resuscitation as she wrongly thought that Jack was the subject of a do-not-resuscitate order. Both were found guilty of gross negligence manslaughter and given suspended prison sentences. Dr Bawa-Garba's appeal was dismissed.

This is a controversial area. In 1995, the Law Commission concluded that it was wrong that the offence of manslaughter should cover deaths caused both deliberately and those that were involuntary. They proposed creating two new offences: (1) 'reckless killing': committed when someone unreasonably and consciously decides to run the risk of causing death, and does in fact cause death; this offence (which would still carry a maximum life sentence) would rarely be committed by a doctor undertaking medical treatment; and (2) 'killing by gross carelessness', a lesser offence that might be committed by a doctor undertaking medical treatment. The recommendations have not been implemented.

In 2007 a new offence of corporate manslaughter was created. Corporate bodies (including NHS Trusts) commit this offence if the way in which their activities are managed or organized: (a) causes a person's death; and (b) amounts to a gross breach of a relevant duty of care owed by the organization to the deceased. To date only one NHS Trust has so far been prosecuted for this offence. In April 2015 Maidstone & Tunbridge Wells NHS Trust was charged in connection with the death of a 30-year-old primary school teacher who died following a Caesarean section. The two doctors responsible for her care were charged with gross negligence manslaughter. The doctor primarily responsible for the errors returned to his native Pakistan before the trial commenced. The trial judge determined at the end of the prosecution case that neither the hospital nor the remaining doctor had any case to answer. He commented that the facts of the case were 'about as far from a gross negligence manslaughter case as it is possible to be'. The decision demonstrates how difficult it will be for a successful prosecution to be brought under this statute.

KEY POINTS—CRIMINAL LIABILITY

Medical treatment which was 'grossly negligent':
- There is no test for 'gross negligence', but conduct must go beyond simple carelessness, and be regarded as reprehensible.
- This offence carries a maximum sentence of life imprisonment.
- NHS trusts can be accused of corporate manslaughter if their activities are so managed that they cause a person's death.

4.6 Product Liability

On occasions, a patient may suffer an injury or a poor outcome as a result of the equipment or drugs used to treat him or her. If the injury results from inappropriate use of the machinery or being given the wrong drugs, then the general principles of negligence discussed will apply. But what if doctor has done nothing wrong, and the injury is caused by faulty equipment or defective drugs? Sadly, this is all too common in medical practice. In the last few years there have been cases of defective hip replacements, dangerous breast implants, and drugs with unforeseen side effects.

If the equipment was faulty because it was not properly maintained, then the ordinary principles of negligence will apply and the hospital (or possibly its contractors) will be liable. Similarly, if drugs are defective because they have not been stored correctly then again the hospital (or possibly its suppliers) will be liable (in the case of a GP surgery, the claim would be brought against the GP partnership or its contractors). But what if the fault is caused by a manufacturing or design defect? In these circumstances the Consumer Protection Act 1987 will apply.

Under this Act where someone suffers death or personal injury as a result of a 'defect' in a 'product', the producer of the product (or someone who holds himself or herself out as the producer by putting his or her name on the product) will be liable to the injured person. The liability is 'strict', meaning that the injured person does not have to prove negligence. Two other categories of person or company may also be liable: (a) the supplier of the product if he or she fails to identify the producer; and (b) the importer of the product if it was manufactured outside the European Union.

A product will be regarded as having a 'defect' if 'the safety of the product is not such as persons generally are entitled to expect'. This is clearly going to depend on the nature of the product; however, in respect of medical devices and products, the standard expected will be high.

The Act contains a number of defences for producers, of which perhaps the most important is the 'scientific knowledge' defence. It is a defence to show that scientific and technical knowledge at the time of supply of the product was not such that the producer of the product might be expected to have discovered the defect. 'Product' means any goods or electricity and includes products comprised within other products. The word has been given a wide definition by the courts. In A & others v National Blood Authority [2001] 3 All ER 289, 'blood' was held to be a product. So when patients were inadvertently infected with hepatitis C as a result of receiving transfusions with infected blood, the National Blood Authority was liable under the Act.

KEY POINTS—PRODUCT LIABILITY

- A patient may be injured by faulty equipment or defective drugs.
- If the injury results from wrongful use of equipment or drugs, then a claim in negligence can be made.
- If injury results from a manufacturing fault or design defect, then the Consumer Protection Act 1987 applies.
- The producer, supplier, or importer of a product may he held liable.
- A defective product is one where its safety is not what a person is generally entitled to expect.
- The term 'product' is given a wide definition by the courts.
- The 'scientific knowledge' defence by producers allows them to claim the defect was undiscoverable at the time.

4.7 Dealing with Untoward Clinical Incidents

What do you do when it all goes horribly wrong? The first and most obvious piece of advice (with apologies to Douglas Adams) is 'Don't panic'. Fleeing the scene is unlikely to help you or the patient. The immediate priority is to take any necessary clinical steps to help the patient. If that involves contacting your supervising consultant or GP partner, or your senior colleague and confessing all, then that is what you need to do, however embarrassing it may be. What next? First of all, some reassurance:

- It is exceedingly rare for any doctor ever to face a criminal prosecution for a clinical mistake.
- It is most unlikely that an isolated error of judgement or clinical mistake will result in disciplinary action either by the GMC, your employer, or any professional body.
- Even in our increasingly litigious society, most patients with a valid claim do not sue. Injured patients who feel that the doctor and hospital have been honest with them in admitting errors are much less likely to bring proceedings.
- In the event of a valid claim or complaint, other than the inevitable embarrassment of being shown to have made an error, there will be few personal consequences for the clinician.
- The claim will be dealt with by NHS Resolution or your medical defence organization and they will be responsible for all legal costs and damages. If you are working in the NHS, it is unlikely that you will even be a party to the proceedings.

With this in mind, please do not be tempted to cover your tracks either by destroying or falsifying medical records. You may get away with it, but if you do not you will be struck off. Be candid both with your employer (or supervising consultant/GP) and the patient. Write a full account of what happened in the patient's notes. If your hospital has a system for reporting adverse incidents, fill in the relevant form and submit it. Tell your patient (and/or his or her family) what has happened and what you have done to put things right. Patients who later discover they have been misled or kept in the dark are far more likely to sue or make a complaint to the GMC. If you think that a complaint or legal action is likely, contact your defence union at an early stage for advice.

KEY POINTS—UNTOWARD CLINICAL INCIDENTS

- When a clinical error occurs, take any necessary steps to help the patient.
- Contact your supervising consultant/GP or senior colleague.
- Do not cover your tracks by destroying or falsifying medical records.
- Be candid with your employer (or supervising consultant) and the patient.
- Write a full account of what happened in the patient's notes.
- Fill in the hospital's relevant adverse incident form.
- Inform the patient or their relatives.
- Contact your defence union for advice.

4.8 NHS Complaints and Referrals to the GMC

Few doctors will retire at the end of a long career having never been the subject of a complaint. In many cases, the complaint will not be valid. Many patients who are not happy with the outcome of their treatment will unfairly blame their treating doctor. Complaints are an occupational hazard of being a doctor. Patients wishing to complain about doctors have a choice of two routes: a complaint to the NHS or a complaint to the GMC, or both. In theory complaints can also be made to the doctor's Royal College, but in practice this is unusual.

4.8.1 NHS Complaints

Patients are encouraged to resolve any complaint they may have informally with their treating doctor. In most cases this will be the quickest and easiest way both for the doctor and the patient to resolve an issue. However, this will only happen if the doctor is open to such an approach. If you are overly defensive, or simply come across as being unapproachable, then it is more likely the patient will go down the formal route. Under the NHS Constitution, all complaints by patients must be investigated and a response given. The complaint may be about a poor medical outcome, but it could be about many other things, such as:

- a doctor's manner;
- a refusal to agree to a particular treatment;
- a refusal to prescribe a particular drug;
- the speed of treatment or referral.

The complaint may be made directly to the NHS trust, hospital, or practice who provided the treatment or, alternatively, to the clinical commissioning group (CCG) which commissioned it.

All NHS hospitals employ staff, and many general practices nominate a senior staff member, to deal with complaints. How a complaint is investigated will vary between trusts and depend on the nature of the complaint. However, it will almost always involve talking to the clinical staff concerned and getting their account of what happened. It may involve a face-to-face meeting with the patient for an explanation to be given or for the situation to be discussed. It may involve other doctors being asked to comment on the care provided. In some cases, it will involve the hospital or practice instructing a doctor outside the organization to provide an independent clinical opinion. In every case, it will involve the person investigating the complaint reaching a conclusion on whether the complaint is valid, and responding to the patient. In some cases, this will mean making an apology to a patient.

If you find yourself the subject of a complaint, however uncomfortable it may be, try to engage with the process. Putting the shutters up is not going to help resolve the patient's concerns, and may lead to disciplinary action by your employer. Many complaints are rejected. This is sometimes because they are found not to be valid or sometimes because they are too late: complaints should normally be made within 12 months of the incident occurring or the patient becoming aware of it; however, this can be extended if there is a good reason. If the patient is unhappy with the outcome of the complaint he or she can refer the matter to the Health Service Ombudsman, who will conduct his or her own investigation.

KEY POINTS—NHS COMPLAINTS

- Complaints are an occupational hazard of being a doctor.
- Complaints can be made to the NHS, CCG, GMC, or relevant Royal College.
- Under the NHS constitution, all complaints by patients within 12 months must be investigated and a response given.
- NHS trusts vary in how they deal with complaints.
- Most complaints should be dealt with informally by the treating doctor, who needs to engage with the process.
- Patients can appeal to the Health Service Ombudsman if their complaint is not upheld by the trust.

4.8.2 Referral to the GMC

A referral to the GMC is potentially the most serious consequence for a doctor following an unexpected clinical outcome. A referral can be made by anyone; however, it is usually one the following:

- The aggrieved patient or their family.
- The doctor's employer.
- Another doctor or other health professional.
- The doctor's Royal College or other professional body.

The GMC will not normally investigate complaints more than 5 years old. The GMC stresses that it deals with only the most serious complaints, and encourages aggrieved patients (at least in the first instance) to complain to the doctor's local clinic or hospital employer. The GMC deals with a much wider range of complaints about doctors than clinical errors. The sort of cases that may be referred to them include:

- Serious or repeated mistakes in carrying out medical procedures or in diagnosis.
- Failing to examine a patient properly or to respond reasonably to a patient's needs.
- Serious concerns about knowledge of the English language.
- Abuse of professional position (for example, an improper sexual or emotional relationship with a patient or someone close to them).
- Discrimination against patients, colleagues, or anyone else.
- Fraud or dishonesty.
- Breach of patient confidentiality.
- Violence, sexual assault, or indecency.
- Any serious criminal offence.

If a complaint is made to the GMC it will decide (usually within 2 weeks) whether the complaint raises serious concerns about a doctor's fitness to practise. If it does not no further action will be taken. If the GMC decides to investigate, the first step will be to write to the doctor to obtain his or her comments on the complaint. This may be the first time you become aware of the complaint, and you should immediately contact your medical defence organization for help and advice on how to respond. The doctor's comments will be sent to the complainant to give him or her an opportunity for further comment. The case will then be considered by two GMC case workers, one of whom will be medically qualified. They will do one of four things:

- Close the case without taking any further action.
- Issue a warning to the doctor.
- Agree undertakings with the doctor to re-train or to work under supervision.
- Refer the doctor to a medical practitioner's tribunal service for a fitness to practise panel.

If there are immediate concerns that a doctor may pose a risk to patients, the doctor may be referred to an Interim Orders Panel, which can suspend or restrict the doctor's practice while the investigation is ongoing. The fitness-to-practise panel will hold an oral hearing (at which the doctor may wish to be represented by a lawyer) to decide whether any action is required. The panel has a wide range of powers, including:

- Permanently erasing the doctor's name from the medical register.
- Suspending the doctor from the register for a set period.
- Putting conditions on the doctor's registration so that he or she is only allowed to do medical work under certain conditions or restricted to certain areas of practice.

The GMC's 2014 report (dealing with its workload in 2013) revealed the following data, summarized as follows:

- The GMC received 8591 complaints.
- It investigated only 3055.
- The majority of the rest were closed immediately.
- A few were referred to the doctor's employer.
- Of those investigated, almost half (1463) were rejected.
- 118 were closed with advice to the doctor.
- A sanction or warning was given in 185 cases.

- 21 were suspended or erased from the register.
- 1289 were still been investigated in June 2014.
- Of the cases investigated, only about 25% related to clinical competence.

KEY POINTS—REFERRAL TO THE GMC

- A referral to the GMC can be made by a patient, employer, healthcare professional, or other professional body.
- The GMC will not normally investigate complaints older than 5 years.
- The GMC deals with a greater range of complaints than clinical errors.
- The GMC usually decides within 2 weeks if a complaint raises concern about a doctor's fitness to practise.
- Initial outcomes include no action, restriction or suspension, a warning, re-training, or referral to fitness-to-practise panel.
- A fitness-to-practise panel can erase a doctor from the medical register, suspend practice, or place restrictive conditions.

4.9 Pearls and Pitfalls

4.9.1 Pearls

- Even when things have gone wrong patients are unlikely to sue.
- Remember your duty of candour and explain honestly to the patient what has happened.
- Many complaints can be dealt with locally and informally. Precipitants for litigation are patients who feel they have been misled, kept in the dark, abandoned, or lied to.
- Failure to follow a guideline is not automatically negligent but should be capable of logical defence.
- Negligence claims can be difficult to prove, but claims involving lack of consent prior to treatment are more likely to succeed.
- Contemporaneous documentation of dialogue with the patient using shared decision-making can be more useful than a signed consent form.

4.9.2 Pitfalls

- Do not assume that the Bolam test will be upheld or considered in cases of clinical negligence. The Bolitho test may override the opinion of an expert witness.
- Do not assume that NHS indemnity provides cover for all NHS practitioners caring for NHS patients.
- Do not assume that all complaints arise from a poor outcome.

4.10 Further Reading

- GMC. *A Guide for Doctors Referred to the GMC*. Available at: www.gmc-uk.org
- Judicial College. (2017). *Guidelines for the Assessment of General Damages in Personal Injury Cases*, 14th edn. Oxford: Oxford University Press.
- Medical Protection Society. *Clinical Negligence Claims—What to Expect*. Factsheet available at: www.medicalprotection.org

- NHS Shared Decision Making. Available at: http://sdm.rightcare.nhs.uk/
- NHS Choices. *Feedback and complaints about the NHS in England.* www.nhs.uk

4.11 Multiple Choice Questions

✓ Interactive multiple choice questions to test your knowledge on this chapter can be found in the Online appendix at www.oxfordmedicine.com/essentiallegalmatters.

CHAPTER 5

The Coroner

Belinda Cheney, Martin Goddard, and David S. Morris

CHAPTER SUMMARY

The Coroner

The coroner investigates deaths that are unnatural, of unknown cause, occurring in state detention, or due to violence.

The coroner has a statutory role to establish who, how, and where a person has died.

The coroner is an independent judicial officer appointed by the local authority and assisted by officers.

Death Certification and Referral

A doctor must certify the medical cause of death 'to the best of his or her knowledge and belief'.

The format I(a), I(b), I(c) and II is designed to show the chain of causation that led to the death.

When in doubt, the best advice is to call and discuss the death with the Coroner's Office.

Post Mortems

Doctors may attend post-mortem examinations as an interested party.

The family have the right to attend or be represented at the autopsy.

The local pathologist performs most hospital post-mortem examinations.

A coroner may instruct an independent pathologist to avoid concerns over conflict of interest.

The Inquest

When a preliminary investigation does not reveal a natural cause of death the coroner will hold an inquest.

An inquest must be held for all deaths in custody or state detention.

An inquest involving a jury occurs after a death in custody, when it is unnatural, or on the say so of the coroner.

There are several short-form conclusions to an inquest that the coroner declares and their use is encouraged.

The Coroner's Court

You have a duty of candour and you are under oath.

Be prepared, avoid flippancy, overly medical terminology, and remember to offer condolences.

Speak clearly and keep it simple.

Be familiar with all relevant reports.

IMPORTANT CASE LAW

- Longfield Care Homes Limited v H.M. Coroner for Blackburn [2004] EWHC 2467XX
- R (Hurst) v London Northern District Coroner [2007] 2 AC 189
- R (Cash) v HM Coroner for Northamptonshire [2007] EWHC 1354 (Admin) at [49]; [2007] 4 All ER 903
- R v Birmingham Coroner ex parte Benton (1997) 162 JP 807
- R v Poplar Coroner ex parte Thomas 1993 QB 610
- R v HM Coroner for Birmingham and Solihull, ex parte Benton [1997] 8 MEDLR 362
- Canning v HM Coroner for the County of Northampton [2006] EWCA Civ 513
- R v HM Coroner for Exeter and East Devon exp Palmer 1997 EWCA 2951
- HM Coroner for North Humberside ex parte Jamieson [1995] QB
- Touche v Inner North London Coroner [2001] QB 1206, CA

RELEVANT STATUTES AND LEGISLATION

- The Coroners and Justice Act 2009. http://www.legislation.gov.uk
- Coroners (Investigations) Regulations 2013. http://www.legislation.gov.uk
- The Coroners (Inquests) Rules 2013. http://www.legislation.gov.uk
- Chief Coroner's Advice, Guidance and Law Sheets. https://www.judiciary.gov.uk/related-offices-and-bodies/office-chief-coroner/guidance-law-sheets
- Births and Deaths Registration Act 1953. http://www.legislation.gov.uk

PROFESSIONAL GUIDANCE

- When a Death is Reported to the Coroner. https://www.gov.uk/after-a-death/when-a-death-is-reported-to-a-coroner
- Medical Protection Society—Reporting deaths to the Coroner. http://www.medicalprotection.org/docs/default-source/pdfs/factsheet-pdfs/ni-factsheet-pdfs/reporting-deaths-to-coroner.pdf?sfvrsn=8

- General Medical Council—*End of Life Care: Certification, Post-mortems and Referral to a Coroner or Procurator Fiscal*. http://www.gmc-uk.org/guidance/ethical_guidance/end_of_ life_certification_post-mortems_and_referral.asp
- Office for National Statistics' Death Certification Advisory Group, Revised July 2010. *Guidance for Doctors Completing Medical Certificates of Cause of Death in England and Wales*. http://www.gro.gov.uk/images/medcert_july_2010.pdf
- Chief Coroners Guidance 23. https://www.judiciary.gov.uk/publications/ chief-coroner-guidance-no-23-report-of-death
- Chief Coroners Guidance 16 on DoLS. https://www.judiciary.gov.uk/wp-content/ uploads/2013/09/guidance-no-16-dols.pdf
- Courts and Tribunals Judiciary: Office of the Chief Coroner. https://www.judiciary.gov.uk/ related-offices-and-bodies/office-chief-coroner

5.1 The Role of the Coroner

The role of the coroner has been documented since 1194. The coroner's original task was the investigation of sudden death with a view to raising revenue for the king. The revenue element is long gone but the coroner must now investigate:

- Violent or unnatural death
- Deaths of unknown cause
- Deaths that occurred in custody or otherwise in state detention.

It is the coroner's role in such situations to establish who was the person who died, as well as how, when, and where they died.

In the majority of cases 'how' is defined as 'by what means'. In what are known as Article 2 cases 'how' is wider and includes not only the means but the circumstances in which the deceased came by his or her death. As has always been the law, neither a coroner nor a jury may express an opinion on any matters other than the four factual questions, nor can any verdict be framed in such a way as to appear to determine any question of criminal or civil liability. No matter how justified, the coroner has no jurisdiction to investigate unless there is a statutory trigger and no duty to hold an inquest where the investigation has revealed a natural cause of death and there is no related and compelling reason to do so.

The coroner is an independent judicial officer, appointed by the local authority and responsible for investigating deaths in certain circumstances. Despite employment by the local authority, the coroner is responsible to the Crown and any complaints about the coroner will come through the Judicial Complaints Investigation Office (JCIO). There are around 98 senior coroners, some of whom are full-time but all of whom have a number of assistant coroners to undertake the same duties and provide cover when the coroner is unavailable. Administrative support comes from the local authority, the police, or a combination of the two in the form of coroners' officers. These people have responsibilities for: (1) phone contact with doctors, police, and families; (2) preparing paperwork; (3) arranging post-mortem examinations; (4) assisting in investigations by taking and collecting statements; (5) sorting witness expenses; and (6) sending out Regulation 28 letters.

In 2014 there were 223,841 deaths reported to coroners, which represents 45% of all registered deaths. The number of inquests opened was 25,889 (12% of all reported deaths), which showed a 14% reduction since the Coroners and Justice Act 2009 came into force in July 2013. This is largely attributable to no longer needing an inquest when the post mortem reveals a natural cause of death. Post-mortem examinations were ordered in 40% of all cases (89,875 post mortems were held), but there is a drive to reduce these and perform more non-invasive examinations. Since 1995, the percentage of post mortems has steadily decreased, from 61% to 40%. The coroner is, however, entirely reliant on such deaths being reported ordinarily by general practitioners (GPs), hospitals, and the police, and an understanding when there is an obligation to report a death.

KEY POINTS—THE ROLE OF THE CORONER

- The coroner investigates deaths that are unnatural, of unknown cause, occurring in state detention, or due to violence.
- The coroner has a statutory role to establish who, how, and where a person has died.
- The coroner is an independent judicial officer appointed by the local authority and assisted by officers.
- If a post mortem reveals a natural cause of death, there is no need for a coroner's inquest.

5.2 Issuing a Medical Certificate of the Cause of Death

Fifty-five per cent of deaths will not require any notification to the coroner, in which case a medical certificate as to the cause of death (MCCD) can be issued by the deceased's GP or a doctor in the treating hospital and the death registered. The MCCD specifies the actual cause of death and should not be confused with the confirmation of death certificate, which confirms that the death has taken place. A medical cause of death must be given. Registered medical practitioners can properly issue a MCCD if:

- They are satisfied that they can state the correct cause of death (which assumes some prior knowledge of the person).
- The cause of death is entirely natural.
- They have treated the deceased in his or her last illness and have seen him or her within 14 days.

When issuing a certificate, a doctor must certify the cause of death 'to the best of his or her knowledge and belief'. This is not to be taken to read 'beyond reasonable doubt'. The test is a great deal less stringent, which avoids unnecessary and quite possibly fruitless post-mortem examinations when common sense should prevail. If a 94-year-old with multiple comorbidities dies, it is acceptable to many coroners to provide as a cause of death 'old age'.

The format used is I(a), I(b), I(c), and possibly even I(d) and II. It is designed to show the chain of causation that led away from death. I(a) refers to the disease or condition leading directly to death; I(b), any other disease or condition that led to the immediate cause of death; and I(c) to any further link in the chain of causation. Example: *I(a). cardiac failure; I(b). myocardial infarction; I(c). coronary atherosclerosis.* There is no legal requirement that a doctor completing a MCCD need go any further than paragraph I(a). Thus *I(a). myocardial infarction* is a perfectly adequate cause of death provided that there is no supervening unnatural cause. However, a fully completed medical certificate of the fact of death takes the following form:

I(a) The disease or condition directly leading to death.

I(b) Other disease or condition, if any, leading to I(a).

I(c) Other disease or condition, if any, leading to I(b).

II Other significant conditions *contributing to the death* but not related to the disease or condition causing it.

With regard to part II, it is worth considering here the case of Longfield Care Homes Limited v H.M. Coroner for Blackburn [2004] EWHC 2467. Mitting J. quoted the post-mortem report, which stated: 'In my opinion the cause of death was: I(a). Bronchopneumonia, I(b). Dementia, II. Traumatic fractures to pelvis and elbow. The cause of death is bronchopneumonia which is a recognised complication of dementing mental states. It is likely the pneumonia was present before the accident and it is likely that the pneumonia would have caused death in spite of the accident. The accident caused fractures to the pelvis and elbow, but the amount of blood loss and trauma is not sufficient to have caused death. It may however have contributed by inducing further stress and immobility, which could have further exacerbated the pneumonic process'. The learned judge made clear in his judgment that, if the fractures were causally related to the pneumonia, they should have been recorded in the first part of the certificate because only significant conditions contributing to death but not related to the disease or condition causing it should appear under part II.

An example of a medical certificate correctly completed might include the following conditions: I(a). *myocardial infarction;* I(b). *ischaemic heart disease;* II. *cancer of the bowel.* In such a case, the patient may have been in a sufficiently weakened condition as a result of the bowel cancer so as not to survive the heart attack, which might otherwise have been survivable. The bowel cancer, however, was not related to the disease or condition in part I and is thus correctly recorded under part II. Once the MCCD is complete and when the doctor is not under any obligation to notify the coroner of the death he or she will ensure the MCCD is sent to the Registrar of Deaths and this is usually achieved by giving it to the relatives.

KEY POINTS—ISSUING A MEDICAL CERTIFICATE OF THE CAUSE OF DEATH (MCCD)

- Fifty-five per cent of deaths will not require any notification to the coroner but, when in doubt, report it.
- A doctor must certify the medical cause of death 'to the best of his or her knowledge and belief'.
- The format I(a), I(b), I(c), and II is designed to show the chain of causation which led to the death.
- Part II records other significant conditions that have contributed to the death but are not related to the disease or condition causing it.
- Contributing factors can result in an inquest, therefore care should be taken to consider carefully what is recorded.
- The MCCD is sent to the Registrar of Deaths, usually by giving it to the relatives.

5.3 When Should a Death Be Reported?

Although there is no statutory obligation on a doctor to report a death to the coroner, the practice and expectation is that any death a doctor judges would need to be referred to the coroner should be. The Chief Coroner has issued guidance no. 23 on referrals (Box 5.1). There is no single list of what deaths are reportable nor any apparent consensus on what is and is not reportable amongst coroners (many of whom appear to produce their own guidance to local hospital trusts), but Box 5.1 contains a list of deaths that would appear to provide a guide for what is reportable.

The coroner is very reliant on doctors to report deaths and there is no doubt that underreporting of deaths to the coroner has significant implications for the identification and investigation of preventable deaths. No example could be more stark than that of Dr Harold Shipman. He managed to murder 215 patients, many of whose deaths were not reported to the coroner. The public inquiry that followed made several recommendations for changes to the coronial system, some of which have been adopted and others not. When in doubt, the best advice is to call and discuss the death with the Coroner's Office. That way you can never be criticized; the decision rests with the coroner whether to make further inquiries or to request a post mortem.

Box 5.1 Reasons to Refer a Death to the Coroner

- No doctor attended the deceased during his or her last illness
- Although a doctor attended during the last illness, the deceased had not been seen in the 14 days before death or after death
- The cause of death appears to be unknown
- The death was sudden or unexpected
- The death cannot readily be certified as being due to natural causes
- The death was due to violence or neglect
- The death was in other suspicious circumstances
- The death occurred or the illness arose in, or shortly after, prison, police custody, or other state detention
- The death may be linked to an accident, whenever it occurred
- The death occurred during an operation or before recovery from the effects of an anaesthetic
- The death may be related to a medical procedure or treatment
- The death may be due to lack of medical care
- The death occurred within 24 hours of admission to hospital (unless the admission was solely for terminal care)
- The death occurred at work or was due to industrial disease or poisoning
- The death is linked with an abortion

The referral of a death to the coroner should be viewed as a neutral act—it implies no criticism of or concern over the care delivered but allows discussion of the case with the coroner or their officer. It should be remembered that these people are not medically qualified and are dependent on the veracity of the information given. This will, however, change with the introduction of the medical examiner system, the details of which are yet to be finalized. The duty of candour that applies to patients and their relatives can equally be applied to the coroner.

KEY POINTS—WHEN SHOULD A DEATH BE REPORTED?

- There is no statutory obligation on a doctor to report a death to the coroner.
- When in doubt, the best advice is to call and discuss the death with the Coroner's Office.
- There is no single list of what deaths are reportable, with many coroners issuing their own guidance to local hospital trusts.
- The referral of a death to the coroner should be viewed as a neutral act.
- All deaths of individuals subject to deprivation of liberty authorizations must be referred to the Coroner's Office.

5.4 Hospital Deaths

In hospital deaths following interventions or procedures, several considerations must be taken into account.

5.4.1 Procedural Deaths

Where death occurs during a procedure, an investigation will often be required. It will not necessarily lead to an inquest, e.g. where the death is due to the severity of the underlying natural condition or a complication arising from the procedure itself. In the case of coronary intervention for an acute ST elevation myocardial infarct, a cardiac arrhythmia may be considered natural; however, the development of an acute coronary dissection or rupture would be a procedural death, albeit a recognized complication and risk.

5.4.2 Postprocedural Deaths

These are those that are related to the operation site. In the case of a bowel resection for carcinoma with an anastomotic leak, the questions that might arise are related to the correctness of the initial procedure, whether the complication was identified in a timely manner, and whether appropriate and timely treatment was given. For example, there is a recognized anastomotic leak rate, but consideration might need to be given to an individual's or unit's complication rate against a benchmark. Other complications may be related to organ systems unrelated to the operative site. Often there may be pre-existing morbidities that should be taken into consideration in assessing the risk to the patient. Thus, the development of a chest infection in a patient with chronic obstructive pulmonary disease might be expected, but again should be identified and treated.

5.4.3 Suspicious Deaths

On occasions, patients are admitted and there are suspicions of violence, trauma, or neglect. In all cases these should be reported to the appropriate bodies prior to death. However, particularly in cases where the police may be involved, a request must be made to the laboratory to store blood samples taken at admission as they may form an important part of the evidence for any subsequent investigation. Likewise, if an accident victim arrives into hospital after a road traffic accident, blood samples should be kept for some time if there is a risk they will die when a blood drug or alcohol level may be relevant.

KEY POINTS—HOSPITAL DEATHS

- Deaths occurring during a procedure will almost always require investigation.
- The cause of death from an underlying condition or from a complication of a procedure needs to be decided.
- Deaths due to violence, trauma, or neglect need reporting to the appropriate bodies.
- Blood samples should be kept if the death could be related to substance misuse.

5.5 Attending a Post Mortem

Any interested party can have a doctor represent them at a post mortem. Doctors may also attend post-mortem examinations as an interested party. Interested party status is usually invited where the conduct of an individual may be called into question, i.e. if the doctor may be criticized. Other doctors and medical students can attend a post mortem, but only with the coroner's permission. It should be noted that the family have the right to attend or be represented at the autopsy, although this is an unusual event. Most post-mortem examinations undertaken on hospital deaths are performed by the local pathologist, which allows good communication with the clinical team. However, the coroner may instruct an independent pathologist not attached to the hospital to avoid any concerns over conflict of interest, and this is becoming increasingly the case.

Second post-mortem examinations are occasionally undertaken. These most commonly occur in the setting of road traffic deaths or possible murders, where a prosecution may be considered and an independent report is required for the defence. Occasionally, a hospital may instruct a second examination by an independent pathologist where the initial findings may lead to a claim against the hospital and they potentially contest the findings. Families may also seek a second examination at their own expense, particularly if they consider a claim against the hospital, although this is rare. In all cases, whilst the body remains under the coroner's jurisdiction, the coroner's permission to attend a post mortem will need to be sought.

The post-mortem report is a medicolegal document produced for the coroner but which is disclosed to the family. Post-mortem reports are often written in a format that may be difficult to understand for the lay person, so families will be advised to discuss the findings with their GP or the hospital. The post-mortem findings are a description of the observations of a single pathologist and with any observational investigation, subject to variations. They may be further refined by the use of histology of tissue samples and microbiological investigations. Reproducibility is generally good; however, part of the role of the pathologist is to interpret the findings together with the clinical information and link them to form a narrative conclusion and ultimately a cause of death. Here, the support of clinical colleagues is often helpful; however, pathologists undertake their role on behalf of the coroner and not the hospital, and they must remain objective to avoid compromising their duty to the coroner. The cause of death is concluded in Office of Population Censuses and Surveys (OPCS) format (*Classification of Interventions and Procedures*), which is often limiting in complex hospital cases.

KEY POINTS—ATTENDING A POST MORTEM

- Doctors may attend post-mortem examinations as an interested party.
- The family have the right to attend or be represented at the autopsy.
- Most hospital post-mortem examinations are performed by the local pathologist.
- A coroner may instruct an independent pathologist to avoid concerns over conflict of interest.
- When a legal claim is being considered, a second post mortem can be undertaken.
- The post-mortem report is a medicolegal document produced for the coroner, although the family are entitled to disclosure.

5.6 Natural and Unnatural Death

The coroner has a duty to conduct an investigation where there is reason to suspect the deceased died from violent or unnatural death, an unknown cause of death (COD), or they died in custody or otherwise in state detention, e.g. under a section of the Mental Health Act, or in an immigration detention centre. Put another way, the duty to investigate is triggered when it appears the death is unnatural.

5.6.1 Definition of Unnatural Death

There is no definition of a natural death, but it is commonly thought to be one where death is caused by the natural progression of a natural illness which is not contributed to, in any degree, by human intervention. Where someone has a pre-existing medical condition, the coroner must decide whether the death was caused by the illness itself or by some unnatural intervention which rendered that condition fatal in circumstances where death would not normally be expected.

Equally, there is no definition of an unnatural death. Historically, it involves suspicion of foul play or some wrongdoing. A recognized complication of a necessary medical procedure does not make a death unnatural. At para 5.74 Jervis says: 'A culpable failure to prevent death from natural causes is an unnatural death; but a non-culpable failure is not. Medical treatment for non-potentially fatal conditions which cause death, will continue to be unnatural. However, appropriate treatment for an otherwise fatal condition resulting in a recognised complication leading to death will not.'.

The following are illustrative examples of some case law where the definition of natural and unnatural death is considered.

5.6.1.1 R v Poplar Coroner ex parte Thomas 1993 QB 610

The late arrival of an ambulance in a patient suffering from an asthmatic attack did not make the death unnatural. Per Simon Brown LJ unnatural is to be given the normal definition; ' ... cases may well arise where human fault can and properly should turn a natural death into an unnatural one'.

5.6.1.2 R v HM Coroner for Birmingham and Solihull, ex parte Benton [1997] 8 MEDLR 362

'Where a person is suffering from a potentially fatal condition and medical intervention does no more than fail to prevent the death, the correct verdict is natural causes even if medical treatment was wrong. A finding of natural causes is not in any way a finding that there was no fault.'

5.6.1.3 R (Touche) v Inner North London Coroner [2001] QB 1206

Death becomes unnatural where it was wholly unexpected and would not have occurred but for some culpable human failing.

5.6.1.4 Canning v HM Coroner for the County of Northampton [2006] EWCA Civ 513

If there is a prima facie case for suspecting some culpable human failure leading to the death, then an inquest should be held.

5.6.1.5 R v HM Coroner for Exeter and East Devon ex parte Palmer 1997 EWCA 2951

Causation test. It is necessary to show the act caused the death in the sense that it more than minimally, negligibly, or trivially contributed to the death.

5.6.2 Death Following Medical Interventions

Death from complications following necessary and appropriately conducted medical procedures does not usually require an inquest. For example, a patient undergoes bowel resection for a malignant tumour; surgery is appropriately carried out yet the patient develops a paralytic ileus postoperatively—a recognized complication. The ileus is appropriately treated but the patient dies. Provided there are no allegations of substandard treatment or neglect that contributed to death, this is not an unnatural death. It starts with a naturally occurring disease process, which runs its course with appropriate and necessary medical intervention. The operation is necessary to save the life of the patient. It carries a known risk, which unfortunately matures. The cancer led to the operation, which led to the risk, which led to the death. The operation and postoperative care being exemplary, established medical practices, there is no break in the chain of causation. Someone who dies from a recognized complication of necessary medical treatment appropriately given for a condition which would otherwise kill him or her is not unnatural. Some coroners would open an investigation if the family raise concerns, and obtain full reports from the clinicians to assess whether an inquest is necessary. If those concerns have validity, there may be a benefit to having an inquest. However, not all family concerns do have validity, and it may be worth exploring in a meeting with the clinicians and the hospital if matters can be resolved at a preliminary stage. Although coroners are always mindful of the interests of the bereaved, their role is not to advocate for them.

Reaching consistent conclusions amongst coroners on what is and is not natural is fraught. A 1999 study showed that, in 16 cases reviewed by 64 coroners, there was consistency in only two. The conclusion was that, 'variation between coroners in whether or not to hold an inquest, and the verdict arrived at, reflect the lack of a definition for natural causes, together with differences in the personal attitudes of each coroner'. This has not changed. Debate continues to rage among coroners on the need to hold an inquest when a fractured neck of femur occurs, is operated on, and at some time later the patient dies of pneumonia. Debate ranges too on the scope of many inquiries in cases of patients with mental health involvement—how far back should the inquiry go. Do not be afraid to challenge the scope of an investigation, but bear in mind the final decision lies with the coroner.

5.6.3 Death from Specific Causes

5.6.3.1 Neglect

If there is reason to suspect that neglect, as defined in HM Coroner for North Humberside ex parte Jamieson [1995] QB, contributed to the death, then the death cannot be considered natural. Neglect requires a gross failure to provide the very basics of life, such as nourishment, liquid, warmth, or medicine to someone in a dependent position. There must be a clear connection between the neglect and the cause of death. Neglect is unlikely to be a verdict in its own right and is likely to be a contributing factor towards another cause of death (for example, 'natural causes contributed to by neglect'). Neglect conclusions are quite rare and, in a medical context, are confined usually to cases where an individual has not been provided with even basic medical attention.

5.6.3.2 Medical Mismanagement

A death, although apparently due to natural causes, will not be so if the death was wholly unexpected and may have resulted from a culpable human failure: Touche v Inner North London Coroner [2001] QB 1206, CA.

5.6.3.3 Alcohol

In the past, it was always the case that, if a person died from the chronic effects of alcohol (for instance, alcoholic cirrhosis, hepatic steatosis, etc.), the death was considered natural. Arguably, the new conclusion of 'alcohol-related' has changed this situation and it will be for individual coroners to reach their own conclusion on this point.

5.6.3.4 Hypothermia

Deaths due to hypothermia or exposure will normally be considered unnatural. However, if it is the case that the body's ability to regulate its temperature has diminished owing, for example, to old age, then such a death may on occasion be naturally occurring.

5.6.3.5 Fractured Neck of Femur

If a traumatic fractured neck of femur appears in either part I or part II of a correctly completed MCCD, then the death cannot be regarded as natural. A fall versus a collapse will always be difficult, but there are clues, such as the way someone was found, their underlying medical condition, previous falls, etc. We could say that, when an old lady has severe osteoporosis and she has what is medically termed a 'pathological fracture', which is consequent upon ordinary stress, and the fracture leads to her death, this would be a natural death. When, however, a similar osteoporotic old lady clearly falls and fractures her femur, this is not a natural death.

However, not all doctors who suggest fractured neck of femur as a contributory cause under part II are correct in so doing. It is necessary to examine the full circumstances of the death to see whether the fracture has in fact played a material part in the death. Thus, the condition of the patient before the fracture needs to be considered, as does the length of time between the fall and fracture and the death. It is to be noted that, except in the case of a pathological fracture, the presence or absence of osteoporosis is not relevant. A traumatic fracture that has a causal effect on death is unnatural whether the patient's bones were robustly strong or fragile.

5.6.3.6 Subdural Haemorrhage

In one view these are always traumatic in origin albeit that in the elderly the trauma may be comparatively trivial and in some cases not even recognized. Some believe the condition of subdural haemorrhage is always due to trauma and there is probably no such entity as spontaneous subdural haematoma.

5.6.4 Postoperative Deaths

The case of Benton (R v Birmingham Coroner ex parte Benton (1997) 162 JP 807) would suggest that it is necessary to look at the whole picture regarding the patient's illness. The argument goes that a person suffering from a bowel obstruction due to bowel cancer who dies after an operation, who would have died around the same time as a result of the obstruction had the obstruction not been surgically removed cannot in reality be said to have died as a consequence of the operation but to have died from the bowel cancer. The operation in these circumstances is said to have failed to save the patient rather than causing the patient's death. Of course, if there has been some element of medical mismanagement, the situation may be different.

The alternative view is that if the patient dies postoperatively from the same condition that they were suffering from in the first place and about the same time as they would have done had the operation not taken place, then that is a naturally occurring death, but that if any other condition supervenes so as to cause the death, whether or not there has been any medical mismanagement (postoperative sepsis for instance), then the death cannot be considered as naturally occurring but due to misadventure.

5.6.5 Preliminary Investigation

The coroner can make whatever enquiries seem necessary to decide whether there is a duty to investigate, and this can include talking to the family, GP, treating hospital, obtaining medical notes, or arranging for a post-mortem examination. What may appear at first as an unknown cause of death can be resolved once the results of the post-mortem examination and/or the deceased's past medical history and/or circumstances are known. If the cause of death is established as being 'natural' without the need for a post mortem, then the matter can be disposed of as requiring no further action. Alternatively, a 100A form can be used. If a post mortem is required and the death is deemed natural then a 100B form can be used to register the death.

If the post-mortem examination is inconclusive and it will take time to get the results of toxicology or histology or to make further inquiries, then a formal investigation will be opened and notified. This next stage of the investigation can take place without opening an inquest. This is new and has decreased the number of inquests and 'natural causes' conclusions substantially. Not only may the inquiries, including the post-mortem examination, be conducted at the preliminary stage without triggering the need to commence a formal investigation, the body can also be released for burial and cremation.

Where the death is deemed natural, there is ordinarily no need to investigate further unless the coroner considers it necessary to do so. By way of example—a family may allege neglect, which could have caused or contributed to the death by natural causes. If this complaint appears to have validity the coroner could investigate further and hold an inquest.

KEY POINTS—NATURAL AND UNNATURAL DEATH

- A coroner must investigate death due to violence, unknown cause, unnatural death, or death in custody.
- There is no definition of an unnatural death, but it usually involves suspicion of foul play or some wrongdoing.
- A recognized medical complication does not make the death unnatural.

- Death from complications following necessary and appropriately conducted medical procedures does not usually require an inquest.
- Death from neglect, medical mismanagement, alcohol poisoning, hypothermia, subdural haematomas, and limb fractures is considered unnatural.
- A coroner cannot express a verdict in such a way as to appear to determine criminal or civil liability.
- The coroner can make whatever enquiries necessary to decide whether there is a duty to investigate.

5.7 The Coroner's Inquest

When a preliminary investigation does not reveal a natural cause of death and/or further tests are required, e.g. toxicology or histology, the coroner will formally open 'an investigation'. At this stage the coroner asks for more information from those involved in the care of the deceased. If it is proven that the deceased died from natural causes, then the investigation can be discontinued. When the cause of death is unnatural, unknown, occurred in custody or state detention, or is due to violence, the coroner must proceed to hold an inquest. An inquest is mandatory for all deaths in custody or state detention. Juries will not be needed if the deceased died from natural causes.

5.7.1 Inquest Conclusions

At the end of an inquest, the coroner (or jury) completes a form entitled the 'Record of an Inquest', which documents the who, how, where, and when determinations. A conclusion (which used to be called a verdict) is then reached. Possible short-form conclusions include:

- Accident or misadventure
- Alcohol-/drug-related
- Industrial disease—most commonly refers to mesothelioma
- Lawful killing—e.g. police shooting of armed assailant
- Unlawful killing
- Natural causes
- Open—where it is impossible to determine what happened and no other conclusion is possible
- Road traffic collision
- Stillbirth
- Suicide—the coroner or jury must be satisfied beyond reasonable doubt that the deceased acted in a manner by which he or she intended to take his or her own life.

There also remains the option of leaving a narrative conclusion. The Chief Coroner issued guidance encouraging coroners to use short-form conclusions. Where coroners opt for a narrative conclusion this should be a brief, neutral, factual statement, which does not express any judgement or opinion.

5.7.2 Reports to Prevent Future Deaths

Reports to prevent future deaths (PFDs—formerly known as Rule 43 letters) are now mandatory, reflecting the importance of the coroner's role in public safety over and above deciding how somebody came by their death. Nevertheless, PFDs are ancillary to the inquest procedure and not its main purpose. A jury has no role in making riders or recommendations that could influence the writing or content of a PFD. The duty to write such a letter arises where:

- A coroner has been conducting an investigation into a death.
- Anything revealed by the investigation gives rise to a concern that circumstances creating a risk of other deaths will occur, or will continue to exist, in the future.
- In the coroner's opinion, action should be taken to prevent the occurrence or continuation of such circumstances, or to eliminate or reduce the risk of death created by such circumstances.

Under the old rules the coroner could only write in relation to matters that arose from the evidence given at the inquest. Now a PFD may address concerns arising from anything revealed in the investigation, which is wider power than under the previous Coroner's Rules. It allows a coroner to write a PFD even before the inquest is concluded. However, the coroner must first have considered all relevant matters, which will include consideration of all documents, evidence, and information that may be relevant. Ordinarily, a PFD will follow the inquest unless there is sufficient evidence revealed by the investigation to warrant earlier action.

The coroner must address a PFD to a person who the coroner thinks may have power to take action. The PFD, which will be delivered in a form prescribed by the Chief Coroner, must rehearse the basic facts, state the medical cause of death, the conclusion of the inquest, the coroner's concerns, and in 'neutral and non-contentious terms' the factual basis for those concerns. The coroner then states the opinion that action should be taken to prevent future deaths. The coroner does not suggest what action should be taken but leaves that to whomever the PFD is addressed. The PFD is not restricted to matters that the coroner has determined at the inquest are either causative or potentially causative. For example, if it is revealed during the course of the investigation that a particular type of drug causes an allergic reaction in some patients which could be fatal, the coroner could write a PFD accordingly despite the deceased in this instant case having died from something wholly unrelated.

The Chief Coroner has issued guidance on the writing of PFDs. This provides that:

- Coroners should be careful, particularly when reporting about something specific, to base their report on clear evidence at the inquest or on clear information during the investigation, to express clearly and simply what that information or evidence is, and to ensure that a bereaved family's expectations are not raised unrealistically.
- Reports should not apportion blame, be defamatory, prejudice law enforcement action or the administration of justice, affect national security, put anyone's safety at risk, or breach data protection, for example, by naming children or breaching medical confidentiality.
- Coroners should not make any other observations of any kind, however well intentioned, outside the scope of the report. Such observations are an expression of opinion wider than is permissible.[1]

The PFD must be copied to various people, including the Chief Coroner. The person receiving the PFD must respond in writing within 56 days of the date on which it was sent. The response must: (a) contain details of action that has been or is proposed to be taken and set out a timetable for this; or (b) explain why no action is proposed. The coroner must copy the response to the Chief Coroner and may sent it to any other person who may find it useful or of interest. The Chief Coroner may publish a summary of the response and may also send a copy to anyone else who may find it useful or of interest.

[1] Reproduced from Guidance no. 5 reports to prevent future deaths. Crown copyright (2016), contains public sector information licensed under the Open Government Licence v3.0 (http://www.nationalarchives.gov.uk/doc/open-government-licence/version/3/)

KEY POINTS—THE CORONER'S INQUEST

- When a preliminary investigation does not reveal a natural cause of death the coroner will hold an inquest.
- An inquest must be held for all deaths in custody or state detention.
- An inquest involving a jury occurs after a death in custody, when it is unnatural, or on the say so of the coroner.
- There are several short-form conclusions to an inquest that the coroner declares and their use is encouraged.
- A narrative conclusion should be brief, neutral, and factual and not express any judgement or opinion.
- A Coroner may write a report to prevent future deaths (PFD) if he or she believes there is a risk of similar deaths occurring.
- The recipient of the PFD must respond to the coroner with an action plan or reason for no action within 56 days.

5.8 Writing Reports for the Coroner

If you have been asked to write a statement for the coroner, remember that the purpose of the inquest is to answer four factual questions—who was the person who died, how, when, and where did he or she die. It is not a review of the totality of the medical care throughout the life of a patient. If they die from a subdural haemorrhage sustained after a fall in hospital no one needs to know about treatment for diabetic ulcers unless these predisposed the patient to fall.

You may well be assisted in writing your statement by the in-house legal team or external solicitors, but it is best to 'own' your report as you will be the one who may be called to give evidence based on it. Use the first person and spell out what you did, why, when, with whom you communicated, and about what—e.g. discussions with the patient, handing over to colleagues, keeping relatives informed. Where referring to others use their names and job titles where possible. The more clear and unequivocal your information is, the less likely is it that you will be called to give evidence. It is usually only the clinicians most involved who will be called. In a hospital death, you might expect the surgeon for a surgical death or the intensivist for an intensive treatment unit (ITU) death to be called to give evidence.

Start by saying who you are, what your qualifications are, what contact you had with the patient, and over what period. Sometimes you will be the most relevant professional involved in the care of the patient, in which case you may remember them; at other times you will be substantially peripheral, in which case you will be reliant on the notes. Either way, ensure you refer to what is in *your* recollection and what comes from the notes. This is a good reminder that notes should be as accurate and contemporaneous as possible! Your report should be a detailed factual account of *your* involvement with the patient. Unless you have been asked to do an overview of all the care received, you should detail your personal involvement rather than that of colleagues when you were not involved and who may well be producing their own reports. Do not criticize others. You are being asked for a factual account and not your opinion.

Recall that you have a duty of candour. If you hold your hand up to any mistakes or treatment that could have been better provided or in a more timely manner or an intervention not taken that would have prevented death or prolonged life—say so. Coroners (and, we hope, families) know that medical professionals do their best but make mistakes, and we have sympathy for those who take responsibility rather than being defensive and aggressive. Never bury or destroy adverse documents. If discovered doing so, your credibility will be in tatters and the coroner may feel compelled to refer you to the General Medical Council (GMC).

Try and write the report for a reasonably intelligent lay person—the majority of coroners now are legally rather than medically qualified; do not assume knowledge of the case nor any medical knowledge, and avoid medical jargon and abbreviations. Even if the coroner has good medical knowledge, the chances are that the families will not, but a copy of your report will normally be disclosed to the family. Spell out what particular conditions are, and if medication is referred put a brief description in parentheses of what it is used for, e.g. mirtazapine (antidepressant), warfarin (anticoagulant).

Organize your report chronologically with numbered paragraphs for ease of reference. Check your spelling, punctuation, and grammar, sign and date the report. A completed report needs to be sufficiently detailed, clear, objective, honest, and factual. Some cases will be long and complex with reports that are likewise, but many can be done quickly, e.g. for deprivation of liberty safeguards, domestic falls, histologically diagnosed mesothelioma. Remember that your report is likely to be disclosed and could well end up in the hands of lawyers for the interested parties or the GMC.

5.8.1 Psychiatric Reports

It is likely that you are writing this report because a patient has committed suicide in hospital or in the community. In rare circumstances, you may also be asked to write a report when someone has died of natural causes. Your report for the coroner is not the same as a discharge summary nor a tribunal report so do not be tempted to cut and paste to save time. If the patient has hanged himself or herself, the coroner will not be greatly aided by details of risks he or she presented to others in the past. Historical information generally will be less relevant than the events leading to the death. You should provide a brief summary of past medical and psychiatric history only, especially if your knowledge comes from previous reports and you had no involvement on this occasion. Think hard about the purpose of the inquest and what is being asked of you. If in doubt, seek clarification. Ask the coroner to set out what it is that he or she wants from you. However, this unfortunately lacks consistency and varies greatly. Ask if there are any specific questions the coroner would like you to address.

KEY POINTS—WRITING REPORTS FOR THE CORONER

- Organize your report chronologically and number paragraphs for ease of reference.
- Start by saying who you are, what your qualifications are, what contact you had with the patient, and over what period.
- Use the first person and spell out what you did, why, when, with whom you communicated, and about what.
- Where referring to others use their names and job titles where possible.
- The more clear and unequivocal your information is the less likely you will be called to give evidence.
- Your report should be a detailed factual account of your involvement with the patient.
- Your report and evidence should be devoid of opinion.
- You have a duty of candour so never bury or destroy adverse documents.
- Try and write the report for a reasonably intelligent lay person without medical jargon and abbreviations.

5.9 Attending and Giving Evidence at the Coroner's Court

When called to the Coroner's Court, remember that you are representing your profession. Your duty of candour means you must be honest even if you have made a mistake. You are under oath. Someone's relative has died and they will want answers. In the first place, answer in a way that someone not medically qualified but of average intelligence could understand. In representing your evidence, you should stick to the facts of the case and, if asked to do so, justify your decisions. Be prepared, avoid flippancy, overly medical terminology, and remember to offer condolences. You should always read the statement you made before going to court and, if possible, look at any contemporaneous notes you made.

Speak clearly and slowly, make sure you can be heard, watch the pen/typing of the coroner because he or she is likely to be trying to take notes. Medical witnesses can speak very quickly and in complex terms, so keep it simple. Everyone will understand if you are nervous—it is not easy appearing in this forum and facing a family filled with grief. Nevertheless, it is understood that doctors do work in difficult environments and must make difficult judgement calls. It is your ability to justify the decision at the time in the circumstances for the patient that matters.

In the event of a serious untoward incident, make sure you are familiar with the report and recommendations. This will inform the areas that you may be questioned about. Admitting that you might have done things better or differently, if this is the case, will often diffuse a situation entirely and does not necessarily admit liability but demonstrates the benefits of hindsight, reflection, and learning. In any event, it is likely that you will have discussed your position with the in-house legal team and possibly their external lawyers. If you consider that there is any possibility of personal liability or criticism, inform your insurers, who may recommend separate legal representation. Do not forget that families often use the inquest as a dress rehearsal for civil action, so protect yourself if you think you are vulnerable.

KEY POINTS—ATTENDING AND GIVING EVIDENCE AT THE CORONER'S COURT

- You are representing your profession.
- You have a duty of candour and you are under oath.
- Be prepared, avoid flippancy, overly medical terminology, and remember to offer condolences.
- Speak clearly and keep it simple.
- Be familiar with all relevant reports.

5.10 Pearls and Pitfalls

5.10.1 Pearls

- When giving evidence in a Coroner's Court, be prepared, avoid flippancy, overly medical terminology, and remember to offer condolences.
- When in doubt about the cause of death, refer a case to the coroner.
- Alert your defence union if you are concerned about your involvement in a case reported to the coroner.
- Respond in a timely fashion to all inquiries from the Coroner's Officers.

5.10.2 Pitfalls

- Destroying documents or being less than truthful with the coroner will result in serious professional consequences. Remember, you have a duty of candour when things go wrong.
- A badly written report for the Coroner's Court will likely prolong proceedings for the family involved. Get help from more senior colleagues.

- Lack of compliance with the coroner's rules on reporting deaths and issuing medical certificates as to the cause of death can have adverse professional consequences.

5.11 Further Reading

- Charles, A. et al. *Under-Reporting of Deaths to the Coroner by Doctors: a Retrospective Review of Deaths in Two Hospitals in Melbourne, Australia.* http://dx.doi.org/10.1093/intqhc/mzm013 232–236 First published online: 6 June 2007.
- Dorries, C. (2014). *Coroners' Courts: A Guide to Law and Practice,* 3rd edn. Oxford: Oxford University Press.
- Knight, B. (1991). *Forensic Pathology.* London: Edward Arnold, a division of Hodder and Stoughton, p. 173.
- Matthews, P. (2014). *Jervis on Coroners,* 13th edn. Andover: Sweet & Maxwell.
- Roberts, I., Gorodkin, L., Benbow, E. (2000). What is a natural cause of death? A survey of how coroners in England and Wales approach borderline cases. *Journal of Clinical Pathology* **53**, 367–73.

5.12 Multiple Choice Questions

✅ Interactive multiple choice questions to test your knowledge on this chapter can be found in the Online appendix at www.oxfordmedicine.com/essentiallegalmatters.

CHAPTER 6

End of Life

Zoë Fritz

CONTENTS

CHAPTER SUMMARY

Capacity and Refusal of Treatment

A capacitous patient can request for treatments—even life-sustaining ones—to be withheld or withdrawn; they can document their desires not to have certain treatments in a written 'advance decision to refuse treatment' or by appointing a 'lasting power of attorney for health and welfare' in England and Wales, or 'power of attorney' in Scotland or Northern Ireland. The right to refuse life-sustaining treatments extends to pregnant women refusing treatment that might save the unborn child.

Best Interests and Incapacity

In a patient lacking capacity treatments can be withheld or withdrawn if it is considered that continuing with those treatments is not in the 'best interests' of the patient. The concept of best interests is laid out in the Mental Capacity Act. To determine best interests, the clinician must consult with those close to the patient and consider the patient's welfare in the widest sense.

Denial of Life-Sustaining Treatment

In making a decision not to offer potentially life-sustaining treatments (for example, attempted cardiopulmonary resuscitation), there is a legal duty to consult with patients, or, where they lack capacity, those close to them. Not to do so is to deprive them of the ability to ask questions and/or to seek a second opinion, and is in breach of their human rights.

Double Effect, Suicide, and Euthanasia

It is illegal to commit any act where the primary intention is to hasten death; the 'doctrine of double effect', however, means that it is legal to treat a symptom even if there is a possible secondary effect of shortening life. Assisting suicide and euthanasia are illegal in all circumstances.

IMPORTANT CASE LAW

- Re F (Mental Patient: Sterilisation) [1990] 2 AC 1
- Airedale NHS Trust v Bland [1993] 1 All ER 821
- Re T (Adult: Refusal of Treatment) [1993] Fam. 95
- R v Louise Collins & Others, *Ex Parte* S (No 2) [1993] 3 WLR 936
- Re MB (Medical Treatment) [1997] 2 FLR 426
- Re JT (Adult: Refusal of Medical Treatment) [1998] 1 FLR 4
- St George's Healthcare Trust v S (No 2) [1998]
- R v Moor (1999) Crim L.R. [2000] Jul 568–590
- Ms B v a NHS Hospital Trust [2002] EWHC 429 (Fam)
- Burke v the General Medical Council [2005] EWCA Civ 1003
- R (Purdy) v DPP (2009) UKHL 45
- Aintree University NHS Trust v James [2013] UKSC 67
- R (Tracey) v Cambridge University Hospital NHS FT and others [2014] EWCA Civ 822
- NHSFT v P [2014] EWHC 1650 (Fam)
- Winspear v City Hospitals Sunderland NHS FT [2015] EWHC 3250 (QB)
- An NHS Trust and others (Respondents) v Y (by his litigation friend, the Official Solicitor) and another (Appellants) [2018] UKSC 46

RELEVANT STATUTES AND LEGISLATION

- Suicide Act 1961 s 2(1)
- Mental Health Act 1983
- The Human Rights Act 1998
- Age of Legal Capacity (Scotland) Act 1991
- Adults with Incapacity (Scotland) Act 2000
- Mental Capacity Act 2005
- Policy for prosecutors in respect of cases of encouraging or assisting suicide, London CPS, February 2010 www.cps.gov.uk

PROFESSIONAL GUIDANCE

- Guidance from the British Medical Association, the Resuscitation Council (UK), and the Royal College of Nursing. (October 2014). *Decisions Relating to Cardiopulmonary Resuscitation*, 3rd edn
- GMC Guidance. (May 2010). *Treatment and Care Towards the End of Life: Good Practice in Decision-Making*
- GMC Guidance. (2015). *When A Patient Seeks Advice or Information About Assistance to Die.* http://www.gmcuk.org
- *The Adults with Incapacity (Scotland) Act Code of Practice.* http://www.gov.scot

6.1 Introduction

'Life is a sexually transmitted disease and the mortality is 100%.'

So said R.D. Laing around 50 years ago—and unfortunately the prognosis has not changed. While many of the chapters in this book deal with things you should be prepared for but will hopefully not have to deal with directly, all practising clinicians will have to deal with the death of their patients, their loved ones, and, eventually, themselves. Cheerful, I know. There is a serious point though: because death is universal, we all come to it with previous experiences and potential biases. It is very important that we are able to acknowledge our own preferences, and then subjugate those to the needs of the individual patient for whom we are caring.

Doctors have the ability to prescribe drugs to alleviate symptoms or to apply organ support to those whose bodies are failing. They can be asked, by patients or families, to provide life-sustaining treatments that they do not believe would offer any clinical relief or to administer drugs to 'end suffering'. At both extremes there are laws to protect both the patient and the doctor. It is this legislation, case law, and some General Medical Council (GMC) cases and guidance that will be reviewed in this chapter: the right to refuse life-sustaining treatment; the role of the Mental Capacity Act (MCA) and respecting 'best interests'; the legal (and philosophical) distinction between withholding and withdrawing treatment; the doctrine of double effect; assisted suicide; and euthanasia. Issues of brain death and organ donation are dealt with in Chapter 7.

6.2 The Right to Refuse Treatment

6.2.1 Capacity

An adult patient with capacity has an absolute right to refuse treatment. There is a

> ' ... fundamental principle, now long established, that every person's body is inviolate.' (Lord Goff in re F (Mental Patient: Sterilisation) [1990] 2 AC 1)

And

> ' ... the patient's right of choice exists whether the reasons for making that choice are rational, irrational, unknown or even non-existent.' (Lord Donaldson in re T (Adult: Refusal of Treatment) [1993] Fam. 95).

This right is absolute.

> ' ... A mentally competent patient has an absolute right to refuse to consent to medical treatment for any reason, rational or irrational, or for no reason at all, even where that decision may lead to his or her own death' (Baroness Butler-Sloss in re MB (Medical Treatment) [1997] 2 FLR 426).

In fact, a doctor providing treatment against a patient's wishes could be charged with battery or assault. In the case that best emphasizes that the right to refuse medical treatment extends to life-sustaining treatment, Ms B took the trust to court on the grounds that the ' ... invasive treatment which is currently being given ... by way of artificial ventilation is an unlawful trespass' (re Ms B v a NHS Hospital Trust [2002] EWHC 429).

Ms B was in her early forties when she became paralysed from the neck down as a result of an intramedullary cervical spine cavernoma. Her life was supported by artificial ventilation through a tracheostomy. She asked her doctors to withdraw her ventilation, knowing that death would almost certainly follow, as she found the idea of living like this intolerable. Although she was initially considered to have capacity to make this decision, the psychiatrists changed their opinion, and started her on antidepressants. In her written statement she said:

> ' ... I felt that I was being treated as if I was being unreasonable by putting people in this awkward position. I fully accept the doctor's right to say, "I personally will not do it", and I respect that position, but I was angered at the arrogance and complete refusal to allow me access to someone that would ... I felt that my rights were being eroded and that is not something I tolerate really.'

In Baroness Butler-Sloss' evaluation she emphasized the right to refuse treatment, even when this would result in the patient's death. She quoted (along with those cases mentioned) Lord Keith of Kinkel in Airedale NHS Trust v Bland [1993] AC 789 (p. 859):

'... the principle of the sanctity of life, which it is the concern of the state, and the judiciary as one of the arms of the state, ... is not an absolute one. It does not compel a medical practitioner on pain of criminal sanctions to treat a patient, who will die if he does not, contrary to the express wishes of the patient.'

After review of the evidence—including written and oral evidence from Ms B and that of her treating anaesthetists, physicians, and psychiatrists—Baroness Butler-Sloss found that the claimant had been treated unlawfully by the Trust. In her summing up, she said (my emphasis):

'... If there are difficulties in deciding whether the patient has sufficient mental capacity, particularly if the refusal may have grave consequences for the patient, it is most important that those considering the issue should not confuse the question of mental capacity with the nature of the decision made by the patient, however grave the consequences. *The view of the patient may reflect a difference in values rather than an absence of competence* and the assessment of capacity should be approached with this firmly in mind. The doctors must not allow their emotional reaction to or strong disagreement with the decision of the patient to cloud their judgment in answering the primary question whether the patient has the mental capacity to make the decision.'

Although the right of a capacitous patient to refuse life-sustaining treatment is well established in case law, as described, it is worth pointing out that the Human Rights Act—which incorporates into domestic law the European Convention on Human Rights (ECHR)—now provides the main legislative weight behind this right, in the form of Articles 3, 5, and 8 (Box 6.1).

6.2.2 Children and Pregnant Patients

Although there is not scope to go into detail on specific cases, it is worth highlighting the law around pregnant women, children, and young people (see also Chapter 9). A pregnant woman with capacity can refuse life-sustaining treatment, including treatment which is intended to save the unborn child. This was emphasized in St George's Healthcare Trust v S (No 2). R v Louise Collins & Others, *Ex parte* S (No 2) [1993] 3 WLR 936. In this case, the hospital was found to have unlawfully admitted and detained under the Mental Health Act 1983 a lady with pre-eclampsia and unlawfully forced her to have a Caesarean section by the order of a court.

A Gillick-competent child (see Chapter 9) under the age of 16 can consent to treatments, but cannot refuse treatments. If clinicians and a child's family are in fundamental disagreement over the child's treatment, the views of the court should be sought. A young person (anyone aged 16/17) can refuse treatments, but, in all of the UK apart from Scotland, a person with parental responsibility or the Court of Protection can overrule their refusal if it would lead to death or

Box 6.1 The European Convention on Human Rights (ECHR)

Articles most relevant to end of life:

Article 2: The right to life and positive duty on public authorities to protect life.

Article 3: The right to be free from inhuman and degrading treatment.

Article 5: The right to security of the person.

Article 8: The right to respect for private and family life.

Article 9: The right to freedom of thought, conscience and religion.

Article 14: The right to be free from discrimination.

severe permanent injury. In Scotland, competent minors have an independent right to consent to or refuse treatment (the Age of Legal Capacity (Scotland) Act 1991).

6.2.3 Advance Decision to Refuse Treatment (ADRT)

An adult with capacity can write an advance decision to refuse treatment (ADRT) if they want to ensure that, in the event of them losing capacity, their wishes not to receive certain treatments are respected. To be legally binding, an ADRT must:

- Comply with the MCA
- Be valid
- Apply to the situation.

An ADRT is considered valid if it:

- Is written by an individual aged 18 or over who had the capacity to make, understand, and communicate the decision when it was made.
- Has clearly specified which treatments they wish to refuse.
- Has explained the circumstances in which they wish to refuse them.
- Is signed by the individual and by a witness if he or she wants to refuse life-sustaining treatment.
- The individual has made the advance decision of their own accord, without any harassment by anyone else.
- The individual has not said or done anything that would contradict the advance decision since it was made.

Some proformas of ADRTs are available online, and the National Health Service (NHS) Improving Quality has published guidance in collaboration with the National Council for Palliative Care.

However, significant problems with ADRTs have been raised. There is no national registry for ADRTs, and so finding whether a patient has one can be difficult. Some general practitioners (GPs) are not aware of the legal constraints on validity, and some lawyers are not aware of the details of medical treatments, so that, of the few ADRTs that are written, many are not valid. A simple wish not to have cardiopulmonary resuscitation (CPR) attempted, for example, may not be considered valid if the circumstances in which the arrest happened are not documented. To be legally binding, it would have to be written: 'should my heart stop, I would not want any attempts at resuscitation, in any circumstance. I understand that this is a refusal of life-sustaining treatment' and then have it dated and signed. But this kind of ADRT may force people into extremes they did not mean to instruct; what about a patient who is choking? So then someone might write: 'I do not wish to have resuscitation attempted unless there is a clear reversible cause'—but then is hyperkalaemia a clear reversible cause? Would you wait until you knew the potassium before stopping CPR?

One approach to this problem is to ensure that an 'advance statement' coexists with the ADRT. While patients do not have the right to request treatments, they can write about their treatment preferences (e.g. 'I would like to die at home if possible' or 'I would like all treatments to prolong life to be considered' or 'quality of life is the most important thing for me: please only give me treatments if you think I have a good chance of retaining my mental functions'). Providing treating clinicians with an 'advance statement' alongside an ADRT allows them to interpret the ADRT for the circumstances that exist. A new charity, 'Advance Decisions Assistance', has mocked up some appropriately legally and medically worded ADRTs and combined them with 'values statements' to go alongside them, to aid patients in understanding what might help ensure their wishes are respected (http://adassistance.org.uk/write-it/).

KEY POINTS—ADVANCE DECISION

- An ADRT is made to ensure that, in the event of losing capacity, a person's wishes not to receive certain treatments are respected.
- An advance statement is a more general indication about acceptable treatment preferences and quality-of-life matters.
- An ADRT must be signed, witnessed, and apply to the patient's circumstance.

6.2.4 Lasting Powers of Attorney for Health and Welfare

Another way for individuals to ensure that their wishes are respected in the event of them losing capacity is to communicate them to a friend or family member and give them 'lasting power of attorney (LPA) for health and welfare' in England and Wales, or 'power of attorney' in Scotland or Northern Ireland. They need to be registered with the Office of the Public Guardian (OPG) at a cost of around £110, but at the moment there is no online registry, and a paper form needs to be completed and sent to the OPG to find out if one exists.

If an individual has both an ADRT and an LPA, then the most recent 'trumps' the other. In other words, if an LPA is appointed, and then an ADRT is written, the LPA cannot ask the doctors to go against what is written in the ADRT; if, on the other hand, the LPA was appointed after the ADRT was written, the LPA has absolute authority. Individuals who felt particularly strongly about some issues, but wanted the LPA to have overall discretion, should therefore appoint an LPA first, and then write a specific ADRT.

Valid ADRTs are rare—at the moment less than 4% of the population have them. Australia has recently undertaken a drive to ensure that they are more widespread. In the UK, a move to ensure that patients consider what outcomes they desire or fear and what treatments they would and would not want—with 'advance care planning' is also afoot, and the need for an online national registry has been acknowledged.

KEY POINTS—THE RIGHT TO REFUSE TREATMENT

- An adult patient with capacity has an absolute right to refuse treatment even if it results in their death.
- A pregnant woman with capacity can refuse life-sustaining treatment, including treatment which is intended to save the unborn child.
- A Gillick-competent child under the age of 16 can consent to treatments but cannot refuse treatments.
- For an ADRT to be legally binding it must comply with the MCA, be valid, and apply to the situation.
- An 'advance statement' should probably coexist with the ADRT to help avoid physician interpretation.
- An LPA given to a friend or relative allows an individual who loses capacity to ensure their wishes are respected.
- An LPA needs to be registered with the OPG for a fee.

6.3 Best Interests and Substituted Judgement

In the UK, when a patient does not have capacity, or an ADRT, or an LPA, physicians must make a decision and act in the patient's 'best interests'. These were enshrined in statute in the MCA in 2005, having previously been established in common law (e.g. Re MB (Medical Treatment) [1997] 2

FLR 426, CA) (see Chapter 1 for explanation of statute and common law). To determine the 'best interests' of a person lacking capacity, the law requires that a process is undertaken, which includes considering, so far as is reasonably ascertainable:

- the person's past and present wishes and feelings (and, in particular, any relevant written statement made by him or her when he or she had capacity);
- the beliefs and values that would be likely to influence his or her decision if he or she had capacity; and
- the other factors that he or she would be likely to consider if he or she were able to do so.

The first case to test this legislation was that of Aintree University NHS Trust v James [2013] UKSC 67. David James was a 68-year-old man who had previously been successfully treated for bowel cancer and chronic obstructive pulmonary disease (COPD). He developed a severe chest infection in May 2012, and required admission to an intensive care unit (ICU) for ventilation. He had a complicated admission, including: episodes of severe sepsis requiring inotropes; a stroke; chronic colonization with *Pseudomonas*; development of contractures and sores; and cardiac arrest, from which he was successfully resuscitated. Following his stroke, and the hypoxic brain injury associated with arrest, he had lost capacity. He was, however, alert, and showed recognition of his family when they came to visit. The clinical team looking after him felt, given his step-wise deteriorating conditions, he had very little chance of recovery and that he would not benefit from further invasive treatments, including renal replacement therapy, attempted CPR, or invasive support of his circulatory problems. The family were in disagreement, and so the hospital sought legal declarations that it would not be in Mr James' best interests to give these treatments. The case went to the Supreme court.

In her judgment, Lady Hale quoted Lord Phillips from R (Burke) v General Medical Council [2005] EWCA Civ 1003, [2006] QB 273:

' ... a patient cannot demand that a doctor administer a treatment which the doctor considers is adverse to the patient's clinical needs'.

She went on to emphasize that the MCA was about whether it was in the best interests to provide certain treatments, not to withhold them:

' ... If a treatment was not in his best interests, the court would not be able to give its consent on his behalf and it would follow that it would be lawful to withhold or withdraw it. Indeed, it would follow that it would not be lawful to give it. It also followed that ... the clinical team would not be in breach of any duty towards the patients if they withheld or withdrew it.'

In determining best interests, she said that the court must:

' ... look at welfare in the widest sense, not just medical but social and psychological; ...try and put themselves in the place of the individual patient and ask what his attitude to the treatment is or would be likely to be; and ... consult others who are looking after him or interested in his welfare, in particular for their view of what his attitude would be.'

Sometimes 'best interests' is contrasted with 'substituted judgement'. Substituted judgement is used widely in the United States, is grounded in respect for autonomy, and instructs the surrogate to make a decision that the person would have made had they had capacity. However, several studies have shown that surrogates are not always accurate predictors of what someone would have wanted. Ideally—as in Hale's Judgment—determining best interests includes an assessment of 'substituted judgement' as part of an objective process to determine what is in the patient's best interests, while not relying too heavily on the surrogate's opinion. Determining 'best interests' is particularly important—as in the Aintree judgment—when it is concerned with withdrawing and withholding treatments.

KEY POINTS—BEST INTERESTS AND SUBSTITUTED JUDGEMENT

- Without a legal instrument to declare one's wishes, a physician will treat an incapacitated patient in his or her bests interests.
- Best interests are elaborated in the MCA 2005.
- Best interests should include a person's past and present wishes, feelings, and any relevant written statement.
- Best interests should include the beliefs and values that would be likely to influence a patient's decision if he or she had capacity.
- A substituted judgement allows a surrogate to make a decision that a person would have made if he or she had capacity.
- Determining best interests should include an assessment of substituted judgement.

6.4 Withdrawing and Withholding Treatment

There is no legal distinction between withdrawing and withholding a medical treatment: if in doubt, the treatment should be started. Patients in respiratory arrest, for example, without a previous Do Not Attempt Cardiopulmonary Resuscitation (DNACPR) should be intubated and ventilated until it is clear that this would not be successful or desired, and then they can be extubated if it is subsequently decided that continued ventilation is not in their best interests. The GMC guidance includes the statement: 'A patient's best interests may be interpreted as meaning that a patient should not be subjected to more treatment than is necessary to allow them to die peacefully and with dignity'. It should be noted that the intent in withdrawing of treatment is not to end the life of the patients, but rather to stop giving them a treatment which is considered adverse to the patient's clinical needs.

6.4.1 Minimally Conscious State

A particular group of patients in which this is the case are those in a permanent vegetative or minimally conscious state. The first case in which this was tested in the courts was that of Tony Bland, a 17-year-old who suffered anoxic brain damage at the Hillsborough disaster in 1989. His family asked that his clinically assisted nutrition and hydration (CANH) be stopped; in 1992 the House of Lords ruled that it was no longer in Mr Bland's best interests to receive CANH and therefore no longer lawful to provide it (Airedale NHS Trust v Bland [1993] 1 All ER 821). They said that similar cases should go through the court 'until a body of experience and practice has been built up which might obviate the need for application in every case'. More than 100 cases have now gone through the courts since that time. In July 2018 the Supreme Court acknowledged that this experience had been gained and ruled that: "If the provisions of the MCA 2005 are followed and the relevant guidance observed, and if there is agreement upon what is in the best interests of the patient, the patient may be treated in accordance with that agreement without application to the court . . . I would emphasise that, although application to court is not necessary in every case, there will undoubtedly be cases in which an application will be required (or desirable) because of the particular circumstances that appertain, and there should be no reticence about involving the court in such cases."

This ruling brings the treatment of those in a Permanent Vegetative State in line with GMC guidance (and wide spread practice) for the withdrawal of CANH in other circumstances—for example, in a patient with dementia who has stopped eating: "Clinically assisted nutrition or hydration may be withheld or withdrawn if the patient does not wish to receive it; or if the patient is dying and the care goals change to palliative care and relief of suffering; or if the patient lacks capacity to decide and it is considered that providing clinically assisted nutrition or hydration would not be in their best interests". As always, such decisions must be discussed with those who are close to the patient, to ensure that The MCA 2005 provisions are followed and that there is agreement about what is in the best interests of the patient.

6.4.2 Communication and Documentation

Up until recently, however, it was common for physicians to make decisions that certain treatments—in particular, attempted CPR—would not be in a patient's best interests, because their chance of survival was low, and yet not discuss that decision with the patient. The most commonly documented reason for not having discussions with patients was that it might cause the patient 'distress'. This practice has been found to be in breach of Article 8 of the Human Rights Act, and it is now illegal to make a decision that a patient should not be for attempted CPR without discussion with the patient, or, where the patient lacks capacity, with those that care for the patient, except in extenuating circumstances. The two cases that have formed the law on this are Winspear v City Hospitals Sunderland NHS FT [2015] EWHC 3250 (QB) and R (Tracey) v Cambridge University Hospital NHS Foundation Trust and others [2014] EWCA Civ 822. The judgments both focused on the decision-making, discussion, and documentation of the DNACPR order.

Janet Tracey had been ventilated following a C-spine fracture that she sustained in a car accident. She had a past medical history of metastatic lung cancer and COPD. She had capacity, and had indicated, via writing, that she wanted to be involved in medical decisions. She had had two failed extubations, and the clinicians looking after her spoke with the family to say that if the third extubation failed they would let her 'slip away'. They did not document a discussion with Mrs Tracey herself and a DNACPR order was written. In fact, the extubation was successful, the first order was rescinded at the family's request, and Mrs Tracey later died with a DNACPR order in place that had been agreed with the family and that she did not want to be 'badgered' about. The case that went to the Supreme Court focused around the first order.

In his judgment, Lord Dyson said that, since a DNACPR order was a decision which would:

'potentially deprive [a] patient of life-saving treatment, there should be a presumption in favour of patient involvement' except in circumstances where a discussion might cause 'physical or psychological harm'.

If a clinician believes that a discussion would cause harm to a patient, then he or she should ensure that he or she clearly documents the justification for this decision. Explaining his reasoning, Lord Dyson said:

'The fact that the clinician considers that CPR will not work means that the patient cannot require him to provide it. It does not, however, mean that the patient is not entitled to know that the clinical decision has been taken. Secondly, if the patient is not told that the clinician has made a DNACPR decision, he will be deprived of the opportunity of seeking a second opinion.'

Lord Ryder, in agreeing with Lord Dyson, highlighted that:

'the duty to consult is integral to the procedural obligation to ensure effective respect for the Article 8 right ... the interest is autonomy, integrity, dignity and quality of life of the patient. It is accordingly critical to good patient care.'

These statements together have important repercussions for clinical practice more generally: if clinicians think a patient would not benefit from a potentially life-saving treatment, they must inform the patient of this decision: not to do so is to deprive the patient of the chance to question the decision or to ask for a second opinion.

The case of Carl Winspear has clarified the law in terms of the duty to consult with those close to the patient who is lacking capacity. Mr Winspear was a 28-year-old with cerebral palsy and spinal deformities, whose mother had been his lifelong carer. He developed a chest infection, and his mother accompanied him into hospital, where he was admitted for treatment for pneumonia. Overnight, the registrar wrote a DNACPR order but with a plan to discuss both with his consultant and Ms Winspear in the morning. This conversation accordingly took place and it was agreed that he would not benefit from invasive ventilation. He continued to deteriorate despite non-invasive ventilation and died later that night. The court found that, while Mr Winspear's treatments were not altered by the order, the hospital had been in breach of Article 8 in not contacting Ms Winspear before placing the DNACPR order. Given that Ms Winspear had accompanied her son into hospital the night before (and had phoned at 10 pm to check on him) it was both 'practicable and appropriate' to contact her before making the decision. Again, this case is likely to alter clinical practice: it was common to make a 'holding' decision while awaiting discussion with those close to a patient who lacks capacity.

One way of counteracting the problem of resuscitation decisions being made without appropriate consultation is to try to make them more routine—for example, as best practice in nursing homes or on admission to hospital. Contextualizing the resuscitation decision within a discussion about overall goals of care is also likely to help make these conversations more useful, so that the wishes of the patient can be aligned with what is clinically possible. Stakeholders from all specialties and across care settings have been working together to build on evidence that this might be a better approach: the Recommended Summary Plan for Emergency Care and Treatment (ReSPECT) has now been adopted in several sites: www.respectprocess.org.uk.

6.4.3 Death as a 'Side Effect'

A crime is *actus reus*—the guilty act—and *mens rea*—the guilty mind—in other words, the intent to bring about the outcome. In particular, murder is the act of killing with the intent to kill. Any act where the doctor's primary intent is to bring about death is therefore unlawful.

Prescribing (or giving) opiates with the intention of alleviating pain, but with the possible 'side effect' of shortening life, is therefore lawful, under the so-called 'doctrine of double effect'. Dr David Moor was acquitted of murder in 1999 on this defence. In fact, opiates given at the correct dose for pain relief would be very unlikely to hasten death; it has been shown that good palliative care might even be associated with longer life expectancy (Temel et al., 2010).

A clinically more likely scenario is a patient in significant respiratory distress—from heart failure or chronic lung disease. Giving the patient both an anxiolytic and morphine will make him or her feel less breathless, and so less distressed, but will also suppress the respiratory drive: the patient may die sooner. The important legal point is that, so long as the primary intention is to alleviate suffering—even with the known potential consequence of hastening death, then the action is legal.

KEY POINTS—WITHDRAWING AND WITHHOLDING TREATMENT

- There is no legal distinction between withdrawing and withholding a medical treatment.
- The intent in withdrawing treatment is not to end the life of the patient but to stop giving him or her unnecessary treatment.
- A Court Order must be obtained to withdraw CANH in a patient in a permanent vegetative state - although this is currently being debated in the supreme court.
- It is illegal to impose a DNACPR without discussion with the patient, or relatives when the patient is incapacitated.
- A clinician must inform a patient or next-of-kin if he or she intends to deny the patient a potentially life-saving or futile treatment.
- Patients and next-of-kin must be given the chance to question the decision or to ask for a second opinion.
- Doctrine of double effect—using opiates with the intention to alleviate suffering despite hastening death—then the action is legal.

6.5 Assisted Suicide

Although killing oneself is no longer a crime,

> '*A person who aids, abets, counsels or procures the suicide of another, or an attempt by another to commit suicide, shall be liable on conviction on indictment to imprisonment for a term not exceeding fourteen years*' (**Suicide Act 1961 s2 (1)**).

Several cases have challenged this legislation. Dianne Pretty had motor neurone disease and was already sufficiently disabled that she would have been unable to bring about her own death. She wanted to *'have a quick death without suffering, at home surrounded by my family so that I can say goodbye to them'*. In 2002 Dianne took her case to the European Court of Human Rights (ECtHR), arguing that not allowing her assistance in committing suicide was infringing her right to self-determination in matters of life and death, and her right not to be subjected to inhuman or degrading treatment. The ECtHR rejected her case, stating that there were:

> *'cogent reasons ... for not seeking to distinguish between those who are able and those who are unable to commit suicide unaided. The borderline between the two categories will often be a very fine one and to seek to build into the law an exemption for those judged to be incapable of committing suicide would seriously undermine the protection of life which the 1961 Act was intended to safeguard and greatly increase the risk of abuse'.*

Dianne Pretty died shortly afterwards.

In 2008, Daniel James, who had been quadriplegic following a rugby accident, travelled to Dignitas in Switzerland. His parents were investigated by the police, but the Crown Prosecution Service said that, while there was 'sufficient evidence' to charge them, it was not in the public interest to do so. In fact, none of the family members of 100 or so people who have gone to Dignitas have been prosecuted; some, however, have been charged, and then had the charges dropped.

In 2008, Debby Purdy, who had multiple sclerosis, argued that the Director of Public Prosecutions (DPP) was infringing her human rights by failing to clarify how the suicide act would be interpreted: *'My wish is to be able to ask for and receive assistance to end my life, should living it become unbearable for me. I wish to be able to make the decision to end my life while I am physically able to do so. I consider that this will probably mean either traveling to Zurich, Switzerland to avail myself of the services of Dignitas (as I do not wish to mess up any attempts, thereby making matters worse for myself), or to go to Belgium...My husband has said he would assist me and if necessary face a prison sentence, but I am not prepared to put him in this position for a number of reasons'.* The case went to the House of Lords, who agreed that clarity was needed, and ordered the DPP to:

> *'promulgate an offence-specific policy identifying the facts and circumstances which he will take into account in deciding, in a case such as that which Ms Purdy's case exemplifies, whether or not to consent to a prosecution under section 2(1) of the 1961 Act'.*

In 2010, the DPP presented 16 public interest factors for prosecution and six against. One of the factors in favour of a prosecution is that

> *'The suspect was acting in his or her capacity as a medical doctor, nurse, other healthcare professional ... and the victim was in his or her care'.*

A doctor, therefore, is more likely to be prosecuted if they were to assist someone to die.

The level of 'assistance' that would be deemed criminally contributory has not been tested in the courts: clearly providing someone with medication that they could use to end their life would be, but what about signing their insurance documents so they could go on a plane to Dignitas? The GMC have published guidance: where patients raise the issue of assisting suicide or ask for information that might encourage or assist them in ending their lives, respect for a patient's autonomy cannot justify illegal action. Limit any advice or information in response, to:

- an explanation that it is a criminal offence for anyone to encourage or assist a person to commit or attempt suicide; and
- objective advice about the lawful clinical options (such as sedation and other palliative care) that would be available if a patient were to reach a settled decision to kill himself or herself.

Assisted suicide is being debated internationally. In Canada in 2015, the Supreme Court ruled unanimously that it should become legal in certain circumstances, stating that it was discriminatory not to assist disabled people of sound mind to kill themselves:

> 'A person facing this prospect [a life of severe and intolerable suffering] has two options: she can take her own life prematurely, often by violent or dangerous means, or she can suffer until she dies from natural causes. The choice is cruel'.

It is legal in Washington and Oregon in the United States, and in Belgium and Switzerland. An 'assisted dying' bill has recently been debated in the UK. The scope of the bill was limited to those expected to die within 6 months; it was defeated by a large majority.

KEY POINTS—ASSISTED SUICIDE

- A person who commits suicide does not commit a crime.
- Assisting a person to commit suicide is a crime.
- A doctor is more likely to be prosecuted if he or she assists someone to die.
- The level of 'assistance' that would be deemed criminally contributory has not been tested in the courts.
- Doctors should warn patients who raise the issue of assisted suicide that it is unlawful and offer objective advice about lawful clinical options.

6.6 Euthanasia

Euthanasia is literally translated from the Greek as 'good death'. Some classifications exist, and it is probably worth going over the different ways the phrases are used, even though some of them are nonsensical categories. The first distinction is between so-called 'passive euthanasia'—where death results from the withdrawal of treatments—and 'active euthanasia'—where a drug is given with the intention of hastening death. As already discussed in this chapter, the withdrawal of treatment is sometimes in the patient's best interests, and is not viewed as euthanasia in UK law.

In addition, a distinction is sometimes made between 'voluntary' euthanasia—where the individual has made the request; non-voluntary euthanasia—where a person is unable to give their consent but has previously expressed a wish to die if he or she was in that state (e.g. those in a vegetative state); and 'involuntary euthanasia'—where a person does not want it, in which case it is murder under any definition. The distinction between 'voluntary euthanasia' and 'assisted suicide' is that the final action—of drinking a medication, or triggering a mechanism that will inject a medication—needs to be taken by the individual wishing to die in assisted suicide. If another individual does the act—even if requested explicitly by the patient—it is euthanasia.

In the current law in the UK all 'active' euthanasia is regarded as either manslaughter or murder and is punishable by law, with a maximum penalty of up to life imprisonment.

Tony Nicklinson challenged this law. He had a stroke that prevented him moving anything from the neck down; he could not speak, but could communicate with his eyes. Unlike Ms B he was not dependent on a ventilator, and so could not request a cessation of treatment to end his life. He could not go to Switzerland, because he could not perform the final act needed for assisted suicide. Instead, after 7 years of living in a dependent state, Mr Nicklinson applied to the High Court for: (i) a declaration that it would be lawful for a doctor to kill him or to assist him in terminating his life, or, if that was refused; (ii) a declaration that the current state of the law in that connection was incompatible with his rights under Article 8 of the Convention of Human Rights. He lost at the

High Court, and subsequently refused food and antibiotics and died shortly after. His wife, joined by two other gentlemen in similar predicaments to her late husband, took the case to the Supreme Court. These appeals were also dismissed, partly on the grounds that this issue needs to be left to an elected parliament to legislate on, rather than be decided on case law.

KEY POINTS—EUTHANASIA

- Passive euthanasia is where death results from the withdrawal of treatments.
- Active euthanasia is where a drug is given with the intention of hastening death.
- Withdrawal of treatment in the patient's best interests is not viewed as euthanasia in UK law.
- Voluntary euthanasia is where the individual has made the request.
- Non-voluntary euthanasia is where a person is unable to give his or her consent but has previously expressed a wish to die.
- Involuntary euthanasia is where a person does not want it—in which case it is murder.
- In the UK all 'active' euthanasia is regarded as either manslaughter or murder and is punishable by law.

6.7 Pearls and Pitfalls

6.7.1 Pearls

- If a patient has both an LPA and an ADRT, the more recent one trumps the older one. Examples of ADRTs and advance statements that can be useful for patients can be found on 'Advance Decisions Assistance' (http://adassistance.org.uk/write-it/).
- There is no legal distinction between withdrawing and withholding treatment: if in doubt start treatment.
- When a patient is sick, have a very low threshold for calling family or loved ones in, even in the middle of the night; not only will it give you the opportunity to talk with them about decisions you may need to make, but it will give them an opportunity to be with their relative/friend.

6.7.2 Pitfalls

- When assessing capacity to refuse life-sustaining treatment, ensure that you do not allow ' ... emotional reaction to or strong disagreement with the decision of the patient to cloud [your] judgment in answering the primary question whether the patient has the mental capacity to make the decision'.
- Do not make a decision that involves withdrawing or withholding life-sustaining treatments (including attempted CPR) without consulting with the patient, or, where the patient lacks capacity, those close to them. The only exceptions are where you think a discussion would cause 'physical or psychological harm' to the patient, or where it is not 'practicable and appropriate' to contact someone close to the patient. In these cases, make sure you document your reasons carefully.
- As a doctor, there is a public interest factor in prosecuting you if you are perceived to have assisted someone's suicide. The GMC advises that, if asked for any advice, doctors tell their patients that it is a criminal offence for anyone to encourage or assist a person to commit or attempt suicide.

6.8 Reference

- Temel, J., Greer, J., Muzikansky, A. et al. (2010). Early palliative care for patients with metastatic non–small-cell lung cancer. *N Engl J Med*, **363**, 733–42.

6.9 Further Reading

- Donchin, A. (2000). Autonomy, independence and assisted suicide: Respecting boundaries/crossing lines. *Bioethics*, **14**(3), 187–204.
- Foster, C. (2009). *Choosing Life, Choosing Death. The Tyranny of Autonomy in Medical Ethics and Law*. Oxford: Hart Publishing Ltd, p. 181.
- Fritz, Z., Cork, N., Dodd, A., Malyon, A. (2014). DNACPR decisions: challenging and changing practice in the wake of the Tracey judgment. *Clinical Medicine*, **14**(6), 571–6.
- Huxtable, R. (2007). *Euthanasia, Ethics and the Law: From Conflict to Compromise*. London: Routledge.
- Huxtable, R. (2013). *Law, Ethics and Compromise at the Limits of Life: To Treat or Not to Treat?* London: Routledge.
- Lewis, P. (2007). *Assisted Dying and Legal Change*. Oxford: Oxford University Press.
- Quill, T.E., Lo, B., Brock, D.W. (1997). Palliative options of last resort: a comparison of voluntarily stopping eating and drinking, terminal sedation, physician-assisted suicide, and voluntary active euthanasia. *JAMA*, **278**, 2099–104. http://www.ncbi.nlm.nih.gov/pubmed/9403426 (accessed 22 July 2015).
- Sterecks, S., Raus, K., Mortier, F. (2013). *Continuous Sedation at the End of Life: Ethical, Clinical and Legal Perspectives*. (Cambridge Bioethics and Law). Cambridge: Cambridge University Press.
- Szerletics, A. (2011). *Best Interests Decision-Making under the Mental Capacity Act*. Essex Autonomy Project Green Paper Report. http://autonomy.essex.ac.uk/best-interests-decision-making-under-the-mental-capacity-act

6.10 Multiple Choice Questions

✓ Interactive multiple choice questions to test your knowledge on this chapter can be found in the Online appendix at www.oxfordmedicine.com/essentiallegalmatters.

CHAPTER 7

Organ Donation and Transplantation

Keith Rigg

CONTENTS

CHAPTER SUMMARY

Legal and Regulatory Framework

The organ donation and transplantation sector in the UK has a comprehensive legal and regulatory framework with some important differences between the UK countries. The key legislative framework includes The Human Tissue Act 2004 and the Human Tissue (Scotland) Act 2006, with the Human Tissue Authority acting as the regulatory body.

Consent

Consent or authorization (Scotland) is the important thread that runs through the legislation and is essential for the removal, storage, and use of organs for transplantation.

Living and Deceased Donor Transplantation

Regulations govern all living donor transplantation, paired/pooled donation, and non-directed stranger donation. The specific requirements of the legislation that cover deceased donor transplantation are consent/authorization, where the wishes of the deceased take precedence. Commercial dealings in human organs remain illegal.

RELEVANT STATUTES AND LEGISLATION

- Coroners Act 1988
- Human Organ Transplants Act 1989

- Human Rights Act 1998
- Human Tissue Act 2004
- Mental Capacity Act 2005
- The Human Tissue Act 2004 (Ethical Approval, Exceptions from Licensing and Supply of Information about Transplants) Regulations 2006
- The Human Tissue Act 2004 (Persons who Lack Capacity to Consent and Transplants) Regulations 2006
- Human Tissue (Scotland) Act 2006
- Human Tissue (Removal of Body Parts by an Authorised Person) (Scotland) Regulations 2006
- Human Organ and Tissue Live Transplants (Scotland) Regulations 2006
- Human Tissue (Scotland) Act 2006 (Maintenance of Records and Supply of Information Regarding the Removal and Use of Body Parts) Regulations 2006
- Quality and Safety of Organs Intended for Transplantation Regulations 2012
- Human Transplantation (Wales) Act 2013
- Quality and Safety of Organs Intended for Transplantation (Amendment) Regulations 2014

PROFESSIONAL GUIDANCE

- GMC (2010). *Treatment and Care Towards the End of Life: Good Practice in Decision Making.* https://www.gmc-uk.org
- Human Tissue Authority Code of Practice A (2017). *Guiding Principles and the Fundamental Principle of Consent.* https://www.hta.gov.uk
- Human Tissue Authority Code of Practice F (2017). *Donation of Solid Organs and Tissue for Transplantation.* https://www.hta.gov.uk
- Human Tissue Authority (2013). *Code of Practice on the Human Transplantation (Wales) Act 2013.* https://www.hta.gov.uk
- NICE (2011). *Organ Donation for Transplantation.* https://www.nice.org.uk
- NHS Blood and Transplant (2017). *Transplantation - Policies and Guidance.* http://www.odt.nhs.uk
- Royal College of Anaesthetists (2011). *Organ Donation: Ethical, Professional and Legal Guidance.* http://www.rcoa.ac.uk

7.1 Introduction

The organ donation and transplantation sector in the UK has a comprehensive legal and regulatory framework, with some important differences between the UK countries. With the first successful deceased donor transplants performed in the UK and the emerging concept of brain death from 1959, there needed to be some clarity about the legality of the process. The Human Tissue Act (HTAct) 1961 and the HTAct (Northern Ireland) 1962 went some way to address this and subsequently there was a steady growth in deceased and living donor transplants.

The Human Organ Transplants Act 1989 was enacted speedily following an inquiry into the trafficking of Turkish peasants to be paid living donors for transplantation. This legislation was aimed primarily at prohibiting commercial dealings in organs for transplantation and restricting transplantation between persons not genetically related. As the complexity of organ donation and transplantation increased, there was a need for further legislative change, which was brought under the umbrella of the HTAct 2004. The main driver for this had, however, come out of the Bristol and Liverpool inquiries, where organs and tissues had often been removed, stored, or used without consent. The HTAct 2004 and the Human Tissue (Scotland) Act 2006 cover the removal, storage, and use of all organs and tissues.

Most recently within the European Community, there has been concern that the quality and safety of organs for transplantation varies between member states. To ensure common standards of quality and safety, the European Union (EU) Organ Donation Directive was published in 2010 and enshrined in UK law in 2012.

KEY POINTS—INTRODUCTION TO DONATION AND TRANSPLANTATION

- The UK has a comprehensive legal and regulatory framework for organ donation and transplantation—The HTAct 2004.
- The HTAct 2004 prohibits commercial dealings in organ transplantations.
- The EU Organ Donation Directive published in 2010 was enshrined in UK law in 2012—it ensures common standards in quality and safety.

7.2 Legal and Regulatory Framework

The specific organ donation transplantation legislation is summarized here along with the associated regulatory framework provided by the Human Tissue Authority (HTA). The Mental Capacity Act 2005 (MCA) and the Human Rights Act 1998 are also of relevance, but will not be discussed in detail.

7.2.1 Primary and Secondary Legislation

A summary of the current primary and secondary legislation covering organ donation and transplantation in the UK is as follows:

- HTAct 2004 and associated regulations.
- The HTAct 2004 (Ethical Approval, Exceptions from Licensing and Supply of Information about Transplants) Regulations 2006.
- The HTAct 2004 (Persons who Lack Capacity to Consent and Transplants) Regulations 2006.

The HTAct 2004 came into force on 1 September 2006 and applies to England, Wales, and Northern Ireland. It provides a legislative framework for regulating the removal, storage and use of human organs and tissue from living and deceased donors for transplantation and research as well as for public display. Consent is the golden thread that runs throughout the Act and is a requirement for the retention and use of body parts, organs and tissue for the purposes specified therein. The Act is also supported by a suite of seven codes of practice. Those relevant to organ donation and transplantation include, Code A: Guiding principles and the fundamental principle of consent and Code F: Donation of solid organs and tissue for transplantation.

The first regulation covers the information that a medical practitioner who removes transplantable material from a donor and who receives the transplantable material is required to submit to NHS Blood and Transplant (NHSBT). The second regulation covers a definition of transplantable material, a list of the requirements for living donor transplantation to proceed, and the approval process of the HTA for these cases.

The Human Tissue Scotland Act came into force on 1 September 2006 and covers Scotland. The Scottish Act includes the following:

1) There is a specific duty on Scottish ministers to promote organ donation and transplantation.
2) It is based on the principle of authorization rather than consent, an expression which is intended to convey that people have the right to express, during their lifetime, their wishes

about what should happen to their bodies after death, in the expectation that those wishes will be respected.

3) The regulation of live donor transplantation will be undertaken by the HTA in line with the HTAct.

The Human Transplantation (Wales) Act 2013 came into force on December 2015. The Act allows for consent to deceased organ donation to be deemed to have been given when a person both lived and died in Wales unless they have opted out, are under 18 years of age, have lived in Wales for less than 12 months, have lived in Wales for more than 12 months but are not normally resident there, or lack capacity. Under these circumstances, a person's consent cannot be deemed to have been given, and express consent should be established or sought. The Welsh Act puts a duty on ministers to promote organ donation, but living donor transplantation remains under the jurisdiction of the HTA.

7.2.2 European Organ Donation Directive

The EU Directive 2010/53/EU on the standards of quality and safety of human organs intended for transplantation was transposed into UK law by The Quality and Safety of Organs Intended for Transplantation Regulations 2012, which was implemented on 27 August 2012. The Directive was put in place to ensure there were common quality and safety standards for the procurement, transport, and use of organs at an EU level. The first objective of the Directive is the safety and quality of organs through common standards, which also facilitates organ exchange between member states. It also contributes indirectly to combating organ trafficking through the establishment of competent authorities, the authorization of transplantation centres, and the establishment of conditions of procurement and systems of traceability.

At a later stage the Commission Implementing Directive 2012/25/EU, which sets out the rules for the transmission of information when organs are exchanged between member states, was transposed into UK law by the Quality and Safety of Organs Intended for Transplantation (Amendment) Regulations 2014. The HTA is the competent authority for the implementation of the Directive across the UK in conjunction with the relevant HTA Codes of Practice. All organizations undertaking procurement and transplantation activities require a licence, which is issued by the HTA in the UK.

7.2.3 Human Tissue Authority

Under the HTAct, the HTA was established to regulate activities concerning the removal, storage, use, and disposal of human tissue in England, Wales, and Northern Ireland. Under the Human Tissue Scotland Act the HTA is responsible for the living donor transplantation regulatory framework in Scotland.

The statutory functions of the HTA include:

- Providing advice and guidance to the Secretary of State for Health, healthcare professionals, and the public.
- Producing codes of practice.
- Regulating live donor transplantation.
- Licensing and inspection.
- Implementation of EU tissue and cells/organ donation directives.

KEY POINTS—LEGAL AND REGULATORY FRAMEWORK

- The HTAct 2004 regulates the removal, storage, and use of human organs and tissue from the living and deceased.

- Consent is required for the retention and use of body parts, organs, and tissue for purposes specified in the Act.
- The Human Tissue Scotland Act is based on the principle of authorization, not consent, and ministers have a duty to promote organ donation and transplantation.
- The Human Transplantation (Wales) Act 2013 allows consent for organ donation to be deemed unless a person has opted out.
- The EU Directive 2010/53/EU ensures common quality and safety standards for the procurement, transport, and use of organs at an EU level.
- The HTA regulates activities concerning the removal, storage, use, and disposal of human tissue in England, Wales, and Northern Ireland.

7.3 Consent

There are specific aspects of consent that relate to organ donation and transplantation. Whilst the term consent will be used throughout this section, the equivalent term in Scotland is authorization. Common law (see Chapter 1) and the MCA cover consent for the removal of organs from the living, whilst the HTAct covers consent for storage and use from the living, as well as consent for removal, storage, and use from the deceased.

7.3.1 Consent for Deceased Donation

In the UK the current model for consent for organ donation is to opt in, where an individual makes a decision in life that they would like their organs to be used for transplantation after their death. In other countries an opt-out model is in place, where everyone is assumed to agree to donate their organs after death unless they made an informed choice to opt out of donation during their lifetime. In reality, a soft opt-out model is used, whereby the family is consulted to see if they were aware of any unregistered objection and, if not, donation would proceed unless the family objected. From 1 December 2015, Wales introduced a soft opt-out system where two types of consent are recognized in law: deemed consent for those people who have not registered to opt out of donating an organ and express consent for those who have registered to say they wish to be a donor. England and Scotland are both currently developing opt-out legislation.

The HTAct makes it clear that, where adults make a decision in life to, or not to, consent to organ donation taking place after their death, then that consent is sufficient for the activity to be lawful. In summary, the wishes of the deceased, in life, should take precedence. The commonest means by which an individual expresses their decision to consent to organ donation in the UK is through the Organ Donor Register (ODR), although individuals may also express their wishes by letting their family know. In practice it is preferable for an individual to do both. If individuals become potential deceased organ donors, specialist nurses in organ donation are able to search the ODR to see if they are registered, and, if so, will ask the family to support the decision. The conversation is facilitated when the individual's decision in life to consent for organ donation does not come as a surprise to their family.

The UK ODR was implemented in 1994, enabling individuals to register their demographic details and to opt to donate all of their organs or specific organs, and there are currently around 25 million registrants. Under the HTAct it was still considered an appropriate vehicle for an individual to consent for organ donation. Critics have argued that the ODR is an inadequate means of expressing informed consent for organ donation, but in terms of the legislation it is deemed appropriate for recording consent for the principle of, rather than for the detailed process and procedure of, organ donation. A new NHS ODR was launched in the UK on 9 July 2015, to make the process of registering and amending details more accessible, and to prepare for the

Box 7.1 Hierarchy of persons in a qualifying relationship as ranked by the Human Tissue Act

- Spouse or partner
- Parent or child
- Brother or sister
- Grandparent or grandchild
- Niece or nephew
- Stepfather or stepmother
- Half-brother or half-sister
- Friend of long standing

implementation of the Human Transplantation (Wales) Act 2013. The new ODR gives registrants across the UK an opportunity to either express their wish to donate or not to donate.

If a potential deceased organ donor had not expressed a wish in life, views will be sought from a nominated representative or a person in a qualifying relationship. Section 4 of the HTAct introduces the rarely used concept of a nominated representative whereby adults may appoint one or more people to represent them after death and to provide a consent decision on their behalf. Otherwise consent would be sought from a person in a qualifying relationship. Box 7.1 lists a hierarchy of persons in a qualifying relationship as ranked by the HTAct. Consent is only needed from one person on the list and this should be obtained from the person ranked highest. There will be situations where there is a differing of opinions from family present, and the Code of Practice F gives some suggestions for resolution.

In the UK, excluding Scotland, adults are defined as 18 years or over, whilst in Scotland it is 16 years or over. Where a child is a potential deceased organ donor, the provisions for consent depend on both the age of the child and whether they were competent to make a decision in life. In Scotland, if the child was aged over 12 and had clearly expressed a wish for organ donation in life, then authorization is not required from a person with parental responsibility. In the rest of the UK, if the child was deemed competent, the person with parental responsibility would still have their views and wishes taken into consideration. Throughout the UK, where the child was not deemed competent or had made no decision, the person with parental responsibility would give consent/authorization. Where there is no one with parental responsibility or, outside Scotland, in a qualifying relationship, then organ donation cannot proceed as consent cannot be given.

UK law establishes that the consent/authorization given by the individual in life should take precedence after death, and that family members cannot legally override the wishes of the individual. However, in the year 2017/18 there were 90 families in the UK who felt unable to honour the wishes of their loved one for organ donation, despite sensitive discussion with a highly trained professional. This is a challenging situation where the law is clear, but where it is not considered appropriate to add to the distress of a recently bereaved family.

7.3.2 Consent for Living Donation

Common law and the MCA cover consent for the removal of organs from living organ donors (usually kidney and liver lobe), and storage and use by the HTAct. In reality the consent process will be combined for the removal, storage, and use. The regulation of living donor transplantation by the HTA is described in Section 7.5 and, as part of the approval process, the HTA will require evidence that consent is voluntary, informed, and given with capacity (see Chapter 2).

7.3.3 Consent for Organ Transplantation

Common law and the MCA cover consent for the recipient transplant operation. This consent should be used in conjunction with the best practice guidelines produced by NHSBT and the British

Transplantation Society Guidelines for consent for solid organ transplantation in adults, which covers informed consent from transplant listing to the transplant operation.

KEY POINTS—CONSENT TO DONATION AND TRANSPLANTATION

- Common law and the MCA cover consent for the removal of organs and tissue from the living.
- The HTAct covers consent for removal, storage, and use of organs and tissue from the living and deceased.
- In the UK the current model for consent for organ donation is opt-in except in Wales where it is opt-out.
- Individuals express consent to organ donation in the UK through the ODR or by letting their family know.
- Without an expressed wish, the highest ranked person in a qualifying relationship may give consent.
- Consent given in life takes precedence after death. Families cannot legally override this but their wishes need to be considered.

7.4 Deceased Donation

There are two types of deceased donors, the donation after brainstem death (DBD) donor and the donation after circulatory death (DCD) donor. The DBD donor, previously known as a heart-beating donor, has an irreversible brain injury with a diagnosis of brainstem death and is maintained on a ventilator in intensive care to maintain circulation and respiration until the time of organ donation. The DCD donor, previously known as a non-heart-beating donor, will have irreversible loss of circulatory and respiratory function following cardiac arrest after planned withdrawal of life-sustaining treatment in the context of severe illness or injury incompatible with life. The majority of DCD donors in the UK are controlled in that withdrawal of treatment takes place within an intensive care or emergency department environment. A minority have been uncontrolled DCD donors, where a witnessed out of hospital cardiac arrest has occurred followed by unsuccessful cardiopulmonary resuscitation.

7.4.1 Diagnosis of Death

The definition of death is considered the irreversible loss of the capacity for consciousness, combined with irreversible loss of the capacity to breathe. There is no legal definition of death in the UK, but the Courts of Law in England and Northern Ireland do recognize brain death criteria as part of the legal framework around the diagnosis of death. Section 26 of the HTAct makes specific provision for the HTA to draw up a Code of Practice on the definition of death for the purpose of the Act, although this has not been undertaken.

The diagnosis of death is clearly described in the *Code of Practice for the Diagnosis and Confirmation of Death*, the second edition of which was published by the Academy of the Medical Royal Colleges in 2008. Unlike the first edition, published in 1998, and previous memoranda on the diagnosis of brain death, the current edition deals entirely with the diagnosis and confirmation of death, whether that is following the irreversible cessation of brainstem function or following cessation of cardiorespiratory function. How that relates to organ donation and transplantation is covered in other documents, such as the HTA Codes of Practice. Deceased donation cannot happen until a diagnosis of death has been made, but for transplantation to be successful the organs need to be viable and therefore donors have to die of the right condition, in the right place, and in the right way.

7.4.2 Donation after Circulatory Death

There has been a fivefold increase in the number of DCD donors in the past decade and, whilst this was initially for kidney transplantation only, it has since expanded to include other organs. The HTAct and the MCA provide the legal framework for DCD donation. With this growth, there has been a more detailed exploration of the associated legal and ethical issues. The Department of Health has produced guidance relevant to England and Wales on legal issues relevant to non-heart-beating organ donation and there is equivalent and similar guidance from Scotland and Northern Ireland. This guidance covers a summary of the relevant legislation, assessing best interests in relation to a potential organ donor, the role of wishes and preferences in assessing best interests, and what specific steps can be taken before death to facilitate donation.

There is a specific provision in Section 43 of the HTAct that relates to uncontrolled DCD donation. This makes it lawful to preserve organs for transplantation whilst awaiting consent, using minimum steps with the least invasive procedure. This raises two specific issues.

Firstly, there was a conflict with the Coroners Act 1988, where the coroner has parallel power when the body of the potential donor also lies within his jurisdiction. This is explained in more detail within the HTA Code of Practice F, but, in essence, organ preservation cannot take place without the permission of the coroner in most causes of sudden death. Good practice guidelines promoting joint working between the transplant team and the coroner in this area are detailed in Annex B of this Code of Practice. Secondly, what constitutes minimum steps with the least invasive procedure? The Code of Practice states that 'minimum steps should be considered in terms of both what is least invasive to the donor, and also in terms of what may be perceived as appropriate by the family.' It states that cold perfusion and intraperitoneal cooling can be considered minimum steps. The Department of Health guidance on legal issues gives further advice.

7.4.3 Storage of Material

Under the HTAct the storage of an organ from a donor intended to be used for transplantation is exempt from licensing requirements. This also includes the storage of other relevant material such as spleen, lymph node, and blood provided the primary purpose is transplantation. If this material is subsequently retained for research purposes, then it becomes a licensable activity. To facilitate certain transplant procedures blood vessels will also be removed from the donor, and, providing these are used within 48 hours, they too are exempt from the licensing requirements.

7.4.4 Requested Allocation of a Deceased Donor Organ

The allocation of organs to recipients is the responsibility of NHSBT, although this must be within the legal framework of the HTAct and the Human Tissue Scotland Act. There are rare occasions where there is a request for allocation of a deceased donor organ to a close relative or friend. A joint policy document published by the four UK health administrations, the HTA, and NHSBT gives advice regarding the exceptional circumstances in which requested allocation can take place. The fundamental principle of all deceased organ donation is that it must be unconditional, and the Scottish legislation does not permit conditions to be attached to authorization for transplantation. A list of other principles that need to be met for requested allocation to proceed are given in the policy document.

KEY POINTS—DECEASED DONATION

- There are two types of deceased donors, those diagnosed with brainstem death (DBD) and those with circulatory death (DCD).
- There is no legal definition of death in the UK but the courts recognize brain death criteria as a diagnosis of death.

- Deceased donation cannot happen until death has been confirmed following cessation of cardiorespiratory function.
- In uncontrolled DCD donation it is lawful to preserve organs for transplantation whilst awaiting consent using minimum interventions.
- The coroner needs to give permission for organ preservation in most causes of sudden death.
- The storage of an organ from a donor intended to be used for transplantation is exempt from licensing requirements.
- It is a fundamental principle that deceased organ donation should be unconditional.

7.5 Living Donation

7.5.1 Summary of Living Donor Types

Living donor transplantation is usually for kidney or liver lobes, although it is possible to transplant the lung lobes. Understanding of the different types of living donation that are permitted under the HTAct has developed. Under the previous legislation living donation was living-related and living-unrelated/emotionally related, but the HTAct specifically allowed paired/pooled donation and altruistic non-directed donation. The current living donor types are:

- **Directed Donation**

  Where an individual donates to a known recipient with a genetic or pre-existing emotional relationship.
- **Directed Altruistic Donation**

  Where an individual donates to a known recipient with no genetic or pre-existing emotional relationship.
- **Non-directed Altruistic Donation**

  Where an individual donates to a recipient unknown to them.
- **Paired and Pooled Donation**

  Where an incompatible donor and recipient are matched with another incompatible pair through the UK Living Kidney Sharing Scheme (UKLKSS) and kidneys exchanged between the pairs. Where two pairs are involved this is paired donation, and where more than two pairs are involved it is pooled donation.
- **Non-directed Altruistic Donor Chain**

  Where a non-directed altruistic donor donates an organ into the paired/pooled scheme, and the organ at the end of the chain goes to the best matched recipient on the national list.
- **Domino Donation**

  Where an organ is removed for the primary purpose of treatment and, where suitable, can be transplanted into another individual. This type of donation is not regulated under the HTAct.

Whilst this section deals primarily with solid organ live donor transplantation, it is also important to note that the HTAct covers the donation of allogeneic bone marrow and peripheral blood stem cells (PBSCs) for transplantation. HTA approval is not required for donation of bone marrow and PBSCs by adults with capacity and children who are competent to give consent, but is required for adults without capacity and children who are not deemed competent to consent. Further details of the HTA approval process and of the arrangements in Scotland can be found in the HTA Code of Practice on Donation of allogeneic bone marrow and PBSCs for transplantation.

7.5.2 Regulation of Living Donation

Under Section 33 of the HTAct it is an offence for an individual to remove an organ from a living person, but the associated Regulations list the requirements for living donor transplantation to proceed, and the approval process of the HTA for these cases.

In summary, the requirements in the Regulations are:

- **Refer the Case to the HTA**

  A registered medical practitioner responsible for the donor must refer the case to the HTA.

- **Show No Evidence of Reward**

  The HTA must be satisfied that there is no evidence of reward, consent has been given, and is otherwise lawful.

- **Report from an Independent Assessor Required**

  The HTA must consider a report from a qualified person (the HTA has developed the role of the Independent Assessor for this purpose) who has interviewed the donor and recipient and which includes specified information listed in the regulations.

- **HTA Must Communicate Decision**

  The HTA must inform the donor, recipient, and referring clinician of their decision.

- **Valid Consent**

  The HTA must be satisfied that the donor has given valid consent.

- **Requirements of the Legislation Satisfied**

  For a living donor to go ahead, the HTA has to be satisfied that the requirements of the legislation are met. The HTA Living Donor Assessment Team considers for approval all straightforward living donor pairs based on the report submitted by the Independent Assessor. Non-directed altruistic donors, paired/pooled donors, and other cases with increased regulatory risk are considered for approval by a panel of three members of the HTA as stipulated in the Regulations.

A more detailed explanation of the regulatory framework and its practical outworking is found in the HTA's *Guidance to Transplant Teams and Independent Assessors*.

7.5.3 Children and Adults Lacking Capacity

The HTAct permits children and adults without capacity to be considered as living donors. In both situations court approval would need to be obtained prior to consideration by an HTA panel. In Scotland the situation is different, as children younger than 16 years of age or adults without capacity are not able to donate organs unless it is part of domino donation.

7.5.4 Paid Donation Is Illegal

Section 32 of the HTAct and Section 20 of the Human Tissue Scotland Act prohibit commercial dealings in human material for transplantation, and the penalty is up to 3 years in prison, a fine, or both. This includes giving or receiving a reward, acting as a broker for reward, and advertising for a reward.

KEY POINTS—LIVING DONATION

- Living donor transplantation is usually kidney or liver lobes.
- Living donor types include directed donation, directed/non-directed altruistic donation, paired/pooled donation, and domino donation.
- It is an offence for an individual to remove an organ from a living person for the purpose of donation without HTA approval.

- Court approval is required prior to consideration by an HTA panel of living donation from incapacitated patients.
- HTA approval is not required for donation of bone marrow and stem cells by competent adults and children but is required if there is incapacity.
- Paid donation is illegal.

7.6 Research, Education, and Training

The removal of organs or tissues from the deceased for research purposes is clearly defined under the HTAct. Consent is always required, but whether the place of removal needs to be an HTA licensed premise depends on the primary purpose for which the organ or tissue was removed. Removal for the primary purpose of transplantation does not require a licensed premise, but is required if the primary purpose is research. If the organ is removed for the primary purpose of transplantation, and then found to be unsuitable for transplantation, it can be used for research provided consent for research had been obtained, irrespective of whether the operating theatre was licensed for removal. However, if an organ is removed for the primary purpose of research even though other organs are removed from the same donor for transplantation, it must be done in an operating theatre that is licensed. The situation is different in Scotland, where the removal of organs for transplantation research only requires the necessary authorization.

Using human bodies or parts of bodies from the deceased for anatomical examination, education, and training are also scheduled purposes under the HTAct, and consent is required for the removal, storage, and use in England, Wales, and Northern Ireland. This does not apply to human cadavers imported into England, Wales, and Northern Ireland, and this includes material that is fresh, frozen, plastinated, dried, embalmed, or preserved in some way. Imported human material is covered by a separate Code of Practice, and it is expected that appropriate consent will have been obtained in the country of origin and that the material is used in accordance with that purpose. The storage of this material is, however, a licensable activity under the HTAct. The code specifies that institutions wishing to import material 'should be able to demonstrate that the purposes for which they wish to import such material cannot be adequately met by comparable material available from sources within those countries, or is for a particular purpose which justifies the import'.

KEY POINTS—RESEARCH, EDUCATION, AND TRAINING

- Consent is always required for the removal of organs or tissues from the deceased for research purposes.
- The place of removal of organs or tissues needs to be an HTA licensed premise if the primary purpose is research, despite using other organs for transplantation.
- Removal for the primary purpose of transplantation does not require a licensed premises.
- Human material imported for education and training is expected to be removed under appropriate consent in the country of origin.

7.7 Pearls and Pitfalls

7.7.1 Pearls

- The HTAct 2004 has been open enough to allow the development of the newer types of living donation that had not been envisaged when the legislation was written.

- There have been repeated calls for opt-out legislation across the UK, and the introduction of deemed consent legislation in Wales will give the opportunity to gauge its effectiveness compared to the existing opt-in legislation across the rest of the UK.

7.7.2 Pitfalls

- The law throughout the UK establishes that the consent/authorization given by the individual in life should take precedence after death, and that family members cannot legally override the wishes of the individual. However, around 10% of families feel unable to honour the wishes of their loved one for organ donation and do override.
- Transplant research has been hindered by the requirement for an organ removed for the primary purpose of research to be done in an operating theatre that is licensed under the HTA, except in Scotland, even though other organs are removed from the same donor for transplantation where a licensed premise is not required.

7.8 Further Reading

- Academy of Medical Royal Colleges. (2008). *A Code of Practice for the Diagnosis and Confirmation of Death* Accessed at http://www.aomrc.org.uk
- Department of Health. (2009). *Legal Issues Relevant to Non-Heart Beating Organ Donation.* Accessed at https://www.gov.uk/government
- Human Tissue Authority. (2017). *Code of Practice A: Guiding Principles and the Fundamental Principles of Consent.* Accessed at https://www.hta.gov.uk
- Human Tissue Authority. (2017). *Code of Practice F: Donation of Solid Organs and Tissues for Transplantation.* Accessed at https://www.hta.gov.uk
- Human Tissue Authority. (2016). *The Quality and Safety of Organs Intended for Transplantation: a Documentary Framework.* Accessed at https://www.hta.gov.uk
- Human Tissue Authority. (2017). *Code of Practice G: Donation of Allogeneic Bone Marrow and Peripheral Blood Stem Cells for Transplantation.* Accessed at https://www.hta.gov.uk
- Human Tissue Authority. (2017). *Code of Practice E: Research.* Accessed at https://www.hta.gov.uk
- Human Tissue Authority. (2017). *Guidance to Transplant Teams and Independent Assessors.* Accessed at https://www.hta.gov.uk/
- Human Tissue (Scotland) Act 2006. *A Guide to its Implications for NHS Scotland.* Accessed at https://www.hta.gov.uk
- NHSBT/British Transplantation Society. (2015). *Guidelines for Consent for Solid Organ Transplantation in Adults.* Accessed at http://www.odt.nhs.uk
- Price D. (2000). *Legal and Ethical Aspects of Organ Transplantation.* Cambridge: Cambridge University Press.
- UK Health Departments. (2010). *Requested Allocation of a Deceased Donor Organ.* Accessed at http://webarchive.nationalarchives.gov.uk

7.9 Multiple Choice Questions

✔ Interactive multiple choice questions to test your knowledge on this chapter can be found in the Online appendix at www.oxfordmedicine.com/essentiallegalmatters.

Elderly Care Law

Richard Biram

CONTENTS

CHAPTER SUMMARY

Geriatric Medicine

This is a branch of medicine concerned with the holistic management of ill-health in older adults.

Equality ACT

Age is one of nine protected characteristics described by the Equality Act. This ensures that older people receive fair treatment in relation to the provision of health or social care.

Elder Abuse

This is a violation of an elderly person's human and civil rights by another person. There are many types of abuse. Elder abuse may be difficult to identify.

Adult Safeguarding

This is a framework via which vulnerable adults may be protected from abuse. It was defined by the Care Act 2014.

Deprivation of Liberty Safeguards

The deprivation of liberty safeguards form part of the Mental Capacity Act. They ensure that people in hospitals and care homes are cared for in a way that does not inappropriately restrict their freedom.

Driver and Vehicle Licensing Agency
It can be difficult for an older adult to determine when they should stop driving. There is no legal age after which driving should cease. There are some medical conditions that preclude driving and which should be reported to the Driver and Vehicle Licensing Agency (DVLA).

IMPORTANT CASE LAW

- HL vs UK (Bournewood)
- P v Cheshire West and Chester Council
- P and Q v Surrey County Council

RELEVANT STATUTES AND LEGISLATION

- European Convention on Human Rights. http://www.echr.coe.int
- The Human Rights Act 1998. http://www.legislation.gov.uk
- The Mental Capacity Act 2005. http://www.legislation.gov.uk
- Deprivation of Liberty Safeguards 2007. http://webarchive.nationalarchives.gov.uk
- The Equality Act 2010. http://www.legislation.gov.uk
- The Care Act 2014. http://www.legislation.gov.uk

PROFESSIONAL GUIDANCE

- Department of Health. (2010). *No Secrets: Guidance on Developing and Implementing Multi-Agency Policies and Procedures to Protect Vulnerable Adults from Abuse.* https://www.gov.uk/government/uploads/system/uploads/attachment_data/file/194272
- Deprivation of Liberty Safeguards—Forms and Guidance. https://www.gov.uk/government/publications/deprivation-of-liberty-safeguards-forms-and-guidance
- British Geriatrics Society. https://www.bgs.org.uk
- DVLA. *Health Conditions and Driving.* https://www.gov.uk/health-conditions-and-driving
- Mental Capacity Act Code of Practice 2016. https://www.gov.uk/government/publications/mental-capacity-act-code-of-practice

8.1 Medicine for the Elderly

The Royal College of Physicians describes geriatric medicine as a branch of general medicine that is concerned with the clinical, preventative, remedial, and social aspects of illness in older age.

8.1.1 Definition

The name geriatric medicine was coined in 1914 by an American physician, Dr Ignatz Nascher. He described it as, ' … derived from the Greek, *geron*, old man and *iatrikos*, medical treatment'. In the UK, geriatric medicine was pioneered by Dr Marjorie Warren. Her enthusiasm stimulated the interest of the Ministry of Health, which recognized geriatric medicine as a speciality in 1948. Since that time, the speciality has grown significantly, and geriatric medicine departments are now found in most UK hospital trusts.

8.1.2 The Need for Specialist Medical Services for Older Adults

- Certain illnesses or syndromes are more common in older adults (e.g. dementia, Parkinson's disease, falls, stroke) and benefit from specialist geriatric multidisciplinary intervention.
- Older adults typically present to hospital with non-specific symptoms, e.g. confusion, falls, incontinence, or immobility.
- Older adults tend to suffer with multiple comorbidities, complicating the clinical picture.
- Older adults are often prescribed a large number of medications, which interact with their illnesses and with each other, adding complexity.
- Older adults are more likely to suffer with cognitive or psychological disorders, making clinical history-taking difficult.
- Older adults are more likely to have functional or social needs in addition to their medical needs.

This constellation of problems requires a holistic, team-based approach to care, utilizing a process known as the 'comprehensive geriatric assessment' (CGA).

8.1.3 Comprehensive Geriatric Assessment—Key Components

CGA is an evidence-based approach to the assessment and treatment of older adults, which returns more patients to their own homes and reduces inpatient mortality compared with standard ward care. The key components include:

- Medical history, functional status, gait and balance, continence, nutrition.
- Cognition, psychological assessment, medication review.
- Social support, financial concerns, home environment, goals of care, advanced care preferences.

The older person must remain central to the process in all aspects of CGA. The aim of CGA is to develop a multicomponent care plan to improve the health, psychological, and physical function of the patient. The result should be to promote wellbeing, enabling the patient to function in as independent an environment as possible whilst meeting their aspirations for care. In the UK, the Department of Health set out guidance for the structure of CGA in their single assessment process documentation (SAP) described in the National Service Framework for Older People 2001. Legal issues in the care of older adults are essentially the same as in younger adults. However, there are some areas that feature frequently on elderly care wards, and it is useful to consider these in more detail.

KEY POINTS—MEDICINE FOR THE ELDERLY

- Geriatric medicine deals with the clinical, preventative, remedial, and social aspects of illness in older age patients.
- Older adults are more likely to have functional or social needs in addition to their medical needs.
- A 'comprehensive geriatric assessment' (CGA) is a process utilizing a holistic, team-based approach to care.
- CGA is evidence-based and returns more patients to their own homes and reduces inpatient mortality compared with standard ward care.
- Legal issues in the care of older adults are *mostly* the same as in younger adults.

8.2 Models of Geriatric Medicine Services

In the UK, geriatric medicine services are organized within secondary care and in community settings.

8.2.1 Geriatric Medicine in Secondary Care

Geriatric medicine is the largest of the UK medical specialities. Sixty-five per cent of people admitted to hospital are aged over 65, and this proportion is rising. Older individuals admitted to hospital are most likely to be frail, cognitively impaired, and are prone to protracted hospital stays and poorer clinical outcomes. Many older adults require social support after discharge and benefit from staff with expertise in discharge planning. Secondary care services for older adults may be organized in a variety of ways.

8.2.2 Geriatric Medicine Service Models

- **Fully integrated:** geriatric medicine team is integrated with the general medicine team or other specialities (e.g. orthogeriatric models).
- **Age-based:** an arbitrary cut-off determining which patients are appropriate for geriatric medicine services. Seventy-five years is the most common marker, but it may vary from 65 to 85 depending upon service structure.
- **Needs-based:** individuals most suitable for CGA are identified, for example, by functional status, rehabilitation needs, or other markers such as frailty or cognitive impairment.

In secondary care, medicine for the elderly services are usually designed around a multidisciplinary team. The evidence base supports a ward-based approach to care, involving geriatricians working with staff from a variety of specialisms, such as physiotherapy, occupational therapy, psychiatry, and palliative care in an environment catering towards the needs of older adults. There is usually close working with community services and an onus on CGA and the development of a care plan via the multidisciplinary framework.

In recent years, there has been increasing recognition of the potential benefits of specialist geriatricians in other areas of care. This includes specialist surgical services (orthogeriatrics or general surgical geriatrics), acute geriatrics, and interface geriatrics. In such services, geriatricians usually work alongside specialists from other teams (surgeons/emergency physicians, etc.) to provide support for the care of frail adults.

8.2.3 Geriatric Medicine in the Community

Outside the acute hospitals there is a variety of primary and intermediate care services provided for older adults around the UK. The nature of services is not homogenous and there is wide variation between localities. In most areas, older adults will access primary care services at their local general practice. In 2014–2015, amendments to the general practice contract require that all over-75-year-olds in England have a named general practitioner (GP) who will oversee their care. By 31 March 2016, this will extend to all patients. Many GP services identify their most vulnerable older adults and offer more proactive care. The aim is to prevent deterioration and hospital admission by undertaking multidisciplinary reviews and developing community health and social care plans.

Most localities provide a range of community services suited to the care of older adults. This includes community matrons, home carers, and intermediate care professionals, who, between them, can provide a range of supervisory, clinical, and caring roles to help maintain individuals' heath and enable them to live safely in their own home. There are a range of allied specialities, such as psychogeriatrics and palliative care, which have strong links into services for older adults. Some services are organized by social services, others by the clinical commissioning group and local health budgets. Local policies and systems are subject to considerable variation, as demonstrated by the National Audit of Intermediate Care.

Older adults may be cared for in bed-based intermediate care units. Most are modelled as rehabilitation units. They may be situated in community hospitals or care homes. Services may be nurse-led, therapy-led, or GP or geriatrician-led, depending upon local availability. Intermediate care may also be provided in a patient's own home or in a care home depending upon a patient's needs or wishes. Community geriatricians play an important role in the management of elderly patients in most areas. Duties include managing intermediate care facilities, performing domiciliary visits, and undertaking peripatetic care in residential and nursing homes.

KEY POINTS—MODELS OF GERIATRIC MEDICAL SERVICES

- Geriatric medicine services are organized within secondary care and in community settings.
- Sixty-five per cent of people admitted to hospital are aged over 65, and this proportion is rising.
- Geriatric medicine service models can be fully integrated, age-based, or needs-based.
- In secondary care, evidence supports a ward-based approach to care, involving geriatricians working with staff from a variety of specialisms.
- Outside the acute hospitals there is a variety of primary and intermediate care services provided for older adults around the UK.
- Intermediate care bed-based units for older adults may be in community hospitals or care homes.

8.3 Age Discrimination

Age discrimination is unfairly treating people differently because of their age. The Equality Act 2010 described nine protected characteristics by which no individual should be subject to discrimination. They are: age, disability, gender reassignment, marriage or civil partnership, pregnancy and maternity, race, religion or belief, sex, and sexual orientation. It may be unlawful if an individual is treated differently because of a protected characteristic. The prohibition on age discrimination in services and public functions came into force on 1 October 2012. It is unlawful for service providers to discriminate, victimize, or harass a person because of their age.

CASE STUDY 1

The NHS Abdominal Aortic Aneurysm Screening Programme offers routine aneurysm screening for men aged over 65. Is a 60-year-old man unfairly discriminated against by this arrangement?

Sometimes it is not unlawful if someone treats an individual differently because of their age. The law says it is possible to justify direct age discrimination if there is a good enough reason to do so. This is described as an objective justification. An objective justification must describe a proportionate means of achieving a legitimate aim and should be able to be tested in court. In Case Study 1, the screening programme could argue that it offers routine aneurysm screening for men aged over 65 because the risk of dying from a ruptured abdominal aortic aneurysm is far greater in that group than any other. Ninety-five per cent of ruptured aneurysms occur in men aged over 65. There is no evidence that routine screening of patients in other groups offers clinical benefit. Routinely screening low-risk individuals might cause unnecessary concern. This is an example of an appropriate reason for treating people differently based on age. Age is the only protected characteristic by which it may be legally possible to discriminate directly. Age is the only protected characteristic that changes during everyone's life. Therefore, all individuals could potentially benefit from preferential treatment at some point due to their age. This is not the case for the other protected characteristics.

8.3.1 Age Discrimination in Clinical Practice

In clinical practice, patients should not be treated differently on the basis of their age.

CASE STUDY 2

A 92-year-old care home resident presents to the emergency department with severe pneumonia. The emergency department team contact the intensive care team (ICU) as they have recognized the impending need for invasive ventilatory support to prevent clinical deterioration. The intensive care doctor responds that the patient is not a candidate for ICU—as they are too old. The ICU never accepts patients aged over 90.

Case Study 2 describes behaviour suggestive of age discrimination, which could be unlawful under the Equality Act legislation. A clinical decision of this nature should not be made on the basis of age. Decisions in relation to the escalation of clinical care require consideration of several factors, including premorbid health status, current clinical condition, likely escalation requirements, potential reversibility of disease, and the wishes of patients and/or their families. In Case Study 2, there is not sufficient information to determine whether intensive ventilatory support is clinically appropriate. Further information is required and might materially affect the decision-making process.

Consider the following possible extrapolations of the scenario:

- The 92-year-old is in a nursing home with severe dementia. He does not recognize his family and is totally dependent upon nursing staff for basic care. He has recurrent chest infections owing to poor swallow and past medical history includes severe aortic stenosis and heart failure.
- The 92-year-old is resident in an assisted living complex. He moved in for company after his wife died. There are no major comorbidities and he is physically robust. He recently underwent general anaesthetic for a hip operation, from which he recovered rapidly. He is an active hobbyist and writes for a local magazine.

The first example describes someone who is extremely unlikely to survive an admission to ICU and seems to be entering the terminal phase of dementia. Given the severity of his current illness, his comorbid heart disease, his poor baseline status, and the high risk of recurrent pneumonia, it would be appropriate to discuss the likelihood of a poor outcome with his family and adopt a more conservative approach to care. The second example describes someone who might well benefit from intensive care treatment. He appears to require single organ support, has a potentially reversible condition, and is otherwise quite fit.

These examples demonstrate that age is not a good sole determinant when making clinical decisions. This is because of the wide variation in clinical presentation of patients of different ages. Older adults may experience worse clinical outcomes than younger adults in some clinical situations. However, this is usually because of the burden of comorbidities, baseline functional status, physical frailty, or cognitive dysfunction. Such issues can also be present in younger adults, whilst some older adults may be remarkably fit. Clinical decisions should take account of this variation.

KEY POINTS—AGE DISCRIMINATION

- Age discrimination is unfairly treating someone differently because of their age. It is covered by the Equality Act 2010.
- It is unlawful for service providers to discriminate, victimize, or harass persons because of their age.

- The law says it is possible to justify direct age discrimination if there is a good enough reason to do so—an objective justification.
- A clinical decision should not be made on the basis of age as it is not a good determinant of outcome.

8.4 Elder Abuse and the Safeguarding of Vulnerable Adults

Elder abuse is a violation of an elderly person's human and civil rights by another person. Abuse was defined by the Department of Health in their 'No Secrets' document:

> 'Abuse may consist of a single act or repeated acts. It may be physical, verbal or psychological. It may be an act of neglect or an omission to act, or it may occur when a vulnerable person is persuaded to enter into a financial or sexual transaction to which he or she has not consented, or cannot consent. Abuse can occur in any relationship and may result in significant harm to, or exploitation of, the person subjected to it.' (© Crown Copyright.)

8.4.1 Types of Abuse

Please see Table 8.1 for information on the types of abuse. A further form of abuse is institutional abuse, including neglect or poor care practices within an institution or care setting, e.g. hospital or care home. Elder abuse can be difficult to detect. The first step in detection is to consider the possibility and enquire. In studies, between 5% and 10% of dependent older adults report some form of abuse. Verbal and psychological abuse is more common than physical abuse.

8.4.2 Risk Factors for Abuse

Abused patients may be physically frail, dependent upon their carer, living in a care home. They may have communication difficulties, cognitive impairment, behavioural problems, aggressive tendencies, and come from lower socioeconomic backgrounds. A carer who abuses is more likely

Table 8.1 Table detailing the various types of abuse

	Example
Physical	Hitting, slapping, pushing, kicking, misuse of medication, restraint, or inappropriate sanctions
Sexual	Rape and sexual assault or sexual acts to which the vulnerable adult has not consented, or could not consent, or was pressured into consenting
Psychological	Emotional abuse, threats of harm or abandonment, deprivation of contact, humiliation, blaming, controlling, intimidation, coercion, harassment, verbal abuse, isolation, or withdrawal from services or supportive networks
Financial or material	Theft, fraud, exploitation, pressure in connection with wills: property or inheritance or financial transactions, or the misuse or misappropriation of property, possessions, or benefits
Neglects and acts of omission	Ignoring medical or physical care needs, failure to provide access to appropriate health, social care, or educational services, the withholding of the necessities of life, such as medication, adequate nutrition, and heating
Discriminatory	Racist, sexist, that based on a person's disability, and other forms of harassment, slurs, or similar treatment

to be suffering from stress, excessive alcohol consumption, changed lifestyle owing to caring role, psychiatric illness, dependence upon the abused (e.g. financial), or suffer isolation.

8.4.3 Detecting Elder Abuse

Elder abuse may be difficult to substantiate and requires careful and sensitive investigation. There is a wide variety of features that may trigger further discussion or review—although many may be present in the absence of abuse. Some warning signs of potential elder abuse include:

- Unexplained falls, injuries, and fractures.
- Burns or bruising in unusual places or of an unusual type.
- Evidence of neglect (poor personal hygiene, malnourishment, dehydration, bed sores).
- Carer withholding or wrongly administering medications.
- Withdrawals of money that are erratic or unusual.
- Level of care or amenities incongruous with known financial status.
- Property is missing, older person 'can't find' jewellery or personal belongings.
- Recurrent genital infections or bruises around breasts, genital area, rectum.
- Patient withdrawn, frightened, or anxious.
- Carer complaining of stress or acting aggressively.
- Carer appearing excessively concerned or unconcerned.
- Difficulty gaining access to patient.
- Refusal by patient or carer to accept appropriate support services.

8.4.4 Managing Abuse

The Care Act 2014 defines adult safeguarding as protecting a person's right to live in safety, free from abuse and neglect. From 1 April 2015, the Department of Health's 'No Secrets' guidance (2000) was replaced in England by Sections 42–46 of the Care Act 2014. Prior to the Care Act, safeguarding was known in England and Wales as 'adult protection'. Under the Care Act, local authorities have new statutory safeguarding duties, including:

- Making enquiries when they think an adult with care needs may be at risk of abuse.
- Establishment of Safeguarding Adults Boards (SABs).
- Arranging for an independent advocate to represent and support a person who is subject of a safeguarding enquiry.
- Cooperating with each of its partners to protect adults experiencing or at risk of abuse.

The Care Act defines a 'wellbeing principle' whereby the local authority must promote wellbeing whilst carrying out their care and support functions, including adult safeguarding. There are six principles of safeguarding within the guidance:

- **Empowerment**—person-led decisions and informed consent.
- **Prevention**—it is better to take action before harm occurs.
- **Proportionality**—least intrusive response appropriate to the risk.
- **Protection**—support and representation for those in need.
- **Partnerships**—local solutions through community services.
- **Accountability**—and transparency in delivery.

Patients who lack capacity to make informed decisions around their preferred outcomes must have a representative or advocate appointed who will act in their best interests. Decisions should be determined according to a 'best interests' approach. Formal mental capacity assessments are required to provide evidence of the patient's ability to make informed decisions. Assessments are decision-specific and must be recorded in the patient's medical record.

CASE STUDY 3

A frail 85-year-old lady is admitted via the emergency department one evening. She suffered a fall and, during examination, admits her husband sometimes drinks too much alcohol and becomes verbally abusive towards her. This has been going on for years. On one occasion, a few months ago, he was physically aggressive and gripped her wrists very tightly whilst shouting at her. There have been no other episodes of violent behaviour. What steps should the clinician take in this scenario?

In Case Study 3, the key issues pertain to the patient's mental capacity and her wishes in reporting the abuse. If the patient is cognitively impaired and lacks capacity to make informed decisions around safeguarding issues, the allegations should prompt a referral to the local adult safeguarding team to undertake a further investigation in the patient's best interests. Where a patient retains capacity to make decisions of this nature, a safeguarding referral should be recommended, and made with his or her consent. All health and social care professionals have a duty to act if they suspect that elder abuse is occurring. Confidentiality can be broken to report abuse, in particular, if a criminal act has occurred. If a health professional is uncertain whether a situation is elder abuse, advice can be sought from the adult safeguarding coordinator. A safeguarding referral is necessary if there is evidence that the person may be at risk of harm.

8.4.5 Safeguarding in Practice

- Record any details in writing. Be accurate and objective.
- Where possible, a person with safeguarding experience should discuss the suspected abuse with the victim.
- If the victim is thought to be unsafe, he or she should be moved to a place of safety (usually by a senior person with safeguarding experience).
- Contact the local social services department and inform them that a safeguarding referral is being made.
- If it is believed that a crime has been committed, the police should be informed (e.g. assault, theft, or fraud).

Victims should be notified of a safeguarding referral unless it is believed that doing so will cause them physical or psychological harm. Some individuals may object to a safeguarding referral being made. If so, an assessment must be made of their capacity to make this decision. Consider whether they are being coerced or intimidated. If so, undertake further discussion in a different environment. An elderly person with capacity has the right to make decisions that comprise a level of risk, e.g. they may choose to continue to live with an abusive partner even if there is a risk of being harmed in the future. Actions resulting from a safeguarding referral may include support for the vulnerable individual (e.g. care package at home), disciplinary proceedings for professionals, or criminal prosecution, depending upon the nature of the abuse.

KEY POINTS—ELDER ABUSE AND THE SAFEGUARDING OF VULNERABLE ADULTS

- Elder abuse is a violation of an elderly person's human and civil rights by another person.
- Abuse can be a single or repeated act. It may be physical, verbal, psychological, an act of neglect/omission, or any form of exploitation.
- Institutional abuse is neglect or poor care practice within an institution or care setting, e.g. hospital or care home.
- The Care Act 2014 defines adult safeguarding as protecting a person's right to live in safety, free from abuse and neglect.

- All healthcare professionals have a duty to act if they suspect elder abuse, and confidentiality can be broken to report it.
- A safeguarding referral is necessary if there is evidence that the person may be at risk of harm.
- Actions resulting from a safeguarding referral may include support, disciplinary proceedings for professionals, or criminal prosecution.

8.5 Deprivation of Liberty Safeguards

The deprivation of liberty safeguards (DoLS) are part of the Mental Capacity Act 2005 and were introduced in 2009 to provide a legal framework for the care and treatment of individuals in care. They apply in England and Wales. The aim is to ensure that people in hospitals or care homes or other supported living environments are cared for in a way that does not inappropriately restrict their freedom.

CASE STUDY 4

The Bournewood Case—HL vs UK

The Bournewood case involved HL, a man with autism. HL was informally admitted to Bournewood Psychiatric Hospital in 1997. A prior resident at the hospital for over 30 years, in 1994 he was discharged to live with two foster carers. One day in July 1997, he became agitated in a day centre and was brought to Bournewood where he was sedated and admitted.

During his admission, he never attempted to leave hospital, but his carers were prevented from visiting and the professional team disagreed with HL's wishes for them to visit and for him to be discharged home. The carers commenced legal action to secure his discharge from hospital.

The case was heard in the High Court, The Court of Appeal, and the House of Lords, but ultimately it was found at the European Court of Human Rights that, in the absence of use of the Mental Health Act, there had been a violation of HL's right to liberty. This case led to the development of the deprivation of liberty safeguards.

The Bournewood Case determined that, where a person is deprived of his or her liberty without any legal authority, then it is a breach of Article 5 of the European Convention on Human Rights, 'No one should be deprived of their liberty unless it is prescribed by law'. The DoLS state that, when a person needs to be deprived of their liberty, there must be safeguards that will ensure that it is in the person's best interests, that he or she has representatives and rights of appeal, and that the DoL is regularly reviewed. The safeguards apply to people in hospitals and care homes registered under the Care Standards Act 2000. They became a statutory obligation on 1 April 2009. Adults in supported living and home settings are covered by the legislation since March 2014.

On 19 March 2014, the Supreme Court presented a judgment on the joint cases of P v Cheshire West and Chester Council and P and Q v Surrey County Council. This judgment has helped to clarify whether care arrangements are in breach of the legislation. In the judgment, the Supreme Court confirmed that, to determine whether a person is deprived of his or her liberty, there are two key questions to ask, described as the 'acid test':

1. Is the person free to leave?
2. Is the person subject to continuous supervision and control?

The Supreme Court determined that it is irrelevant whether the person objects to the care arrangements. It is also irrelevant whether the arrangements are felt to be in the person's best interests. This means that, if a person lacks capacity to consent to their care or treatment, is not free to leave, and is subject to continuous supervision and control, they are deprived of their liberty. The judgment advises that a low threshold should be used in applying the acid test given the vulnerability of people likely to be deprived of their liberty, and the intention that the DoLS should be protective of such people.

8.5.1 Identifying a Deprivation of Liberty

A person must lack capacity—as defined by the Mental Capacity Act. Apply the acid test—is the person subject to continuous supervision, are they free to leave? Each case should be considered individually; however, some factors might indicate that a DoL application would be particularly worthwhile:

- Use of physical restraints or sedation to control behaviour.
- The individual is confined to a particular area of their care environment (e.g. a ward with a locked door).
- Objections or possible challenges to the confinement, e.g. family expressing concern regarding sedation, or Court of Protection order expected.
- The individual is subject to an existing DoL authorization which is due to expire.

Anyone can request a DoLS assessment. Usually it is the role of the managing authority (i.e. care home or hospital) to alert the supervisory body, who then instruct and authorize assessments from a best interests assessor and mental health assessor.

8.5.2 Standard and Urgent Authorizations

8.5.2.1 Standard Authorizations

These should be used where a managing authority identifies that it is likely that currently, or within the next 28 days, someone will be in a hospital or care home in circumstances that amount to a DoL. Where possible, a standard authorization should be sought in advance. The managing authority must fill out a form requesting a standard authorization. This is sent to the supervisory body, which has 21 days to determine whether the person can be deprived of his or her liberty. This is usually undertaken via the same processes as the local safeguarding team. The supervisory body will appoint assessors to consider whether the individual may remain deprived of their liberty under the safeguards. If the assessors determine that the DoL cannot be authorized (e.g. if the current arrangements are not found to be in the individual's best interests), alternative arrangements may need to be made by the care home or hospital so that the patient can be cared for in a less restrictive way. If the DoL is authorized, it may be valid for up to 1 year and must be reviewed regularly.

8.5.2.2 Urgent Authorizations

These are valid for 7 days but may be extended. The managing authority can give an urgent authorization for a DoL where it believes the need is immediate (i.e. to provide care before the supervisory body are able to respond). This should only normally be used where there are sudden unforeseen needs. Any decision to authorize a DoL must be considered to be in the person's best interests. All patients with an active DoL authorization will have a representative—this can be a family member, friend, or paid representative if no family/friends are identified to take on this role. Independent mental capacity advocates (IMCAs) will represent a person being assessed by a best interests assessor if they have no friends or family to represent them. An IMCA can also be available to provide support to friends or family acting as representatives.

CASE STUDY 5

A 79-year-old gentleman with dementia is admitted to hospital after suffering a fall. He wandered from his home and was found collapsed by a passer-by. No cause for his collapse was identified and the patient was deemed medically fit for discharge. The multidisciplinary team were concerned that, due to his cognitive impairment, the patient was at risk of wandering from home again and kept him on the ward for his own safety until appropriate discharge arrangements could be made.

The patient consistently asked whether he could go home, and on two occasions was prevented from leaving the ward by nursing staff. On one occasion he became aggressive when he couldn't leave and security were called to the ward to prevent him from leaving. The psychiatry team report that he has no insight into the dangers he presents to himself and does not have capacity in terms of making discharge decisions. Is this patient being deprived of his liberty?

In Case Study 5, the patient meets the criteria for a DoL referral. He does not have capacity to make discharge decisions. He is not free to leave the ward. He is under a form of continuous supervision and, despite the fact that he is not being sedated or physically restrained, his persistent attempts to leave the ward are an indication of his wishes and suggest that a DoL referral would be appropriate in this case.

KEY POINTS—DEPRIVATION OF LIBERTY SAFEGUARDS

- If a person is unlawfully deprived of their liberty, it is a breach of Article 5 of the European Convention on Human Rights.
- The deprivation of liberty safeguards (DoLS) is a legal framework to protect patients from unlawful restriction to their freedoms.
- The safeguards apply to people in hospitals, care homes, supported living, and home settings.
- A DoLS authorization ensures that liberty restrictions are in the person's best interests, they are represented, have rights of appeal, and are kept under regular review.
- Two key questions determine if liberty is curtailed. (1) Is the person free to leave? (2) Is the person subject to continuous supervision and control?
- Anyone can request a DoLS assessment. The facility manager alerts the supervisory body (local authority) who then deploy a best interests/mental health assessor.
- Standard or urgent authorizations can be applied for and, if a DoLS is authorized, it may be valid for up to 1 year and must be reviewed regularly.

8.6 Driving and Older Adults

There is no legal age after which an individual should cease driving. When to stop driving is an individualized decision. In the UK, a driving licence must be renewed at the age of 70. It must then be renewed every 3 years on completion of a declaration of good health. In addition, an older driver may be required to undergo a medical examination by their insurer. A driver must notify the DVLA about any medical conditions that may affect their ability to drive safely. This might include pre-existing conditions or new ones.

Patients might wish to consider whether they remain safe to drive if they notice their reactions are slower than they used to be, if they find driving increasingly stressful, if their eyesight is getting worse, or if they have a medical condition that may affect their driving. If patients are uncertain whether a medical condition may affect driving ability, they should consult their GP.

There are a large number of medical conditions that will render an individual unfit to drive. The DVLA website has a comprehensive list of medical conditions and details about which conditions confer driving restrictions. There is also an advice line for medical professionals seeking assistance. Some conditions that cause concern about driving in older adults include:

- Conditions causing loss of consciousness (epilepsies, syncope, poorly controlled diabetes, etc.).
- Paroxysmal cardiac arrhythmias/severe ischaemic heart disease.
- Severe Parkinson's disease.
- Cognitive impairment.
- Uncorrectable visual impairment (it is illegal to drive if you cannot read a number plate from a distance of 20.5 m).
- Some acute conditions have definitive short-term restrictions, e.g. stroke, myocardial infarction, pacemaker insertion.

Some considerations where there is concern about an older person driving:

- Is any impairment permanent or temporary?
- Are there any vehicle adaptations that would reduce a disability?
- If patients or their families have concerns in relation to driving, they should seek advice from a medical professional (GP or relevant specialist).
- A formal assessment of driving ability can be undertaken in a driving assessment centre if a patient so wishes, or if concerns remain after medical review.
- If a medical professional believes a patient is driving despite advice to stop, where doing so is a danger to public safety, the doctor has a duty to inform the DVLA.

KEY POINTS—DRIVING AND OLDER ADULTS

- There is no legal age after which an individual should cease driving.
- In the UK, a driving licence must be renewed at the age of 70 and then every 3 years thereafter on completion of a declaration of good health.
- Drivers must notify the DVLA about medical conditions that may affect their ability to drive safely.
- The DVLA website has a comprehensive list of medical conditions and details about which conditions confer driving restrictions.
- If a patient is driving despite advice to stop, where doing so is a danger to public safety, the doctor has a duty to inform the DVLA.

8.7 Pearls and Pitfalls

8.7.1 Pearls

Most older adults are able to participate in decision-making around their care. They should not be excluded from the process. Remember to take a person-centred approach in all aspects of clinical practice. Where necessary, undertake and document the findings of a test of mental capacity in relation to individual decisions (e.g. discharge destination, escalation of care, etc.).

8.7.2 Pitfalls

Age is not a good sole indicator of likely benefit from treatment. Some older adults will experience very good clinical outcomes, even with invasive treatment. When considering the level of care to provide an older adult, a thorough history and consideration of baseline function and clinical status is vital.

8.8 Further Reading

- Action on Elder Abuse, PO Box 60001, Streatham, London, SW16 9BY. Accessed at https://www.elderabuse.org.uk
- AgeUK. Tavis House, 1–6 Tavistock Square, London, WC1H 9NA. Accessed at https://www.ageuk.org.uk
- Barton A et al. (2003). History of geriatric medicine in the UK. *Postgraduate Med J*, 79, 229–34.
- Bonnie RJ (2003). *Elder Mistreatment: Abuse, Neglect and Exploitation in an Aging America.* Washington, DC: National Academies Press.
- Clarfield M (1990). Dr Ignatz Nascher and the birth of geriatrics. *Can Med Assoc J*, 143(9), 944–5.
- Ellis G et al. (2011). Comprehensive geriatric assessment for older adults admitted to hospital: meta-analysis of randomised controlled trials. *BMJ*, 343, d6553.
- Royal College of Physicians. (2012). *Hospitals on the Edge, The Time for Action.* London: RCP.
- Lachs M et al. (2004). Elder abuse. *Lancet*, 364, 1263–72.
- NHS England. (2014). *National Audit of Intermediate Care.*
- Office of the Public Guardian. (2013). *Safeguarding Policy.* Nottingham: OPG.
- RCP Specialities Pages. Royal College of Physicians. Accessed at https://www.rcplondon.ac.uk
- The Supreme Court of the United Kingdom, Parliament Square, London, SW1P 3BDT. Accessed at http://supremecourt.uk
- World Health Organization. (2002). *World Report on Violence and Health.* Geneva: WHO.

8.9 Multiple Choice Questions

✔ Interactive multiple choice questions to test your knowledge on this chapter can be found in the Online appendix at www.oxfordmedicine.com/essentiallegalmatters.

Child Health Law

Roddy O' Donnell

CHAPTER SUMMARY

Parens Patriae

    It is the State's duty to protect dependent persons from harm.

Reasonableness

    A reasonable doctor should consider what a child and those legally responsible for the child should expect to know about the child's care, especially in matters of consent.

The Parents Speak for the Best Interests of the Child

    The starting point assumes that the parents speak for the best interests of the child. If there is disagreement between the parents or between the treating team and the parents, formal legal advice may need to be sought.

The Transition to Adult Decision-Making

    A child, although a minor, may have sufficient understanding and intelligence to make decisions about treatment that is not determined by a judicially fixed age limit.

Parental Responsibility

Parental responsibility can be acquired by many legal methods and is not automatically conferred by a biological relationship.

Abuse and Neglect

Abuse and neglect of children is a serious global issue, although there are signs that it is reducing in the developed world over recent decades.

IMPORTANT CASE LAW

- Bolam v Friern Hospital Management Committee [1957] 1 WLR 582
- Gillick v West Norfolk and Wisbech AHA [1986] AC 112
- 'Marion's Case' [1992] 175 CLR 189
- Bolitho v City & Hackney Health Authority [1997] 3 WLR 1151 House of Lords
- Re MB [1997] EWCA Civ 3093 26 March 1997
- Montgomery v Lanarkshire Health Board [2015] UKSC 11

PROFESSIONAL GUIDANCE

- General Medical Council. (2004). *Withholding or Withdrawing Life Sustaining Treatment in Children: A Framework for Practice*, 2nd edn. https://gmc-uk.org
- Royal College of Obstetricians and Gynaecologists. (2005). *Guidance on the Registration of Stillbirths and Certification for Pregnancy Loss Before 24 Weeks of Gestation*. https://rcog.org.uk
- BMA. (2006). *The Law and Ethics of Male Circumcision: Guidance for Doctors*. https://www.bma.org.uk
- BMA. (2008). *Parental Responsibility*. https://www.bma.org.uk
- BMA. (2008). *Working Together to Safeguard Children*. https://www.bma.org.uk
- MPS. (2008). *Guide to Ethics: A Map for the Moral Maze*. http://www.medicalprotection.org
- BMA. (2010). *Children and Young People Toolkit*. https://www.bma.org.uk
- BMA. (2011). *Female Genital Mutilation—Caring for Patients and Safeguarding Children*. https://www.bma.org.uk
- GMC. (2012). *Protecting Children and Young People: the Responsibilities of All Doctors*. https://www.gmc-uk.org
- Faculty of Forensic and Legal Medicine. (2012). *Guidelines on Paediatric Forensic Examinations in Relation to Possible Child Sexual Abuse*. https://fflm.ac.uk
- Royal College of Paediatrics and Child Health. (2014). *Child Protection and the Anaesthetist. Safeguarding Children in the Operating Theatre*. https://rcpch.ac.uk
- Royal College of Paediatrics and Child Health. (2014). *Guidance on Clinical Research Involving Infants, Children and Young People: an Update for Researchers and Research Ethics Committees*. https://rcpch.ac.uk

9.1 Consent in Children

9.1.1 Definition of a Child

Article 1, Convention on the Rights of the Child, 1989 (ratified in 1991 in the UK)

'every human being below the age of eighteen years unless, under the law applicable to the child, majority is attained earlier'

English law on the consent to treatment has continuously evolved over the past 50 years through the principles of common law (see Chapter 1) and changes in societal attitudes. In children and young adults, it has meant that laws overlap in such a way that, although there are clear age boundaries, there are complexities. Also, there are some differences between the laws of Scotland, England, and Northern Ireland. In the legal concept known as *parens patriae* it has for centuries been accepted that ultimately it is the state's duty to protect dependent persons from harm. The concept originally developed to assist adults that lacked what is now known as capacity. Over the past 200 years it came to include the protection of children, including in some cases from their parents. In the past 20 years, the consideration of when children should be considered capable of making informed choices about their medical treatment, and when the state should decide, has changed considerably.

9.1.2 Reasonableness

The principles of what is reasonable information that a patient should be told when giving informed consent are changing. The long held legal principle established in the Bolam test (Bolam v Friern Hospital Management Committee 1957), which is 'the standard of a responsible body of medical opinion', and which was refined in Bolitho (Bolitho v City and Hackney Health Authority 1997) so that a judge may reject a medical opinion that is 'logically indefensible', has received criticism over time that reflects changing societal attitudes. Information about medicine is now becoming much more readily accessible to the wider population. On 11 March 2015 the UK Supreme Court ruling in Montgomery v Lanarkshire Health Board made a specific departure from previous rulings by placing more responsibility on clinicians, stating 'the doctor's duty of care takes its precise content from the needs, concerns and circumstances of the individual patient, to the extent that they are or ought to be known to the doctor', and in explaining the risk that 'The test of materiality is whether, in the circumstances of the particular case, a reasonable person in the patient's position would be likely to attach significance to the risk, or the doctor is or should reasonably be aware that the particular patient would be likely to attach significance to it'. The test is therefore: to be a reasonable doctor one must consider what a reasonable patient should know and is establishing a significantly higher standard for consent, perhaps especially in children.

9.1.3 Parents Speak for Their Child's Best Interests

It must be the intention of the clinician to act in the child's best interests and the child's welfare must be paramount. In almost all circumstances it should be expected that the people who speak for their child's best interests will be their parents or legal guardians. The standard should therefore be collaborative: between the professionals, the child, and their parents. In some circumstances, where parents are not available, do not have parental responsibility, or lack capacity, it may be reasonable to ask the child to give his or her permission to the team to give treatment or undertake investigations. The standard at which the clinician will be judged is that of reasonableness; there are therefore going to be nuances that may take considerable experience to negotiate. If clinicians are aware that they may not have this experience they should ask themselves whether it is reasonable that they should be seeking consent under these circumstances. When obtaining consent from children there are many additional considerations that must be made, which include:

- The age and ability of the child.
- The nature of the treatment or investigation.
- Any other barriers to a free informed choice.
- The urgency of the need for consent.

Commonly a clinician has only one parent who is with the child with whom to discuss consent. In almost all circumstances it is reasonable and therefore lawful that informed consent is given by that parent and, where appropriate, on discussion with the child (Children Act Section 2(7), 1989). The clinician is explicitly expected to act in good faith and for the benefit of the child. There may be circumstances, however, where a sensible person might feel a conflict of opinion between parents who are either in an antagonistic relationship or where societal views may be polarized: one example might perhaps be male circumcision, where the consent of both parents with parental responsibility should be sought. Knowledge of the social situation of the child is therefore often essential. A small number of cases may arise where relatively unproven treatments or those with serious side effects are proposed where a reasonable clinician would be expected, if time allows, to discuss the options and get the informed consent of both parents. If there is disagreement between the parents in these circumstances it would be sensible to obtain formal legal advice.

KEY POINTS—CONSENT IN CHILDREN

- A child is defined by the law as those under 18 years old.
- In the legal concept known as *parens patriae* the state has a duty to protect dependent persons from harm.
- Parents or legal guardians will usually speak for their child's best interests, but the age and ability of the child also need to be taken into account.
- It is lawful that informed consent is given by one parent.
- The law in relation to consent for children will be judged on what a reasonable parent would expect to know.
- If there is disagreement between the parents it would be sensible to obtain legal advice.

9.1.4 Adulthood and Decision-Making

In England, Wales, and Northern Ireland until 1969 the age of majority was reached when one became 21 years old and applied to the right to vote, own property, get married, and make a legal will, amongst other rights of adulthood. Through the Family Law Reform Act 1969, the age at which one became considered legally an adult was reduced to 18; and explicitly the right to give consent to medical treatment or investigation. The Act also directly stated that young people aged 16 and 17 must too be presumed competent to give consent, and permission of a parent to treatment is not necessarily required. The act is careful, however, not to invalidate parents' rights to consent on behalf of their child aged 16 or 17, and it does not direct what is lawful where the child withholds consent when parents wish treatment to be undertaken. Teenagers and parents frequently do not see the world in the same way, and differences of opinion may sometimes therefore occur that leave the treating doctor in a difficult position that may require referral to a court to determine what the right action is. In Scotland, the law was enacted in the Age of Legal Capacity (Scotland) Act 1991, and adulthood, excluding the right to vote but including marriage and property ownership, is at 16 years of age and this includes the right to give or withhold consent to treatment or investigation.

9.1.5 Gillick Competence

In 1980 Mrs Gillick sought an assurance from West Norfolk and Wisbech Area Health Authority that her daughters would not be prescribed contraceptives without her consent. The action came as a response to a Department of Health and Social Security circular to area health authorities that contained advice that it would not be unlawful for doctors seeing a girl under 16 to prescribe contraception if they were acting in good faith and that confidentiality could be maintained if she did not want her parents to be informed. Mrs Gillick was unsuccessful in her challenge, and Lord Scarman commented that 'a minor's capacity to make his or her own decision depends upon the minor having sufficient understanding and intelligence to make the decision and is not to be determined by reference to any judicially fixed age limit'. The legal situation had been clarified and in other countries where common law principles apply, the ruling was received sympathetically, including Australia ('Marion's Case' (1992) 175 CLR 189), Canada, and the USA. Lord Fraser indicated that doctors will be justified in prescribing contraception without the parents' consent or knowledge provided they are satisfied that:

- The girl under 16 years of age will understand their advice.
- The doctor cannot persuade her to inform her parents.
- She is very likely to have sexual intercourse with or without contraception.
- Unless she receives contraception her physical or mental health are likely to suffer.
- Her best interests require the doctor to give contraception or advice without parental consent.

The guidance about contraception became known as Fraser guidelines. The concept of those under 16 giving informed consent has evolved and is now more commonly known as 'Gillick competence'. It is not the intention of the legislation that Gillick competence is used as a device to remove parents from the process for the convenience of the clinician. In the same way, it is not good practice to obtain consent from the parents or guardians without reasonable steps being taken to involve the child in what it is proposed is done to them and why.

A child's understanding of language and risk changes with age and varies from individual to individual. Although it is a continuous variable, clinicians must make a categorical decision: am I reasonable to say I have consent to treat or investigate this person or not? Capacity to make an informed decision can be adversely affected, for example, by pain, fear, low mood, and separation from family, all of which are common in medical settings. The use of play therapy and specialist psychologist input may be needed. A clinician's knowledge of the child's background, a relationship that is sympathetic to the child, and the presence of a family member or other trusted independent person may enhance the child's capacity to give consent (see also Chapters 2 and 3).

KEY POINTS—CONSENT IN CHILDREN

- At 18 years one has the right to give consent to medical treatment or investigation.
- Young people aged 16 and 17 are presumed competent to give consent and permission of a parent to treatment is not *necessarily* required.
- Gillick competence—a minor must have sufficient understanding and intelligence to make a decision and this is not determined by a judicially fixed age limit.
- A child's understanding of language and risk changes with age and varies from individual to individual.

9.1.6 Suggested Criteria for Establishing Competence

The child:

- Understands the nature, purpose, and necessity of what is proposed.
- Understands the potential consequences of not having the treatment.
- Understands that the information applies to them.
- Retains and uses information to make a decision.
- Communicates their decision.

The situation:

- Autonomy is not significantly impaired by barriers, including pressure, pain, or fear.

The person seeking consent:

- Is acting reasonably in asking for consent.
- Is acting in the best interests of the child and their welfare is paramount.
- Has given the information needed for the child to make a reasonable decision.

9.1.7 Where Refusal of Consent May Lead to Death or Serious Harm

It was established in Re MB [1997] EWCA Civ 3093 26 March 1997, in which the Gillick ruling was cited, that a person who has capacity may 'for rational or irrational reasons or for no reason at all, choose not to have medical intervention, even though the consequence may be ... her own death'. Although not yet tested formally in the courts, it has been widely accepted today that Gillick competence is not intended to cover refusal of treatment that is intended to prevent serious harm or death (see Chapter 6).

9.1.8 Consent to Organ and Blood Donation

In England, Wales, and Northern Ireland the age at which a person may register as an organ donor is 18 and the age at which they may become a blood donor is 17. In Scotland, the age at which a child may register as an organ donor without parental consent is 12 and the age at which he or she may become a blood donor is 17. The Mental Capacity Act 2005, which deals with deciding those who may be deemed to lack capacity, also applies to patients aged 16 or over.

9.1.9 Research Involving Infants, Children, and Young People

The Royal College of Paediatrics and Child Health has recently created guidance to assist those involved in undertaking medical research in children. Some of the key principles as quoted in the document include:

- **Risk**

  Research should ideally carry no greater than minimal or low risk. However, research that involves greater than minimal risk may be acceptable if the interventions involve diagnostic procedures or treatments that are important for the individual child.
- **Assent or Consent**

  In most instances, the child's assent or consent should be underpinned by parental consent. However, in the context of research, dissent should be respected, even if parental consent continues.
- **Sedation**

  Researchers must justify the use of sedation, and provide evidence that appropriate monitoring will be in place during the procedure, and that they possess the necessary competencies and skills to carry out the procedures, and to deal immediately with any adverse effects.
- **Rewards**

  The nature of any token of thanks should be in proportion with the age of the child, approved by the research ethics committee, and made clear in the parent/patient information sheets.

9.1.10 Who Has Parental Responsibility?

A mother who has given birth to a baby always automatically acquires parental responsibility for that child from birth. It can only be lost through the decision of a court of law, for example, at adoption. A man or civil partner of the mother giving birth acquires parental responsibility by being registered as such on the birth certificate. He can also acquire parental responsibility by:

- Entering into a 'parental responsibility agreement' with the child's mother.
- Applying to the court for parental responsibility.
- Applying to the court for a residence order.
- Marrying the child's mother.
- Being appointed as the child's guardian.
- Adopting the child.

A step-parent who is the spouse or civil partner of a parent who has parental responsibility may also acquire parental responsibility by:

- Making a parental responsibility agreement with all parents with parental responsibility.
- Obtaining a residence order or parental responsibility order from the court.
- Adopting the child.
- A step-parent cannot appoint a guardian for the child or change the child's surname, although he or she may have parental responsibility.
- Both parents with parental responsibility must agree before a child is removed from the UK for a period exceeding 1 month and for such things such as a change of name. If this agreement is not forthcoming the question should be referred to the court.
- Not having parental responsibility does not relieve a father of his obligation to maintain his child and pay maintenance.
- A person with parental responsibility may not surrender or transfer any part of that responsibility, unless the child is adopted.

Others who may have parental responsibility include:

- A local authority designated in a care order.
- Courts may appoint a guardian for a child who has no parent with parental responsibility (Section 5 of the Children Act 1989).
- Parents with parental responsibility may also appoint a guardian in the event of their own deaths.
- A local authority or other authorized person who holds an emergency protection.
- A person who has parental responsibility for a child 'may arrange for some or all of it to be met by one or more persons acting on his or her behalf', e.g. a child minder, the staff of a boarding school.
- Foster parents do not usually have parental responsibility.

KEY POINTS—CONSENT IN CHILDREN

- Gillick competence is not intended to cover refusal of treatment that is intended to prevent serious harm or death.
- In England, Wales, and Northern Ireland the age at which a person may register as an organ donor is 18.
- The Mental Capacity Act 2005 applies to patients 16 years or over.
- For research purposes, a child's assent or consent should be underpinned by parent consent. A child's dissent should be respected despite parent wishes.
- A mother who has given birth to a baby automatically acquires parental responsibility. It can only be lost through a decision of a court of law.
- Parental responsibility can be acquired by many legal methods.

9.2 Child Protection

9.2.1 Child Abuse and Neglect—an International Problem

About 3500 children under 15 die from physical abuse or neglect every year in the industrialized world. For every week, two die in Germany and the UK, three in France, four in Japan, and 27 in the USA. Those under 1 are at much greater risk, and the risk declines with age. The risk of death doubles for those aged 1–4, compared with 5–14-year-olds.

In Europe, Spain, Greece, Italy, Ireland, and Norway all have a relatively lower incidence of child maltreatment deaths. Belgium, the Czech Republic, New Zealand, Hungary, and France have levels that are four to six times higher, and the USA, Mexico, and Portugal have rates 10–15 times higher than the countries with the lowest rates. It can be assumed that these statistics are likely to underestimate the true rates of maltreatment. The data do suggest, however, that the rates of death from maltreatment are falling in the industrialized world. Poverty, stress, and drug or alcohol abuse are related factors consistently found in association with physical abuse and neglect.

In the UK, physical abuse registrations fell from 11,400 to 5800 children between 1994 and 2009, and sexual abuse registrations declined from 7500 to 2200, whereas registrations for neglect increased from 7800 to 16,900. The number of children who are the subject of child protection plans is rising: from 30,700 (2004–5) to 37,900 (2008–9) to 44,500 (2009–10) in England and Wales.

9.2.2 Childhood Sexual Abuse

Worldwide, 7.9% of men and 19.7% of women reported having experienced sexual abuse before the age of 18. By continent the highest prevalence rate of child sexual abuse geographically was found in Africa (34.4%), America and Asia (between 10.1% and 23.9%), followed by Europe (9.2%). It is suggested that South Africa has the highest rates of any country for both men (60.9%) and women (43.7%). For boys: after S. Africa, Jordan has the second highest rate (27%), followed by Tanzania (25%), Israel (15.7%), Spain (13.4%), Australia (13%), and Costa Rica (12.8%); the remaining countries all have rates below 10%. For girls, after S. Africa, seven countries reported rates above 20%: Australia (37.8%), Costa Rica (32.2%), Tanzania (31.0%), Israel (30.7%), Sweden (28.1%), the USA (25.3%), and Switzerland (24.2%). In the UK, one in 20 children (4.8%) had experienced contact sexual abuse. Over 90% were abused by someone they knew, and a high proportion of these did not tell anyone else about it.

Safeguarding children creates dilemmas that can be difficult to handle, especially in primary care, where both child and potentially abusive parent may be your patient. In the hospital environment, the most common environments in which information becomes known to suggest abuse is likely to be in paediatrics, the emergency department, and psychiatry. All National Health Service (NHS) organizations are supposed to employ a designated lead in nursing and medicine for child protection. The leads are available for advice and training, but the responsibility to undertake the measures to protect the child remains with the doctor. In any local authority area, there is an emergency social worker available who should be contactable 24 hours a day for child protection matters. If a crime has been or is likely to have been committed, the local authority has a legal duty to carry out an urgent investigation.

9.2.3 Disclosure of Information

In the context of child protection, confidentiality is not an absolute duty. Where harm is likely or has occurred, delays in disclosing or sharing information have been shown in distressing and well-publicized cases to cause further harm. The standard legal test is that of reasonableness, putting the child's interests first. In whatever setting it is uncovered, there is an explicit obligation in UK law that requires disclosure and effective action to protect the child or children that overrides the duty to maintain confidentiality. You should also inform those with legal responsibility for the child about information you are disclosing even where they have given their consent (see also Chapter 3).

9.2.4 Female Genital Mutilation

Female genital mutilation has been a crime in the UK since 1985, reinforced in The Female Genital Mutilation Act 2003. The 2003 act was amended and in 2015 it became a statutory duty for medical professionals to notify police of female genital mutilation. The British Medical Association (BMA) has also produced very helpful guidance for doctors who have concerns that a child may be at risk of abuse or neglect.

9.2.5 Making an Urgent Referral

At present in the UK there is no uniform referral process, and different local authorities have differing forms and procedures. There are usually two forms of referral: urgent and non-urgent. Non-urgent referrals are often made using a multidisciplinary approach and the documentation is widely known as a common assessment framework, or CAF, form. Medical practitioners may reasonably be expected to contribute to completing a CAF form to allow special provision, for example, arising at home, school, or elsewhere as a result of their illness or family circumstances.

The CAF is not usually appropriate in the urgent situation where the child has suffered harm or is likely to do so. In the emergency setting, telephone contact is usually made to social services or the police by the referring doctors and nurses. The referring team should be able to outline their concerns and report if abuse is likely or has actually been suffered. This level of concern then requires a formal emergency referral under Section 47 of Chapter 41 of the 1989 Children Act. 9.25. In this section of the Children's Act the law details the local authority's duty to investigate. Children's services must carry out an investigation when they have reasonable cause to believe that a child living in their area has suffered, or is likely to suffer, significant harm. After a Section 47 inquiry is started, the following things should usually happen:

- There must be contact within 1 day with the police.
- Immediate measures should be undertaken to protect the child.
- An alleged abuser may agree to leave the home.
- There may need to be removal of the alleged abuser by police.
- An arrangement can be made for children, including siblings, to be cared for in a safer place.

9.2.6 Legal Orders

A number of legal orders can be invoked under the Children Act 1989.

- **Police Protection Order**

  This can be placed by the police in case of an emergency; it has a maximum duration of 72 hours; the child is removed to suitable accommodation or there is prevention of removal from safety (e.g. hospital ward).

- **Emergency Protection Order**

  This is usually by social services; the maximum duration is 8 days but it can be extended by 7 days on one occasion only.

- **Child Assessment Order**

  This is undertaken by an authorized person under the Act, usually the local authority, to allow clinicians to examine a sibling, for example, when parents are uncooperative. It is little used but its duration is a maximum of 7 days.

- **Interim Care Order**

  This is undertaken by the local authority usually (or the National Society for the Prevention of Cruelty to Children [NSPCC]). Before 2014 its duration was limited to a maximum of 8 weeks and it gives joint parental responsibility to social services.

- **Supervision Orders**

  These are undertaken by social services or the NSPCC. They last 12 months in the first instance and are usually reviewed annually. The courts have powers to authorize or prohibit medical examination of a child.

Within a short period of referral, usually 24–48 hours, a strategy meeting should have taken place, with input from health, social services, and the police. It is led and chaired by a social worker. At the end of the investigation a child protection conference and a child protection plan is created. Where serious harm or death has taken place, a serious case review is undertaken, leading to a report that is published and available to the public.

9.2.7 The Role of Different Courts and the Standard of Proof

Since the 2014 Children and Families Act, there is now a single entity known as 'the Family Court' that exercises jurisdiction over family proceedings. The Family Court sits in different locations across the country. The standard of proof required by the court is at the civil level; that is, on the 'balance of probability' (see Chapter 1). The 'balance of probability' is also the standard of proof required for cases before the coroner and the General Medical Council, in contrast to the standard of 'beyond reasonable doubt' required in criminal cases. The 2014 Children and Families Act also directs courts to presume that parents' continued involvement in their life is usually in the child's best interests even where they are not living with them after neglect or abuse. It also prohibits smoking in private vehicles when a child under 18 years is a passenger.

KEY POINTS—CHILD PROTECTION

- All NHS organizations are supposed to employ a designated lead in nursing and medicine for child protection.
- The responsibility to undertake measures to protect the child remains with the doctor.
- In any local authority area, an emergency social worker should be contactable 24 hours a day for child protection matters.
- In UK law, disclosure and effective action to protect children overrides the duty to maintain confidentiality.
- There is a statutory duty for medical professionals to notify police of female genital mutilation.
- Non-urgent referrals for child protection require completing the CAF form. When urgent, telephone contact is required with social services or police.
- After referral ± protection/interim care orders, a social worker chairs a multidisciplinary team meeting and a child protection plan is put in place.

9.3 Withholding and Withdrawing Treatments

There are circumstances when paediatricians and general practitioners have to consider that the end of a child's life is approaching. The Royal College of Physicians has put together a short document addressing what is best practice legally and ethically in these distressing situations. There are five situations in which it may be ethical and legal to consider withholding or withdrawing a child's treatment:

- The brain-dead child and permanent vegetative state.
- The 'no chance' situation.
- The 'no purpose' situation.
- The 'unbearable' situation.

9.3.1 Brainstem Death and the Permanent Vegetative State

These are very rare and require specialist expertise to make a diagnosis. Relatively few paediatricians even at consultant level will have encountered these situations frequently enough to be comfortable in making the diagnosis. The permanent vegetative state requires a specialist consultant paediatric neurologist with the appropriate expertise to make the diagnosis. Brainstem death is most frequently diagnosed by those with considerable experience in paediatric intensive care or neurology. The law requires a diagnosis of brainstem death to be made to allow organ donation from a beating heart donor to be undertaken. Management of the much less frequently undertaken non-beating-heart solid organ donation is even more complex and requires considerable resources and expertise, but is not dependent on a diagnosis of brainstem death.

More commonly, paediatric teams consider withholding or withdrawing treatments on the basis of three situations.

9.3.2 The 'No Chance' Situation

The child has such severe disease that life-sustaining treatment simply delays death without significant alleviation of suffering. Treatment to sustain life is inappropriate.

9.3.3 The 'No Purpose' Situation

Although the patient may be able to survive with treatment, the degree of physical or mental impairment will be so great that it is unreasonable to expect him or her to bear it.

9.3.4 The 'Unbearable' Situation

The child and/or family feel that, in the face of progressive and irreversible illness, further treatment is more than can be borne. They wish to have a particular treatment withdrawn or to refuse further treatment irrespective of the medical opinion that it may be of some benefit.

In a situation where the conditions for one of these categories are not met, where there is disagreement, or where there is uncertainty over the degree of future impairment, the Royal College of Paediatrics and Child Health advises that the child's life should always be safeguarded until these issues are resolved. The guidance notes make clear that withdrawal or withholding of life-sustaining treatment does not imply that the child will receive no care and highlights the need for provision of palliative care to ensure that the remainder of the child's life is as comfortable as possible.

KEY POINTS—WITHOLDING AND WITHDRAWING TREATMENT

- Witholding and withdrawing treatment in children can proceed after brainstem testing as in adult patients.
- Where life-sustaining treatment delays death or treatment is too burdensome in the face of progressive and irreversible illness, then withdrawal of treatment is permitted.
- Where there is uncertainty over the degree of future impairment, it is advisable to safeguard the child's life until these issues are resolved.
- The provision of palliative care is instituted once a decision is made to withdraw treatment.

9.4 Registration of Births and Deaths

In England, Wales, and Northern Ireland, the live birth of a child must be registered within 42 days. In Scotland, the time limit is shorter, at 21 days. If the parents are legally married or in a civil partnership, whether of opposite or same sex, either parent can register the birth. If the parents are not married or in a civil partnership, the mother may register the birth. The mother may also authorize the other partner to register the birth and obtain parental rights by signing the register together or by completing a statutory declaration (or acknowledgement) of parentage form. Male couples must obtain court authority to register the birth.

If no parent is available through medical or other reasons to register the birth, some others may do this for them: someone who was present at the birth, someone who is responsible for the child, or a member of the administrative staff at the hospital where the child was born. Where the infant's gender is ambiguous a delay in registering the birth is advised and in some cases a deferment of birth registration may be applied for.

9.4.1 Death Certification

9.4.1.1 Stillbirth

The Births and Deaths Registration Act 1953 Section 41 as amended by the Stillbirth (Definition) Act 1992 Section 1(1) defines stillbirth as 'a child which has issued forth from its mother after the 24th week of pregnancy and which did not at any time breathe or show any other signs of life'. Many parents find it distressing that infants delivered after labour before 24 weeks, but who show no signs of life, are not able formally to register death. A local certificate is often offered by the hospital. There was an unsuccessful Private Members' Bill in 2014 intended to alter the definition of stillbirth to be based on the experience of giving birth. The Royal College of Obstetricians and Gynaecologists has produced a good practice guide on this matter.

9.4.1.2 Neonatal Death

Infants that are born with signs of life but who do not survive up to 28 days have a separate Neonatal Death Certificate (form 65) that must be completed.

9.4.1.3 Deaths after 28 days of life

After 28 days of life a medical certificate of cause of death (form 66) should be completed.

9.4.2 Child Death Overview Panels

From 2008 it became the statutory responsibility of local safeguarding children's boards to establish child death overview panels (CDOPs). The legislation followed the publication of the Laming Report into the death of Victoria Climbié and the subsequent Working Together to Safeguard Children (2006). All deaths from birth to 18 years, excluding stillbirths, must be referred for review by the local CDOP panel. Where the death is unexpected, referral should be made within 24 hours.

KEY POINTS—REGISTRATION OF BIRTHS AND DEATHS

- In England, Wales, and Northern Ireland, the live birth of a child must be registered within 42 days.
- If the parents are legally married or in a civil partnership, whether of opposite or same sex, either parent can register the birth.
- Male couples must obtain court authority to register the birth.
- All stillbirths after 24 weeks of pregnancy need to be registered.
- A neonatal death certificate needs completing for infants born with signs of life but who do not survive up to 28 days.
- All deaths from birth to 18 years, excluding stillbirths, must be referred for review by the local child death overview panel (CDOP) panel.

9.5 Pearls and Pitfalls

9.5.1 Pearls

- Assume that children should be involved in decisions about their care whenever possible.
- Except in very unusual circumstances the parents speak for the best interests of the child.

9.5.2 Pitfalls

- Be cautious of assumptions about parental responsibility.
- Child abuse and neglect exist within all socioeconomic, racial, and cultural groups.
- Child abuse and neglect are missed when the clinical team do not consider it.

9.6 Further Reading

- Pereda N et al. (2009). The prevalence of child sexual abuse in community and student samples: a meta-analysis. *Clin Psychol Rev*, 29(4), 328–38.
- Radford L et al. (2011). *Child Abuse and Neglect in the UK Today*. London: NSPCC. https://www.nspcc.org.uk

9.7 Multiple Choice Questions

✓ Interactive multiple choice questions to test your knowledge on this chapter can be found in the Online appendix at www.oxfordmedicine.com/essentiallegalmatters.

CHAPTER 10

Mental Health Law

Anthony Holland, Elizabeth Fistein, and Cathy Walsh

CHAPTER SUMMARY

Mental Health

This is 'a state of complete physical, mental, and social wellbeing, and is not merely the absence of disease' (WHO, 2006).

Mental Ill-Health

This includes abnormal thoughts, emotions, behaviour, and cognition, affecting ability to function and relationships with others.

Mental Capacity

The Mental Capacity Act 2005 and the Mental Health Act 1983 govern the legal basis of mental health treatment in England and Wales.

Detention Under the Mental Health Act

To detain a person under the Mental Health Act, the process set out in law must be followed and there must be a ready means of appeal—mental health review tribunals.

Human Rights

Interference with one's human rights is only lawful when conducted within a regulatory framework, which provides patients with a means of challenging decisions.

Deprivation of Liberty

If treatment involves a deprivation of liberty, then independent review and authorization will be required—the deprivation of liberty safeguards.

Liability in Relation to Capacity

If a clinician has followed the recommendations in determining capacity and best interests, they will be free from liability if later challenged.

- Schloendorff v Society of New York Hospital 211 NY 125 (1914)
- S v S, W v Official Solicitor [1970] 3 All ER 107; 111, [1972] AC 24, at 43
- Winterwerp v the Netherlands (1979)
- Malette v Shulman (1990) 67 DLR (4th) 321 (Ont CA)
- Secretary, Department of Health v JWB and SMB (1992) 66 ALJR 300
- Re: MB Caesarian section [1997] EWCA Civ 1361
- Litwa v Poland (2000)
- Keenan v the United Kingdom [2001]
- Pretty v the United Kingdom (2002)
- R(N) v M and others [2003] 1 WLR 562
- Nevmerzhitsky v Ukraine (2003)
- Glass v the United Kingdom (2004)
- HL v the United Kingdom (2004)
- Storck v Germany (2005)
- Ciorap v Moldova (2007)
- UKSC 19 On appeal from: (2011) EWCA Civ 1257; [2011] EWCA Civ 190

RELEVANT STATUTES AND LEGISLATION

- European Convention for the Protection of Human Rights 1950
- Criminal Procedure (Insanity and Unfit to Plead) Act 1991
- Mental Capacity Act 2005
- Mental Health Act 1983 (Amended 2007)

PROFESSIONAL GUIDANCE

- BMA (2016). *Mental Capacity Act Tool Kit.* www.bma.org.uk
- BMA (2016). *Deprivation of Liberty Safeguards.* www.bma.org.uk
- Department of Health (2015). *Code of Practice: Mental Health Act 1983.* www.gov.uk
- Department of Health (2015). *Reference Guide to the Mental Health Act 1983.* www.gov.uk
- GMC (2008). *Consent: Patients and Doctors Making Decisions Together.* www.gmc-uk.org
- RCGP (2014). *Care of People with Mental Health Problems.* www.gmc-uk.org
- The Law Society (2015). *Deprivation of Liberty: a Practical Guide.* www.lawsociety.org.uk

10.1 Introduction

Mental health is everyone's concern, an idea epitomized by the campaign tag line of the Royal College of Psychiatrists, 'No Health Without Mental Health'. The aim of this chapter is to demonstrate how an understanding of a patient's mental health within his or her particular social and family context is central to clinical practice across all of medicine. We will consider the legal basis for the treatment of mental ill-health and how it can complicate the treatment of physical illness by contributing to circumstances that may lead to ethical and legal concerns. The general legal principles that govern health interventions are explored and two specific statutes for England and Wales—the Mental Capacity Act (MCA) 2005 and the Mental Health Act (MHA) 1983 (as amended 2007)—are both considered in some detail. It will be shown how a sound appreciation of the clinical issues, an understanding of the law, and an ability to apply that law in clinical settings are essential when faced with situations involving mental ill-health.

KEY POINTS—INTRODUCTION

- Mental health is everyone's concern—'no health without mental health'.
- Concern for mental ill-health is central to clinical practice across all of medicine.
- Mental ill-health can complicate treatment of physical illness.
- Ethical and legal issues arise from the treatment of mental ill-health.
- The MCA and the MHA govern the legal basis of mental health treatment in England and Wales.

10.2 Definitions and Prevalence

10.2.1 What is Mental Health?

Mental health refers to the mental wellbeing component included in the World Health Organization's (WHO) definition of health: 'a state of complete physical, mental and social well-being, and not merely the absence of disease' (WHO, 2006). Interventions relating to mental health are therefore about the promotion of wellbeing, the prevention of mental disorders, and the treatment and rehabilitation of people affected by mental disorders.

10.2.2 What is Mental Ill-Health?

Mental disorders are defined in diagnostic and statistical manuals such as *The Diagnostic and Statistical Manual of Mental Disorders* (DSM-5) (APA, 2013) and *The International Statistical Classification of Diseases and Related Health Problems* (ICD-10) (WHO, 1992), and include a broad range of syndromes, which are generally characterized by some combination of abnormal thoughts, emotions, behaviour, and/or cognitive impairments that have an effect on a person's ability to function and may also affect his or her relationships with others.

The term 'mental disorder' is often used to refer to:

1. The major mental illnesses (e.g. schizophrenia, bipolar affective disorders, depression, generalized anxiety disorder, phobias, obsessive-compulsive disorders, eating disorders, dementias, and delirium).
2. Conditions of developmental origin (e.g. intellectual/learning disabilities, autism spectrum conditions, and personality disorders).
3. Substance dependency (e.g. alcohol or other mind-altering substances).
4. Symptoms associated with physical illnesses (e.g. affective disorders in Parkinson's and Huntington's diseases).

10.2.3 The Prevalence of Mental Disorders

This broad range of mental disorders is common in primary care, with prevalence rates reported in the range of 30–50%. Many of these very varied disorders can be successfully treated or managed in a way that reduces and minimizes their impact on a person's life. Mental disorders that are serious enough potentially to complicate the management of physical health problems are also common. Accident and emergency (A&E) departments frequently see patients who have self-harmed or have suffered injuries owing to substance abuse. A person dependent on alcohol who is admitted for surgery may develop withdrawal symptoms and delirium tremens some days after admission to hospital because of forced abstinence from alcohol. Other examples are anxiety and depression, both of which may arise on a general medical ward in the context of a diagnosis of a life-limiting physical illness. People may also present with symptoms that are not readily explained in which anxiety and depression may be a significant factor.

Dementia is common in older people admitted acutely to hospital and in most cases it has not been previously diagnosed. According the Alzheimer's Society, 80% of people living in UK care homes have a form of dementia or severe memory problems. If these patients are admitted to an unfamiliar hospital environment, their behavioural problems can worsen and they may suffer a sense of bewilderment or psychological distress. Similar symptoms may be associated with an organic confusional state (delirium) that requires investigation and treatment in its own right. Studies have reported that perhaps 40% of people on a general medical ward have impaired decision-making capacity, much of which is likely to be secondary to a comorbid mental disorder. Thus, in all health settings and across all health disciplines, practitioners will be faced with clinical situations in which the co-occurrence of mental ill-health or the presence of cognitive impairments might result in, or contribute to, difficulties in clinical management that are ethically and legally challenging.

KEY POINTS—DEFINITIONS AND PREVALENCE

- Mental health is 'a state of complete physical, mental and social well-being, and not merely the absence of disease' (WHO, 2006).
- Mental ill-health includes abnormal thoughts, emotions, behaviour, and cognition, affecting ability to function and relationships with others.
- Between 30% and 50% of patients seen in primary care have a mental disorder.
- Mental disorders may emerge *de novo* or worsen in hospital during treatment for a physical illness.
- Mental health issues can lead to difficulties in clinical management that are ethically and legally challenging.

10.3 Mental Ill-Health and Impaired Capacity

10.3.1 Understanding the Law of Consent

The reliance on the notion of consent as the sole justification for medical interventions creates difficulties in cases where a patient, who is thought to be in need of treatment, is unable to give (or withhold) meaningful consent. For example, patients admitted to hospital unconscious, with advanced dementia, those who have suffered a cerebral vascular accident, or patients with profound intellectual disabilities will not be able to understand, retain, or use information about a proposed treatment. The influence of past and present circumstances, anxiety, and pain on a person's ability to understand, reason, and communicate a choice may be much more subtle and not easily determined in a cursory examination in the emergency department. A patient, for the above reasons or for reasons unknown, may act in ways that impede the therapeutic process, which may or may not be a genuine reflection of what they wish for.

Under these circumstances, determining whether a patient has the capacity to make the necessary decisions will be critically important. Health staff have an obligation to make it clear that failing to treat will have serious consequences and may be fatal. The ethical and legal question that arises is whether it is ever appropriate to treat patients in the absence of a valid consent and, if so, under what circumstances this may happen. To fail to intervene in the case of a patient who is apparently refusing treatment that is clearly necessary for his or her survival, health, or wellbeing could be grounds for severe criticism or even a subsequent claim of negligence. On the other hand, a paternalistic imposition of life-saving treatment upon a patient who is able to understand the consequences of his or her refusal would amount to an unlawful assault. In the final analysis, the clinical imperative is to treat the person in a manner that is lawful, recognizing that imposing treatment may well involve judicial sanctioning to keep the person in hospital against his or her will, including using sedation and/or physical interventions to undertake investigations or give treatment. For more information on consent see Chapter 2.

KEY POINTS—UNDERSTANDING THE LAW OF CONSENT

- Obtaining valid consent from all patients prior to treatment is not always possible when capacity is impaired.
- When indicated, determining a patient's capacity prior to obtaining consent is sometimes necessary.
- When patients refuse treatment, health staff must make clear the consequences that may arise.
- Patients who refuse life-saving interventions must be treated in a lawful manner, which may require a court decision.

10.3.2 Human Rights

10.3.2.1 Article 2

The broader context in relation to treatment when capacity is impaired is that of a person's human rights with tensions arising between different and competing rights. On the one hand, Article 2 of the European Convention on Human Rights (ECHR) establishes a right to life. This has been interpreted in case law to create an obligation on public bodies to provide care to patients with mental disorders to reduce the risks of suicide (Keenan v the United Kingdom [2001]). However, the obligation to take action to preserve life threatened by the effects of mental ill-health must be balanced against obligations arising from Articles 3, 5, and 8 of the ECHR.

10.3.2.2 Article 3

Article 3, the right to freedom from torture, has been interpreted to find the unnecessary use of physical force to deliver psychiatric treatment as an infringement of this right. To be lawful, treatment administered without the patient's consent must be both medically necessary and in the patient's 'best interests'—R(N) v M and others [2003] 1 WLR 562, Nevmerzhitsky v Ukraine (2003), Ciorap v Moldova (2007).

10.3.2.3 Article 5

Article 5, the right to liberty, states: 'Everyone has the right to liberty and security of person. No one shall be deprived of his liberty save in the following cases and in accordance with a procedure prescribed by law [including] (e) the lawful detention of persons for the prevention of the spreading of infectious diseases, of persons of unsound mind, alcoholics or drug addicts or vagrants'. Article 5(1)(e) appears, therefore, to provide fairly wide-ranging legal justification for detention in hospital for psychiatric treatment. However, a body of case law has been used to develop important safeguards that are directly enforceable in England. There must be objective medical evidence of mental ill-health or disability of a nature or degree warranting confinement, and there must be periodic review of the continued need for detention (Winterwerp v the Netherlands (1979)). Moreover, detention must be a proportionate response to the circumstances (Litwa v Poland (2000)). In addition, inebriation by itself is not sufficient grounds for detention in hospital.

10.3.2.4 Article 8

Article 8, the right to privacy, grants the 'right to respect for private and family life'. This article has been interpreted through case law as conferring a right to personal integrity. The provision of medical treatment without valid consent may prima facie represent an infringement of this right (Pretty v the United Kingdom (2002), Glass v the United Kingdom (2004), Storck v Germany (2005)). However, Article 8(2) permits infringements 'necessary in a democratic society in the interests of national security, public safety or the economic well-being of the country, for the prevention of disorder or crime, for the protection of health or morals, or for the protection of the rights and freedoms of others'.

10.3.2.5 Qualified Rights

The rights to liberty, freedom from degrading treatment, and personal integrity are all 'qualified rights'. This means that although, on the face of it, they seem to prevent interventions such as medical treatment in the absence of consent, they can be overridden in certain circumstances, such as the provision of treatment that is necessary for the health of people who are unable to make the decision to give or withhold consent. The ECHR has, through its judgments, made clear that such interference is only lawful when conducted within a regulatory framework, which provides patients with a means of challenging decisions to treat them without their consent (Glass v the United Kingdom [2004], HL v the United Kingdom [2004]). Therefore, doctors may only treat without consent when they follow guidance from case law or relevant legislation, and it is obligatory for doctors to be fully aware of the law in this regard.

KEY POINTS—HUMAN RIGHTS

- Article 2 requires public bodies to take action to preserve life threatened by mental ill-health balanced against obligations arising from Articles 3, 5, and 8.
- Under Article 3, treatment administered without the patient's consent must be both medically necessary and in the patient's 'best interests'.
- Under Article 5, there must be objective medical evidence of mental ill-health warranting confinement and periodic review of the need for detention.
- The provision of medical treatment without valid consent can represent an infringement of Article 8, but there are exceptions.
- Interference with one's human rights is only lawful when conducted within a regulatory framework, which provides patients with a means of challenging decisions.

10.3.3 Mental Health and Legal Statutes

Different factors impact on a person's ability to make decisions, including, for example, profound anxiety, a confusional state associated with the onset of a physical illness, the presence of a thought disorder, delusions and/or hallucinations owing to the onset of a serious mental illness, depression, or suicidal ideation. An understanding of the presence and impact of a person's mental health on his or her behaviour may likely lead more readily to a resolution of challenges in relation to compliance with treatment. However, where decisional capacity is impaired and treatment is necessary, the law provides some guidance and authority in this area.

In the UK, case law concerning treatment for those who lack capacity to consent and for the provision of compulsory treatment for mental disorders when in hospital has been consolidated into the following statutory frameworks:

1. MCA 2005, and the Adults with Incapacity (Scotland) Act 2001 in Scotland.
2. MHA 1983 (amended by the MHA 2007) and the Mental Health (Care and Treatment) (Scotland) Act 2003.

These two Acts of Parliament are there to deal with distinct situations but also overlap. Guidance on when to use the MCA and when to use the MHA is detailed in the MHA Code of Practice issued by the Department of Health. The MCA is discussed in detail in Chapter 2.

> ## KEY POINTS—MENTAL HEALTH AND LEGAL STATUTES
>
> - Many different factors impact on a person's ability to make decisions.
> - The MCA 2005 provides a legal basis for treatment of patients who lack capacity.
> - The MHA 1983 details the law on the provision of compulsory treatment for mental disorders when in hospital.
> - Guidance on when to use the MCA and when to use the MHA is detailed in the MHA Code of Practice issued by the Department of Health.

10.3.4 Deprivation of Liberty Safeguards

In general, before treatment is undertaken, regard must be given to whether some other as-effective treatment is less restrictive of the person's rights and freedom of action. If physical force or restrictions on that person's liberty are required to administer treatment, it is only permissible if it is necessary to prevent harm to the patient and proportionate to the likelihood and seriousness of the patient suffering harm.

In cases where the care of the person lacking capacity involves a 'restriction' on his or her freedom of movement, it can lawfully take place providing it is in his or her interests and is the least restrictive option. However, if the 'restriction' amounts to a 'deprivation of liberty' (for example, if a patient is required to remain in hospital against their wishes for a period of recovery post-surgery, and/or then to be moved into a nursing home that will not allow him or her to go out whenever they wish), then independent review and authorization, known as the deprivation of liberty safeguards (DoLS) will be required.

Legal safeguards for people lacking capacity have been considered necessary by courts as any restriction to the right to freedom of movement (contrary to Article 5 of the ECHR) is considered very serious and only to take place under particular circumstances and with appropriate levels of legal protection. The European Court and the UK Supreme Court have considered what determines a 'deprivation of liberty' as opposed to a simple 'restriction of liberty'—this is a complex matter but a judgment in the Supreme Court in 2014 (UKSC 19 On appeal from: 2011, EWCA Civ 1257; [2011] EWCA Civ 190) arrived at a wide definition—in essence it is whether or not others have complete and absolute control of a person's life.

A DoLS authorization under the MCA is given by a 'supervisory body' (e.g. a local authority), following a request from a 'managing authority' (the hospital or care home at which the individual is placed or is likely to be placed). Best practice would be for an authorization to be in place at the time the deprivation of liberty occurs. The six qualifying requirements for a DoLS are summarized as follows:

- **Age**—is the individual aged 18 or over?
- **Mental health**—does the individual have a mental disorder as defined by the Act?
- **Mental capacity**—does the individual lack capacity to decide whether or not he or she should be accommodated in the care home or hospital specified at the material time (i.e. the time of the assessment)?
- **Best interests:**
  - Is it in the best interest of the individual for him or her to be deprived of his or her liberty?
  - Is it necessary for him or her to be deprived of his or her liberty to prevent harm to himself or herself?
  - Is the deprivation of liberty a proportionate response to the likelihood of the individual suffering harm and the seriousness of that harm?
- **Eligibility**—this qualifying requirement is met unless the person is ineligible to be deprived of their liberty by the MCA.

- **No refusals**—has the person made a valid and applicable advance decision to refuse some or all of the treatment in question or is there a valid and conflicting decision by a donee or deputy? If so, they may not meet the qualifying criteria for DoLS.

A DoLS authorization should be regularly reviewed, amended, or revoked when required. Where a DoLS authorization is refused, the clinicians involved in the patient's care must ensure that deprivation of the patient's liberty does not occur as unlawful deprivation of liberty exposes a hospital to potential liabilities and is a breach of the patient's human rights. All deaths of patients that occur where a DoLS authorization is in place should be reported to the coroner.

KEY POINTS—DEPRIVATION OF LIBERTY SAFEGUARDS

- Treatment that is least restrictive of the person's rights and freedom of action must always be considered first.
- If treatment involves a deprivation of liberty, then independent review and authorization—DoLS will be required.
- There is an 'acid test' for deprivation of liberty—if a person is under continuous supervision and control and is not free to leave, then this constitutes an objective DoL.
- A DoLS authorization should be regularly reviewed, amended, or revoked when required.
- Unlawful deprivation of liberty exposes a hospital to potential liabilities and is a breach of the patient's human rights.
- All deaths of patients that occur where a DoLS authorization is in place should be reported to the coroner.

10.4 The Mental Health Act 1983 (Amended 2007)

The MHA 1983, as amended 2007, applies when a person has a 'disorder or disability of the mind' of a 'nature or degree' that warrants detention in hospital for assessment or makes it appropriate for him or her to receive medical treatment in hospital. The detention must be deemed necessary in the interests of the patient's health or safety or for the protection of others. Detention for treatment of a mental disorder is only permissible if it is not possible to provide the necessary treatment without the patient being detained. Once detained, medical treatment, including nursing, psychological intervention, and specialist mental health rehabilitation, can be given without the consent of the patient.

In contrast with the MCA, the MHA cannot be used as a legal framework to justify compulsory treatment for physical conditions in the absence of consent; it can only be used to authorize treatment for mental disorders, its causes, or consequences. Such treatment is only authorized for people who are formally detained in hospital, following assessment by two doctors and an approved mental health practitioner. The MHA 1983 (amended 2007) for England and Wales set out in Part II and Part III the different 'Sections' that can be used to detain a person in hospital, for how long, and what conditions have to be met (for example, 'civil sections' include Section 2 for assessment of up to 28 days and Section 3 for treatment up to 6 months). If, during the course of a person's detention in hospital, the necessary criteria are no longer met, the responsible clinician must remove the Section and the patient either remains in hospital informally, having given valid consent, or is allowed to leave. Once detention under the MHA is authorized, there is no requirement for a DoLS authorization. Unlike the MCA, the MHA can also be applied to people who retain the capacity to make decisions about their treatment and it can be used to impose treatment in the interests of the protection of people other than the patient.

Under Part III of the MHA there are also provisions for courts, on the basis of expert evidence, to authorize detention in hospital (referred to as hospital orders) for assessment and treatment for a mental disorder if someone is suspected or convicted of an offence punishable by imprisonment. In the context of the criminal justice system, where someone is considered unfit to plead, the Crown Court can also use the Criminal Procedures (Insanity and Unfit to Plead) Act 1991 for a trial of the facts and determine what should then happen in the event that the facts of the case are proven. This was what had been proposed in the recent high-profile case of Lord Janner, given that he was considered unfit to plead owing to his advanced dementia. He died before this process could be undertaken.

The fundamental principle behind the MHA is that such a statute provides protection against arbitrary detention and provides a ready means of appeal. Psychiatrists and others who use it are responsible for interpreting the law and will have to satisfy those challenging their decisions that the necessary requirements have been met.

KEY POINTS—THE MENTAL HEALTH ACT 1983 (AMENDED 2007)

- The MHA 1983 (amended 2007) provides the legal means for assessing and/or treating a person's mental disorder in hospital in the absence of consent.
- The MHA cannot be used as a legal framework to justify compulsory treatment for physical conditions in the absence of consent.
- Formal detention in hospital must follow assessment by two doctors and an approved mental health practitioner.
- The MHA can be applied to people who retain capacity and to impose treatment in the interests of the protection of people other than the patient.
- To detain a person under the MHA the process set out in law must be followed and there must be a ready means of appeal—mental health review tribunals.
- The MHA provides for courts to authorize detention in hospital of a suspected criminal for assessment and treatment for a mental disorder.

10.5 Mental Capacity in Clinical and Social Care Contexts

Under what circumstances is it appropriate to treat in the absence of patient consent and what actions can and should be taken when someone is resisting treatment? The MCA makes it clear that what might be seen as 'an unwise decision' does not in itself indicate the lack of capacity. When there is non-compliance with treatment, an appropriate early task for the clinical team is to try and understand why the person is behaving in the way that he or she is. This will require an understanding of that person's mental state as much as the physical state. Ultimately, judgements have to be made on the balance of probabilities that the person lacks the relevant decision-making capacity and that a particular course of action is in his or her best interests. If clinicians have followed the necessary process and documented what they have done in determining capacity and best interests, they will be free from liability if later challenged. In urgent situations, clinicians must act to save life unless it is very clear that the patient had made an advance directive to refuse treatment and it is valid and applicable to that particular situation. We conclude the chapter by considering case examples and the demands of applying the law in clinical settings in what may be complex situations in which it may not be clear which is the most appropriate legal framework.

KEY POINTS—MENTAL CAPACITY IN CLINICAL AND SOCIAL CARE CONTEXTS

- According to the MCA, what might be seen as 'an unwise decision' does not in itself indicate the lack of capacity.

- The clinical team should try to understand why a person is behaving in a way that may seem irrational.
- If a person lacks the relevant decision-making capacity, a particular course of action by a physician should be in the patient's best interests.
- If clinicians have followed the recommendations in determining capacity and best interests, they will be free from liability if later challenged.
- In urgent situations, clinicians must act to save life unless there is a valid and applicable advance directive to refuse treatment.

CASE STUDY 1

Mrs Y is aged 87 years. She was diagnosed with Alzheimer's disease some years ago and, having previously lived independently, she now lives in a nursing home where she requires help with all aspects of her care. She is brought into A&E, having fallen, and is suspected of having a fracture of the head of the femur. She appears to be in pain and is clearly distressed. She is actively resisting a physical examination and will not lie still for an X-ray. How do you best understand her behaviour? Under what conditions can she and should she be treated and what laws are potentially relevant?

Commentary

The priority from the health staff's perspective is to relieve her suffering through the use of appropriate treatments. In this example, the person concerned has a mental disorder and is very likely to be confused, possibly made worse by pain and being in a strange environment. She may lack the capacity to consent to the assessment and treatment plan, and her behaviour is making this very difficult such that staff consider that sedation and restrictions on her movements may be necessary. Clinically, the challenge is to confirm or not the presence of confusion, whether it is worse now, and, if so, why, and what might be done to alleviate it. Will having familiar family members present be helpful? Is it appropriate to treat any pain with analgesics in her best interests as this might also improve her distress? Are there any other factors that might be contributing to her confusion, such as an infection? The staff may also be confused! Can we treat or not? If the discussed measures do not improve the patient's understanding and behaviour, what legislation should be considered?

The MHA would not provide justification for the treatment of the fracture, as this is not medical treatment for a mental disorder. If, as a result of dementia, the patient lacked the capacity to make this decision, then the MCA would apply. If, subsequently, severe depression developed whilst the patient was recovering in hospital, and if the patient refused the necessary treatment, then detention in hospital for treatment under the MHA might be considered. In this case it would be the depression that was being treated. The MHA can only be used to authorize treatment for a mental disorder in hospital (not at home), and, if the patient lacked capacity to make a decision about this treatment, then consideration should be given to whether the MCA was sufficient for giving the treatment for her depression in her 'best interests', without detaining the patient in hospital. However, in circumstances where a patient who lacks capacity is objecting to treatment in hospital for a mental disorder, the Codes of Practice indicate that the MHA, which provides easy access to a means of appeal, should be used to authorize treatment. If, by the time the patient is well enough to leave hospital, it becomes clear that she will need to live in a nursing home under circumstances that amount to a deprivation of liberty, then it is the MCA that provides the framework for this decision in the absence of the patient's consent owing to lack of capacity. A DoLS authorization would be required if these new care arrangements gave others complete and effective control of this person's life. In one episode of 'treatment', therefore, these different frameworks are needed at different times and circumstances to justify the provision of the different kinds of care and treatment needed by the patient. Please see Chapter 2 for more on adults who lack capacity.

CASE STUDY 2

The use of both the MCA and the MHA is also illustrated by the case example discussed involving an adult with a rare genetically determined neurodevelopmental disorder associated with mild learning disabilities, hyperphagia, and significant behavioural and psychiatric problems, including a high risk of psychotic illness in one specific genetic subtype.

Mr R, aged 24, has Prader–Willi Syndrome. He has severe obesity (his BMI is 45) and has developed type 2 diabetes mellitus. He does not accept that he is at risk of the complications of his poorly controlled diabetes.

Commentary

Subsequent assessments of his understanding of his health problems and his eating behaviour indicate that he lacks the capacity to make decisions about his social care and his diabetes treatment, and therefore the MCA applies. As this is treatment for a physical disorder the MHA does not apply. With time he accepts supervision of his eating and he loses weight. He also accepts treatment for his diabetes. As a result, his blood sugar control improves. However, his behaviour and mental state suddenly deteriorates and he appears confused and has auditory hallucinations and delusional ideation. His blood sugar levels are in the normal range and the onset of a comorbid psychotic illness is diagnosed. He is refusing treatment for this and his deteriorating behaviour and mental state is putting him at risk. As this is treatment for a mental disorder and it is decided that this needs to take place in hospital, the MHA is used to admit him to hospital and to treat his mental disorder in the absence of his consent. His mental state improves on treatment with antipsychotic medication and he is discharged within 4 weeks. He agrees to continue on his medication and also accepts treatment for his diabetes. The justification for treatment is that he now has the capacity to make such decisions and is consenting to the treatment and living arrangements. If he lacked the capacity to consent, the DoLS would have to be considered because he would be considered to be under continuous supervision.

CASE STUDY 3

Mrs S, aged 60, is brought to A&E by her family in a confused and disorientated state. Her family advise the health staff that she has advanced metastatic breast cancer and periodically becomes very confused and distressed. This has now happened on many occasions but each time she receives treatment her confusion improves and she is able to return home. On this occasion her family produce a letter written and signed by her, saying that in the event of another admission she wants to be kept comfortable but that no active steps should be taken, such as treatment of any intercurrent infections with antibiotics.

Commentary

The patient remains very confused and lacks the capacity to consider any specific course of action at the present time and therefore the MCA applies. The family, although distressed, are supportive of her previously stated wish and the staff in A&E agree that this written advance directive refusing treatment is valid and applicable and should be respected. She receives palliative care and dies a few days later. Please see Chapter 2 for more on advance decisions to refuse treatment.

Mr J is admitted to hospital for tests prior to major surgery. On the third day in hospital he becomes agitated, scratching his skin and reaching out at things that are not there. It is obvious that he is disorientated and he appears unaware that he is in hospital. Findings on his initial physical examination had indicated possible abnormal liver function. This is confirmed by blood tests. Evidence of a marked tremor together with his abnormal mental state result in a likely diagnosis of delirium tremens due to alcohol withdrawal. Urgent contact with his family confirms that he has been a longstanding heavy drinker of alcohol.

Commentary

He lacks the capacity to consent to treatment for his abnormal mental state. As he lacks capacity the MCA could apply but as this is a mental disorder that requires treatment the MHA could also be used. As sedation and restriction on his freedom of movement is required, because of the risk he poses to himself and others, the MHA is used and he is detained under Section 3, remaining in the general hospital in a side room because of concerns about his physical state and the potential adverse effects of treatment. He makes a good recovery from the delirium tremens and is taken off his Section. He now has full capacity and has consented to the surgery that initially led to him coming into hospital.

Whilst understanding the law is essential, the problems described in the case examples are best managed by:

1. A sound understanding of the patient and his or her circumstances.
2. Decisions that are informed by a wider understanding of the issues.
3. A sound clinical approach with accurate identification of the mental health component to the patient's presentation.
4. The establishment, where possible, of a good therapeutic relationship with the patient concerned.

There is also the question as to what is in reality possible. What actions are now justified to ensure that treatment takes place and a positive outcome ensues? In these circumstances it is concepts such as 'proportionality' and judgements as to the likelihood and severity of the potential harm, if such treatment is not given, that become important.

10.6 Conclusion

The presence of one or other of many known mental disorders may impact on a person's understanding and ability to communicate, or may lead to behaviour that makes assessment and treatment problematic. This impact on a person's capacity to interact with others may be of a nature and severity that their capacity to make specific decisions is compromised. This chapter has focused on the jurisdiction of England and Wales using the MCA and the MHA as examples of legislation that are there to provide a statutory framework and a ready means of challenge. Detaining and treating persons without their consent, or sedating persons when they are mentally disturbed, must be taken very seriously, as such action can amount to infringement of those persons' human rights, which must never be taken lightly. A thorough understanding of the clinical, ethical, and legal challenges that a disturbance in mental health can bring is essential to ensuring a successful outcome for those patients who depend on our care and compassion.

10.6.1 Pearls

- When patients refuse treatment, health staff must make clear the consequences that may arise.
- Mental ill-health can complicate treatment of physical illness.
- Guidance on when to use the MCA and when to use the MHA is detailed in the MHA Code of Practice issued by the Department of Health.
- To detain a person under the MHA the process set out in law must be followed and there must be a ready means of appeal—mental health review tribunals.
- If a clinician has followed the recommendations in determining capacity and best interests, he or she will be free from liability if later challenged.
- Detaining and treating persons without their consent, or to sedate persons when they are mentally disturbed, must be taken very seriously, as such action can amount to infringement of those persons' human rights, which must never be taken lightly.

10.6.2 Pitfalls

- Mental ill-health can complicate treatment of physical illness.
- Patients who refuse life-saving interventions must be treated in a lawful manner, which may require a court decision.
- Ethical and legal issues arise from the treatment of mental ill-health.
- Interference with one's human rights is only lawful when conducted within a regulatory framework, which provides patients with a means of challenging decisions.
- Unlawful deprivation of liberty exposes a hospital to potential liabilities and is a breach of the patient's human rights.
- The MHA cannot be used as a legal framework to justify compulsory treatment for physical conditions in the absence of consent.
- A thorough understanding of the clinical, ethical, and legal challenges that a disturbance in mental health can bring is essential to ensuring a successful outcome for those patients who depend on our care and compassion.

10.7 References

- American Psychiatric Association. (2013). *Diagnostic and Statistical Manual of Mental Disorders*, 5th edn. Washington, DC: APA.
- World Health Organization. (1992). *International Statistical Classification of Diseases and Related Health Problems* (ICD-10).
- World Health Organization. (2006). *Constitution of the World Health Organization*. Geneva: WHO.

10.8 Further Reading

- Ansseau M, Dierick M, Buntinkx F, et al. (2004). High prevalence of mental disorders in primary care. *J Affect Disord*, 78(1), 49–55.
- Cairns R, Hotopf M, Owen G (2014). Deprivation of liberty in healthcare: UK Supreme Court judgment has changed the rules. *Br Med J*, 348, 3390.

- Fistein EC, Holland AJ, Clare ICH, Gunn MJ (2009). A comparison of mental health legislation from diverse Commonwealth jurisdictions. *Int J Law Psychiatry*, 32, 147–55.
- Fistein EC, Clare ICH, Redley M, Holland AJ (2016). Tensions between policy and practice: a qualitative analysis of decisions regarding compulsory admission to psychiatric hospital. *Int J Law Psychiatry*, 46, 50–7.
- Keene AR. (2015). *Assessment of Mental Capacity: A Practical Guide for Doctors and Lawyers*, 4th edn. London: Law Society Publishing.
- Timmons S, Manning E, Barrett A et al. (2015). Dementia in older people admitted to hospital: a regional multi-hospital observational study of prevalence, associations and case recognition. *Age Ageing*, 44, 993–9.
- Toft T, Fink P, Oernboel E, Christensen K, Frostholm LO, Olesen F (2005). Mental disorders in primary care: prevalence and co-morbidity among disorders. Results from the Functional Illness in Primary care (FIP) study. *Psychol Med*, 35, 1175–84.

10.9 Multiple Choice Questions

✔ Interactive multiple choice questions to test your knowledge on this chapter can be found in the Online appendix at www.oxfordmedicine.com/essentiallegalmatters.

Medical Regulation

Anna Curley

CONTENTS

CHAPTER SUMMARY

GMC Sets and Maintains Standards

The General Medical Council (GMC) sets and maintains standards of education and training as well as entry into practice, and ensures competence of practising physicians.

Medical Act 1983 Governs Statutory Purpose of GMC

The Medical Act 1983 covers the statutory purpose of the GMC, its governance, responsibilities in relation to the medical education, registration, and revalidation of doctors, and gives guidance to doctors on matters of professional conduct, performance, and ethics.

Revalidation

The purpose of medical revalidation is to bring all licensed doctors into a governed system that prioritizes professional development and strengthens personal accountability.

Professional Standards

'Maintaining High Professional Standards in the Modern NHS' provides a framework document for the handling of concerns about doctors and dentists employed in the National Health Service (NHS) in England.

Whistle-Blowers and the Public Interests Disclosure Act 1998

Statutory protection for whistle-blowers is provided by the Public Interests Disclosure Act 1998. NHS staff, including general practitioners (GPs), are covered by the Act. To gain protection provided by the Act the disclosure must be made in good faith, the whistle-blower must reasonably believe that the information is substantially true, and that he or she is making the disclosure to the right prescribed person.

Medical Practitioners Tribunal Service

The Medical Practitioners Tribunal Service (MPTS) is a statutory entity distinct from the GMC and is directly accountable to parliament. The Medical Act 1983 sets out the general powers and responsibilities for MPTS to hold hearings into a doctors' fitness to practise.

IMPORTANT CASE LAW

- Madan v General Medical Council (GMC) [2001] EWHC 577 (Admin)
- Kay v Northumberland Healthcare NHS Trust [2001]
- Vento v Chief Constable of West Yorkshire Police [2002] EWCA Civ 1871
- R (George) v General Medical Council (GMC) [2003] EWHC 1124 (Admin)
- Virgo Fidelis Senior School v Boyle [2004] IRLR 268
- Babula v Waltham Forest College [2007] EWCA Civ 174; [2007]
- BP Plc v Elstone & Petrotechnics Ltd UKEAT/0141/09
- Houshian v General Medical Council (GMC) [2012] EWHC 3458 (Admin)
- Harry v General Medical Council (GMC) [2012] EWHC 2762 (QB)
- Abdullah v General Medical Council [2012] EWHC 2506 (Admin)
- Patel v General Medical Council [2012] EWHC 3688 (Admin)
- Bhatnagar v GMC [2013] EWHC 3412 (Admin)
- Brew v General Medical Council [2014] EWHC 2927 (Admin)
- Dr Bawa-Garba v the General Medical Council [2015] EWHC 1277 (QB)
- PSA for Health and Social Care v GMC & Anor [2015] EWHC 1304

RELEVANT STATUTES AND LEGISLATION

- Medical Act 1983 (as amended by the Professional Performance Act 1995)
- The European Primary Medical Qualifications Regulations 1996
- The NHS (Primary Care) Act 1997
- Public Interest Disclosures Act 1998
- The Medical Act (Amendment) Order 2000
- The Medical Act 1983 (Provisional Registration) Regulations 2000
- The Medical Act 1983 (Amendment) Order 2002
- Health Care Professionals Act 2002
- The European Qualifications (Health Care Professions) Regulations 2003
- The European Qualifications Regulations 2004
- The Medical Act 1983 (Amendment) Order 2006
- The European Qualifications (Health and Social Care Professions Regulations) 2007
- The Health Care and Associated Professions (Miscellaneous Amendments) Order 2008
- The Medical Professions (Miscellaneous Amendments) Order 2008
- Health and Social Care Act 2008
- The General and Specialist Medical Practice Order 2010
- The Medical Act 1983 (Amendment) (Knowledge of English) Order 2014
- The Health Care and Associated Professions (Indemnity Arrangements) Order 2014
- Professional Standards Authority for Health and Social Care (References to Court) Order 2015

PROFESSIONAL GUIDANCE

- Department of Health. (2005). *Maintaining High Professional Standards in the Modern NHS. Doctors and Dentists Disciplinary Framework.* www.nationalarchives.gov.uk
- Department of Health. (October 2006). *Handling Concerns about the Performance of Healthcare Professionals: Principles of Good Practice.* www.ncas.nhs.uk/publications
- GMC. (November 2006). *Good Medical Practice.* www.gmc.co.uk

- NCAS guidance (2006). *Handling Concerns about the Performance of Healthcare Professionals.* www.ncas.nhs.uk
- ACAS. (2009). *The ACAS Code of Practice on Disciplinary and Grievance Procedures.* www.acas.org.uk
- NCAS. (December 2010). *The Back on Track Framework for Further Training; Restoring Practitioners to Safe and Valued Practice.* www.ncas.nhs.uk
- NCAS. (Jan 2011). *Handling Concerns about a Practitioner's Health—a Guide for Managers.* www.ncas.nhs.uk
- GMC. (2012). *Raising and Acting on Concerns about Patient Safety.* www.gmc.co.uk
- NHS Employers. (2012). *Staying on Course—Supporting Doctors in Difficulty Through Early and Effective Action.* www.nhsemployers.org
- GMC. (updated 2014). *Fitness to Practise Rules.* www.gmc.co.uk

11.1 Background to Medical Regulation

Regulation of the medical profession is to ensure that medicine is only practised by appropriately qualified individuals. Regulatory systems set and maintain standards of education and training as well as entry into practice, and ensure competence of practising physicians. Medical regulators can also identify and take action against incompetent, unethical, or immoral practices by physicians. In the UK, these regulatory roles are carried out by the General Medical Council (GMC).

The history of regulating doctors in the UK dates back as far as 1421, when physicians petitioned parliament to ask that nobody without appropriate qualifications be allowed to practise medicine to reduce the 'great harm and slaughter of many men'. By the early 16th century statutory regulation of the medical profession and elimination of unqualified practitioners had become the responsibility of the church. The establishment of the College of Physicians in 1518 led to a dual system of licensing between church and the medical profession, which was still the case a century later when nearly a quarter of doctors received their licences from archbishops. Further progress in medical regulation came with the 1815 Apothecaries Act, which introduced compulsory apprenticeship and formal qualifications for apothecaries, the equivalent of modern-day general practitioners (GPs), under the licence of the Society of Apothecaries. The Medical Act 1858 marks the start of the modern period of medical regulation in the UK. The 1858 Act created The General Council of Medical Education and Registration of the United Kingdom, which was renamed the General Medical Council (GMC) in the 1950 Medical Act. This formally recognized the rights of doctors to self-regulate the profession in return for a guarantee of professional competence and integrity in their actions. The 1950 Medical Act also introduced disciplinary boards, a right of appeal to the GMC, and a compulsory year of training for doctors after their university qualification. Although this compulsory year currently remains in place, a recent review of postgraduate medical education and training in the UK, 'The Shape of Training', recommended that doctors should be fully registered to practise on leaving medical school rather than completing a year working under supervision. The recommendations from the report are currently being considered by the GMC.

The Medical Act 1983 provides the current statutory basis for the GMC's overall duties. Its role in education has since evolved, and in 2010 it took over the functions of the Postgraduate Medical Education and Training Board, which, up to then, was the body responsible for medical education and training in the UK. The GMC is responsible for developing combined standards for undergraduate and postgraduate education.

KEY POINTS—BACKGROUND TO MEDICAL REGULATION

- Regulation of the medical profession is to ensure that medicine is only practised by appropriately qualified individuals.
- Medical regulators can also identify and take action against incompetent, unethical, or immoral practices by physicians.
- In the UK, the regulatory roles are carried out by the GMC.
- The Medical Act 1983 provides the current statutory basis for the GMC's functions.

11.2 The General Medical Council

There are 270,000 doctors on the UK medical register. The role of the GMC is to ensure that the medical register is accurate and up to date, and that practitioners are suitably qualified to practice. The GMC has multiple additional roles: setting out the educational standards for all UK doctors, approving postgraduate medical education and training, supporting continuing professional development, and investigating and acting on concerns about doctors' behaviour, health, or performance.

The Medical Act 1983 covers the statutory purpose of the GMC, its governance, responsibilities in relation to the medical education, registration, and revalidation of doctors, and giving guidance to doctors on matters of professional conduct, performance, and ethics. The Medical Act 1983 sets out the basic legislative framework for the composition and governance of the GMC, including its powers, duties, proceedings, and committees.

The Medical Act gives the GMC powers and responsibilities for taking action when questions arise about doctors' fitness to practise. The GMC (Fitness to Practise) Rules 2004 set out how these matters are investigated and adjudicated upon, and have the force of law. These rules are a version of the 2004 Rules, incorporating amendments made in 2009, 2013, and 2014—The General Medical Council (Fitness to Practise) (Amendment) Rules Order of Council 2014. Additional relevant European legislation affecting medical regulation includes Directive 2005/36/EC, which sets out the GMC's obligations for recognizing the medical qualifications held by doctors from within the European Economic Area (EEA). This directive has now been amended by Directive 2013/55/EU and was transposed into UK law through the European Communities (Recognition of Professional Qualifications) Regulations 2007, and the European Qualifications (Health and Social Care Professions) Regulations 2007. The relevant sections of these regulations have now been incorporated into the Medical Act 1983. Figure 11.1 highlights the review process once a complaint has been made to the GMC.

KEY POINTS—THE GENERAL MEDICAL COUNCIL

- A major role of the GMC is to ensure that the medical register is accurate and practitioners are suitably qualified to practise.
- Other roles include setting educational standards, approving postgraduate training, supporting continuing professional development, and investigating performance.
- The Medical Act 1983 sets out the basic legislative framework for the GMC's composition, governance, powers, duties, proceedings, and committees.
- The Fitness-to-Practise Rules 2004 set out how matters on performance are investigated, adjudicated, and have the force of law.
- European legislation sets out the rules the GMC can apply to the recognition of medical qualifications from within the EEA.

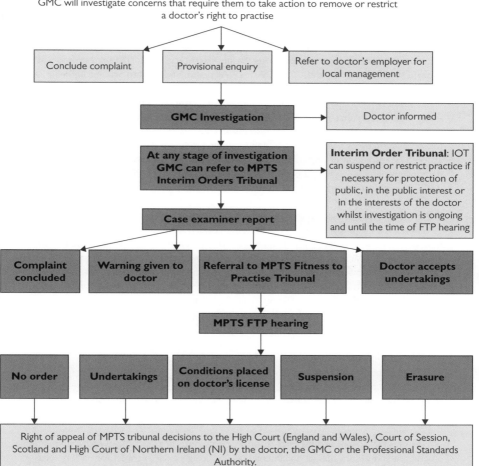

Figure 11.1 Flow chart to highlight the initial General Medical Council review process. FTP, Fitness to practice; GMC, General Medical Council; IOT, Interim Orders Tribunal; MPTS, Medical Practitioners Tribunal Service.

11.3 Revalidation

The purpose of medical revalidation is to improve the safety, quality, and effective delivery of care for patients by bringing all licensed doctors into a governed system that prioritizes professional development and strengthens personal accountability.

In December 2012 the GMC launched revalidation in the UK. This followed years of discussion and a number of high-profile cases in the 1990s where there was public concern that issues raised by patients, doctors, and other healthcare practitioners had not been adequately investigated. Revalidation aims to give extra confidence to patients that their doctor is being regularly checked by their employer and the GMC. Revalidation has been designed to support professionalism and to identify doctors in difficulty early to facilitate their remediation and thus assure patient safety. Revalidation is statutory and is linked to the appraisal process (annual medical appraisals were brought in for consultants and GPs in 2001–2). All doctors licensed to practise in the UK are now required to demonstrate every 5 years that they are up to date and fit to practise.

Each practising doctor is allocated a responsible officer, who is the senior medical officer in every organization that employs doctors. Responsible officers have a statutory duty to ensure that appraisal and clinical governance systems are adequate. They also make a recommendation for revalidation every 5 years for each doctor to the GMC based on satisfactory annual appraisals, absence or resolution of any concerns, compliance with local clinical governance processes, and demonstration of professional practice according to agreed specialist standards. The GMC then decides whether to renew a doctor's licence based on the recommendation from the responsible officer.

Annual appraisals are conducted against a framework of best practice. Doctors are encouraged to reflect on their practice and approach to medicine, reflect on the supporting information they have gathered, and consider what that information demonstrates about their practice. They must identify areas of practice where they could make improvements or undertake further development and demonstrate that they are up to date and fit to practise. Within each appraisal there is a core module, which is divided into four domains that cover the spectrum of medical practice (Box 11.1).

The GMC specifies which attributes must be achieved to be revalidated. In 'Good Medical Practice', the GMC also sets out what is intended by the words 'must' and 'should'. They describe 'you must' for an overriding duty or principle and use the term 'you should' when providing doctors with an explanation of how to meet the overriding duty. For example, doctors 'must' work in partnership with their patients. To achieve this, they 'should' discuss their condition and treatment options with them in a way that they can understand and respect their right to make decisions about their care. The GMC makes it clear in its guidance that serious or persistent failure to follow their directives will put a doctor's registration at risk. The GMC acknowledges, however, that there may be external factors outside of a doctor's control that affect whether they can follow the guidance.

Doctors must maintain their professional performance and apply knowledge and experience to practise and ensure that all documentation (including clinical records) formally recording their work is clear, accurate, and legible. They must contribute to and comply with systems to protect

---

Box 11.1 Revalidation: Appraisal Domains

- Knowledge, skills, and performance
- Safety and quality
- Communication, partnership, and teamwork
- Maintaining trust

patients. In particular, they must take part in systems of quality assurance and quality improvement and comply with risk management and clinical governance procedures.

They must ensure that systems are in place for colleagues to raise concerns about risks to patients and respond to risks to safety. Doctors must also protect patients and colleagues from any risk posed by their health. Doctors must communicate effectively, work constructively with colleagues, delegate effectively, and establish and maintain partnerships with patients. They must show respect for patients, and treat patients and colleagues fairly and without discrimination and act with honesty and integrity. Supporting information that doctors must provide to achieve revalidation includes evidence of continuing professional development, quality improvement activity, details of significant events, feedback from colleagues and patients, and also review of complaints and compliments.

KEY POINTS—REVALIDATION

- Revalidation is designed to improve the safety and quality of patient care by ensuring that doctors prioritize professional development and personal accountability.
- It also aims to identify doctors in difficulty early to facilitate their remediation and thus assure patient safety.
- Revalidation is statutory, linked to the appraisal process and has a 5-year cycle.
- Each hospital appoints a responsible officer to ensure that appraisal and clinical governance systems are adequate.
- The responsible officer recommends revalidation for every doctor to the GMC based on appraisal outcomes.
- The GMC's domains that must be satisfied include knowledge, skills and performance, safety and quality, communication and teamwork, and maintaining trust.

11.4 Investigating Poor Professional Standards

Individual practitioners have a personal responsibility for their own health, conduct, and capability, and are expected to work in accordance with 'Good Medical Practice' and other relevant GMC guidance. Although the vast majority of doctors provide good quality, safe, and effective care, inevitably problems will arise. Organizations must have measures in place to identify problems and reduce risk when they occur. Patient safety is the primary consideration, but fairness to doctors is also paramount. Employers should have policies in place which link to 'Maintaining High Professional Standards in the Modern NHS' (a framework document for the handling of concerns about doctors and dentists employed in the National Health Service [NHS] in England) and the 'Performers List Regulations'. They should also understand these policies and train key members of staff on their content and, importantly, look at concerns in the context of underlying systems or organizational problems.

Concerns at work fall into three main categories: health, conduct, and capability. The employer's Code of Conduct should set out details of acts that will constitute gross misconduct or a serious breach of contractual terms potentially leading to dismissal. There are several documents available to guide those responsible for managing medical staff. The Advisory, Conciliation and Arbitration Service (ACAS) statutory code on disciplinary procedures (introduced in 2009) is a principles-based good practice approach rather than a mandatory procedural requirement. It aims to encourage early and informal resolution of concerns at work to reduce the necessity for formal procedures. Minor misconduct or early indications of unsatisfactory performance, for example, may be handled informally (Figure 11.2). Where cases require formal investigation, there are specific pathways that should be followed (Figure 11.3). In the vast majority of cases when action other than immediate exclusion can ensure patient safety, the clinician should always initially be dealt with using an informal

INFORMAL PROCESS

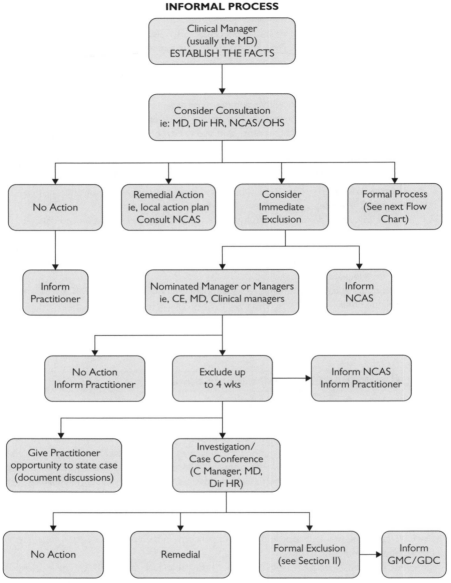

Figure 11.2 The informal process to investigate poor professional standards. CE, Chief Executive; Dir, director; GMC/GDC, General Medical Council/General Dental Council; HR, human resources; MD, medical director; NCAS/OHS, National Clinical Assessment Service/Occupational Health Service.

FORMAL PROCESS

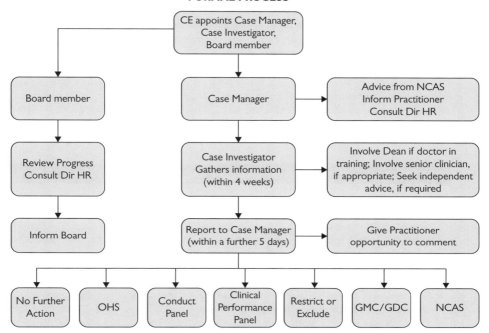

Figure 11.3 The formal process to investigate poor professional standards. Abbreviations are as Figure 11.2.

approach. Only where a resolution cannot be reached informally should a formal investigation be instigated.

At any stage in the handling of a case, consideration should be given to the involvement of the National Clinical Assessment Service (NCAS). The National Clinical Assessment Authority (NCAA) was established to improve arrangements for dealing with poor clinical performance of doctors. In 2005 it became a division of the National Patient Safety Agency, now known as the NCAS. The NCAS provides 24-hour telephone advice, supports local case management and performance assessment, with implementation of recommendations arising from assessment. Any practitioner undergoing assessment by the NCAS must cooperate with a request from the NCAS to give an undertaking not to practice in the Health and Personal Social Services (HPSS) or private sector other than their main place of HPSS employment until the assessment has been completed. If the practitioner chooses not to cooperate in the absence of a causal underlying health problem, disciplinary action may be needed. Support from external organizations may also be required from time to time, and the medical Royal Colleges can often give competency advice and assistance. Where the concerns involve a doctor in training, postgraduate deaneries should be involved.

The key individuals who may have a role in the formal investigation process include the Chief Executive, a non-executive member of the Board appointed by the Chairman of the Board, to oversee the case, a case manager (usually the Medical Director), and a case investigator. The Director of Human Resources role is to support the Chief Executive and the Medical Director.

Employers must maintain confidentiality at all times, and should be familiar with the guiding principles of the Data Protection Act. The guiding principles of Article 6 of the Human Rights Act must be strictly followed. If an employing body is considering exclusion or restriction from practice, NCAS must be notified, so that alternatives to exclusion can be considered. An immediate time-limited exclusion can be considered to protect the interests of patients or other staff. The case investigator should complete the investigation within 4 weeks of appointment. The investigator's report to the case manager should then provide sufficient information to make a decision on whether further action is needed, whether restrictions on practice or exclusion from work should be considered, and whether concerns warrant referral to the GMC. If exclusion occurs and it is decided that the exclusion should come to an end, there should be formal arrangements for the return to work of the practitioner in a timely and managed fashion.

KEY POINTS—INVESTIGATING POOR PROFESSIONAL STANDARDS

- Concerns at work fall into three main categories: health, conduct, and capability.
- The Advisory, Conciliation and Arbitration Service (ACAS) has a statutory code on disciplinary procedures.
- Minor misconduct or performance issues are usually handled informally, but some require a formal investigation.
- The National Clinical Assessment Service (NCAS) provides 24-hour telephone advice, supports local case management, and performance assessment.
- Medical Royal Colleges can give competency advice and assistance while postgraduate deaneries deal with doctors in training.
- If an employing body is considering exclusion or restriction from practice, the NCAS must be notified, so that alternatives to exclusion can be considered.
- A case investigator should report within 4 weeks and the case manager should then make a decision on whether further action is needed.

11.5 Whistle-Blowing

Recent events, most notably the Stafford Hospital scandal in England in the late 2000s, have highlighted the need for greater openness and support of individuals raising concerns about patient safety. Statutory protection for whistle-blowers is provided by the Public Interests Disclosure Act (PIDA) 1998, a private members bill originally put forward by conservative MP Richard Shepherd, which came into force in July 1999. PIDA gives automatic protection to those raising a concern internally with an employer and also to prescribed regulators, for example, the Care Quality Commission (Box 11.2). NHS staff, including GPs, are covered by the Act. However, as the law stands, junior doctors in training do not appear to have full whistle-blowing protection (Day vs Lewisham and Greenwich NHS Trust [2016] ICR 876).

Whistle-blowing law only provides protection from detriment carried out by employers. Deaneries do not constitute employers for the purposes of whistle-blowing legislation, and removal of a doctor from a training programme following a whistle-blowing event, as occurred in the case of Dr Day, cannot be contested under whistle-blowing legislation. Many will argue that this failure to protect thousands of trainee doctors, many of whom work at senior level with significant responsibility, undermines the original purpose of the Whistleblowers Act. Whether postgraduate deaneries (Health Education England) who recruit doctors, supply them to various trusts, and monitor the terms of engagement via appraisal, act as an employment agency for the purposes of Section 43K(1) (a) and (2) of the Employment Rights Act remains to be determined.

Box 11.2 Public Interest Disclosure Act 1998

- Whistle-blowers do not lose statutory protection because they are mistaken. Disclosure must have been made in good faith, the whistle-blower must reasonably believe that the information is substantially true, and that he or she is making the disclosure to the right prescribed person. Babula v Waltham Forest College [2007] EWCA Civ 174; [2007].
- A whistle-blower does not necessarily lose PIDA protection if he or she goes to the media. Kay v Northumberland Healthcare NHS Trust (2001)24.
- PIDA protection also applies to post-employment victimization. BP Plc v Elstone & Petrotechnics Ltd UKEAT/0141/09.
- Subjecting a worker to a detriment for making a protected disclosure is a form of discrimination and that injury to feelings should be compensated accordingly. Virgo Fidelis Senior School v Boyle (2004) IRLR 268.
- Damages are uncapped and awards for injury to feelings are assessed in the same way as for other forms of discrimination. Vento v Chief Constable of West Yorkshire Police [2002] EWCA Civ 1871.

Whistle-blowing is officially defined as 'making a disclosure that is in the public interest'. PIDA is described as an 'Act to protect individuals who make certain disclosures of information in the public interest, to allow such individuals to bring action in respect of victimisation and for connected purposes'. To amount to whistle-blowing, the disclosure must be in relation to serious activity, such as illegal activity, miscarriages of justice, threats to individuals, and/or damage to the environment. It usually occurs when employees disclose to a public body, often either the police or a regulatory body, that their employer is involved in unlawful practices.

To gain the protection afforded to whistle-blowers, the disclosure must have been made in good faith, the whistle-blower must reasonably believe that the information is substantially true, and that he or she is making the disclosure to the right prescribed person. The good faith test is used to prevent unmeritorious claimants: the government stated in the Bristol Royal Infirmary Enquiry that it had intended good faith to mean 'honestly and not maliciously'. Whistle-blowing protection results in the right to take a claim for unfair dismissal or detriment (for example, not being promoted on account of whistle-blowing) to an employment tribunal. Claimants must notify ACAS if they wish to take a case to an employment tribunal, and claims of unfair dismissal must be raised within 3 months of the end of employment. The usual employment law restrictions on minimum qualifying period and age do not apply to this Act. ACAS offer a free 'early conciliation' service. The deadline for making a claim to the tribunal is extended by the amount of time spent in conciliation. Claims made to the employment tribunal are not made public, but regulations enable the employment tribunal service to forward claims to the appropriate regulator where the claimant consents.

Clauses that attempt to prevent an individual from making a PIDA-protected disclosure are void. If healthcare professionals report concern to the media, in most cases they will lose their whistle-blowing law rights, but this is not always the case. Disclosure to the media can be protected under the act. Wider disclosures are protected if they are reasonable in all circumstances and not made for personal gain (Kay v Northumberland Healthcare NHS Trust (2001)). The whistle-blower must reasonably believe that he or she would be victimized if he or she raised the matter internally or with a prescribed regulator; or the concern had already been raised with the employer or a prescribed regulator; or the concern was of an exceptionally serious nature. It is unclear whether PIDA applies to proceedings before a regulatory body; for example, the case of Margaret Hayward, who carried out secret filming for a BBC documentary to expose the neglect of elderly patients, but was removed from the nursing register by the Nursing and Midwifery Council for her 'whistle-blowing' actions.

KEY POINTS—WHISTLE-BLOWING

- Statutory protection for whistle-blowers is provided by the Public Interests Disclosure Act 1998.
- Whistle-blowing is officially defined as 'making a disclosure that is in the public interest'.
- It must be in relation to illegal activity, miscarriages of justice, threats to individuals, and/or damage to the environment.
- The disclosure must have been made in good faith honestly and not maliciously.
- Whistle-blowing protection results in the right to take a claim for unfair dismissal or detriment to an employment tribunal.
- If healthcare professionals report concern to the media, in most cases they will lose their whistle-blowing law rights.
- A whistle-blower must raise matters internally or with a prescribed regulator and only in exceptional circumstances to other bodies or the media.

11.6 Fitness-to-Practice Hearings at Undergraduate Level

In 2009, the GMC and the Medical Schools Council (MSC) produced a document relating to the professional behaviour expected of medical students and the scope, threshold, and practical application of student fitness to practise ('Medical Students: Professional Values and Fitness to Practise, Guidance from the GMC and the MSC', GMC, 2009). From the perspective of the GMC's statutory role, this guidance was advisory rather than mandatory. However, the guidance makes it clear that students must be aware that unprofessional behaviour during their medical education, or serious health issues affecting their fitness to practise, can result in the GMC refusing to grant provisional registration with a licence to practise.

Medical schools, not the GMC, are responsible for determining the fitness to practise of individual medical students, and GMC guidance explicitly states that it does not have any direct authority to deal with or advise on individual cases of medical student fitness to practise or disciplinary issues. All decisions, however, should follow guidance set out by the GMC and be consistent with the regulations and procedures of the medical school. Decisions should be based on the balance of probabilities that the student's fitness to practise is impaired. The panel should consider mitigating factors, give clear reasons if they impose a sanction, ensure it is proportionate, and issue a written determination. They should also indicate whether the outcome of the hearing should be declared to the GMC when applying for registration with a licence to practise. GMC guidance states that medical schools should make it clear that they may pass personal information to other organizations, including the GMC, if a student receives a warning or a sanction. There should also be a clear formal appeals process.

Medical schools and those involved in education and training at undergraduate level must have clear guidelines on the disclosure of information where a student's fitness to practise has raised concern. According to the Information Commissioners Office, students are not protected from disclosure to external bodies under the Data Protection Act 1998. This applies especially when a real issue is raised about a student's fitness to practise and it represents a risk to patients or the public. All students should be informed that this information may be shared with medical and educational supervisors, and there should be clear procedures for sharing information between medical schools and other organizations.

11.7 Medical Practitioners Tribunal Service

The Medical Practitioners Tribunal Service (MPTS) was launched in 2012, and its role is to protect patients by making independent decisions about a doctor's fitness to practise, measured against professional standards set by the GMC. Although the MPTS is part of the GMC, it provides a hearings service that is fully independent in its decision-making and separate from the investigatory role of the GMC. It is led by a chair with senior judicial experience, who is accountable directly to parliament. Tribunals hear fitness-to-practise and interim order hearings. The Medical Act 1983 sets out the general powers and responsibilities for MPTS to hold hearings into doctors' fitness to practise. The more detailed arrangements of how tribunals work are set out in the GMC Fitness-to-Practise Rules 2004. The tribunal is made up of three members, one of whom will act as chair. There will be at least one doctor (medically qualified with a licence to practise) and at least one lay person (not medically qualified). The tribunal members hear the evidence and make decisions on a case.

11.7.1 Interim Orders Panel

The GMC will refer cases to an Interim Orders Tribunal (IOT) of the MPTS (previously known as an Interim Orders Panel, or IOP) where it is deemed that a doctor's ongoing unrestricted practice could undermine public confidence in the profession or cause harm to patients while the allegations are investigated. IOTs can make:

- No order
- An order of suspension
- Impose conditions of practice
  - restrictions on the doctor's practice
  - restrictions to the doctor's behaviour
  - commitments to practise under clinical supervision
  - commitments to undergo retraining.

Findings of fact are not made by IOTs when considering whether to make an order for public protection. Sufficient corroborating evidence on initial examination (a prima facie case) will be sufficient to justify an order upon initial examination, e.g. R (George) v General Medical Council (GMC) [2003] EWHC 1124 (Admin). Doctors can appeal the decisions of the IOT to the High Court. The IOT must take a proportionate approach to the allegations and evidence, balancing the interests of the practitioner and public protection (Madan v General Medical Council (GMC) [2001] EWHC 577 (Admin), Houshian v General Medical Council (GMC) [2012] EWHC 3458 (Admin), Harry v General Medical Council (GMC) [2012] EWHC 2762 (QB)). However, in Bhatnagar v GMC [2013] EWHC 3412 (Admin), the judge opined that the panel had to ask itself what a reasonable onlooker would think if the allegations were subsequently to be proved at a fitness-to-practice hearing and the panel had not suspended the doctor while the case was being investigated. This judgment has made it more likely that a doctor will be suspended at an IOT hearing in certain types of cases.

The tribunal has to justify its decisions in light of the history and give reasons and assess ongoing risk and whether there is a real risk of repetition. Length of order has to be proportionate and the High Court found in Abdullah v General Medical Council [2012] EWHC 2506 (Admin) that IOP panels should not be imposing 18-month duration orders at the outset of a case. The High Court has also upheld appeals where the order of suspension by the IOP was deemed excessive and conditions of practice were sufficient (Dr Bawa-Garba v the General Medical Council [2015] EWHC 1277 (QB)) or where the absence of an interim order could not be said to create a risk to the public interest or public protection (Patel v General Medical Council [2012] EWHC 3688 (Admin)).

11.7.2 Fitness-to-Practice Hearings

There are a number of procedural stages within a fitness-to-practice hearing, and hearings can last several days to weeks depending on the amount of evidence presented. Case management has been introduced in an attempt to reduce the overall length of hearings and the time taken to reach fitness-to-practice hearings.

- **Stage 1**: Findings of fact (are the facts proved?).
- **Stage 2**: Decision on impairment (is the doctor's fitness to practise impaired?).
- **Stage 3**: Decision on the sanction (should registration be restricted or removed and is an immediate order required?).

11.7.2.1 Stage 1: Fact Finding

If a doctor denies the factual allegations, as set out in the GMC charges, the GMC barrister will call witnesses and present documentary evidence to prove the case against the doctor. Doctors have a right to come to the hearing, to be represented by a lawyer or another person, to present evidence, and to call and cross-examine witnesses. There is no 'misconduct' procedural stage in conviction cases, as criminal convictions are deemed proven on the facts. This means that, if a criminal court has already convicted a doctor, the tribunal will not enquire into the events leading to conviction to establish misconduct—it is automatically assumed. Matters concerning a doctor's health will be kept confidential by the GMC. Any public determination will not make express references to a doctor's health. In matters of health, a fitness-to-practise tribunal can go into private session, excluding the press and public for that element of oral evidence and the section of judgment on the case that relates to health.

The fitness-to-practise tribunal determines where the truth lies on the balance of probabilities using the civil standard of proof. Evidence can be called at all three stages of the hearing. Submissions and legal arguments can also be made. The tribunal might find at any stage that the case brought by the GMC is not substantiated. Not all factual allegations, even if proved, constitute misconduct or deficient performance. If the case against the doctor is not proved at any stage of the proceedings, the case will be closed. The Code of Conduct for doctors set out in 'Good Medical Practice' is used by MPTS tribunals to assess whether a doctor has fallen below the standards expected.

11.7.2.2 Stage 2: Impairment

The tribunal asks 'Is the doctor's fitness to practise currently impaired?' If the doctor's fitness to practise is not deemed impaired but there has been a significant departure from the guidance set out in the GMC's guidance, the tribunal may issue a warning and these are published against a doctor's registration for 5 years.

11.7.2.3 Stage 3: Sanction

The tribunal has the following options:

- To end the case with no change to the doctor's registration.
- To accept undertakings.
- To impose a sanction of specified conditions for up to 3 years.
- Suspension or erasure from the medical register (except in cases that relate solely to a doctor's health).

The tribunal's decision is not intended to be punitive, but it may have a punitive effect. The main reason for imposing sanctions is to protect the health, safety, and wellbeing of the public, maintain public confidence in the profession, and promote and maintain proper professional standards and conduct for the members of the profession.

Where a sanction of conditions or suspension is imposed, a review hearing will usually be convened at a later date. The sanction must be proportionate and fair, and the panel has access to an 'Indicative Sanctions' guide for use in decision-making. The tribunal will consider future risk of repetition and a doctor's level of insight into their decision-making process. A doctor can, in certain circumstances, appeal the tribunal's decision. Grounds of appeal need to be identified and lodged within 28 days of the MPTS determination. Where the tribunal imposes a sanction, they will be required to consider whether to make an immediate order to cover the appeal period of 28 days set out in the statute (the Medical Act 1983, as amended). Appeal courts will not easily interfere with a decision of the MPTS (Brew v General Medical Council [2014] EWHC 2927 (Admin)). The Professional Standards Authority, an independent body accountable to parliament, which monitors organizations that register and regulate healthcare personnel, can also appeal a decision of the MPTS to the High Court, if they feel that the MPTS was unduly lenient in their sanctioning of a doctor (Professional Standards Authority for Health And Social Care v General Medical Council & Anor [2015] EWHC 1304).

KEY POINTS—MEDICAL PRACTITIONERS TRIBUNAL SERVICE

- The Medical Practitioners Tribunal Service (MPTS) makes independent decisions about a doctor's fitness-to-practise, measured against standards set by the GMC.
- MPTS tribunals hear fitness to practise and interim order hearings.
- The Interim Orders Tribunal (IOT) will determine if a doctor's practice could undermine public confidence or cause harm to patients while allegations are investigated.
- An IOT can order suspension or impose conditions of practice. It must justify its decisions and assess ongoing risk.
- There are three stages to a fitness-to-practise hearing—stage 1: findings of fact; stage 2: decision on impairment; stage 3: decision on the sanction.
- The fitness-to-practise tribunal determines where the truth lies on the balance of probabilities, and evidence can be called at all three stages of the hearing.
- Fitness-to-practise tribunal sanctions include: accepting undertakings, imposing conditions for up to 3 years, and suspension or erasure from the medical register.

11.8 Pearls and Pitfalls

11.8.1 Pearls

- Although the MPTS is part of the GMC it provides a hearings service that is fully independent in its decision-making and separate from the investigatory role of the GMC. MPTS decisions can be appealed by the doctor, the GMC and the Professional Standards Authority to the High Court (England and Wales), Court of Session, Scotland and High Court of Northern Ireland (NI).

11.8.2 Pitfalls

- Not all NHS staff are covered by the Public Interests Disclosure Act 1998. Junior doctors in training do not have full whistle-blowing protection. Whistle-blowing law only provides protection from detriment carried out by employers. Deaneries do not constitute employers for the purposes of whistle-blowing legislation.
- Medical students undergoing university fitness-to-practise hearings are not protected from disclosure to external bodies under the Data Protection Act 1998 if there is deemed to be a

real issue about their fitness to practise or where this represents a risk to patients or members of the public.

11.9 Further Reading

- General Medical Council. (2006). *Good Medical Practice*. London: GMC. www.gmc-uk.org
- General Medical Council. (2010). *Revalidation: the Way Ahead*. London: GMC. www.gmc-uk.org
- Porter R (1999) [1997]. *The Greatest Benefit to Mankind: A Medical History of Humanity from Antiquity to the Present*. New York: W. W. Norton & Company, pp. 316–17.
- Raach JH (1944). English medical licensing in the early seventeenth century. *Yale Journal of Biology and Medicine*, 16(4), 267–88.
- Report of the Mid Staffordshire NHS Foundation Trust Public Inquiry, chaired by Robert Francis QC. http://www.midstaffspublicinquiry.com

11.10 Multiple Choice Questions

Interactive multiple choice questions to test your knowledge on this chapter can be found in the Online appendix at www.oxfordmedicine.com/essentiallegalmatters.

CHAPTER 12

Healthcare Management

William R. Roche

CONTENTS

CHAPTER SUMMARY

Rationing

All healthcare systems have to ration the availability of care. A medical manager has to deal with a range of competing priorities and influences in making difficult decisions around the provision of care.

Corporate Manslaughter

Legally, organizations are held to account when a death results from gross failings by senior management.

Intellectual Property

Intellectual property can be generated by research activity, innovative delivery or management of care, including information management. If it is produced by employees in the course of their employment or normal duties it generally belongs to the employer.

Dealing with the Media

The criticism of a colleague in social media may breach professional standards and lead to a claim of defamation. The General Medical Council (GMC) advises doctors who identify their professional status on social media to identify themselves.

Due Diligence

The concept of due diligence in relation to medicine places a duty on employers to undertake proper background checks. Employers must ensure that doctors have appropriate qualifications, experience, suitable references, and have English language competence.

Corporate Duty of Candour

The GMC requires doctors to make full and open disclosure to patients when something untoward happens in the course of their care.

Hospitality and Commercial Interests

The law prohibits the promotion of medicinal products to any healthcare professional by gift, pecuniary advantage, or benefit unless it is inexpensive.

Student and Trainee Liability

Employers have responsibility for the adverse effects on patients of negligent acts by students and trainees. An organization has a duty of care to staff and students with regard to their health, safety, and wellbeing.

IMPORTANT CASE LAW

- R v Secretary of State for Social Services, West Midlands Regional Health Authority and Birmingham Area Health Authority (Teaching), *ex parte* Hincks and others (1980) 1 BMLR 93
- Lee v South West Thames Regional Health Authority [1985] 2 All ER 385
- Coughlan v. North and East Devon Health Authority *ex parte* Coughlin [2001] QB 213
- R (On the Application (ota) of Condliff) v North Staffordshire Primary Care Trust [2011] EWHC 872 (Admin)
- R (ota AC) v Berkshire West Primary Care Trust [2011] EWCA Civ 910, 2011
- Rose, R (on the application of) v Thanet Clinical Commissioning Group [2014] EWHC 1182 (Admin)
- R [Health and Safety Executive] v. Mid Staffordshire NHS Foundation Trust 2014. www.judiciary.gov.uk
- R v Cornish and Maidstone and Tunbridge Wells NHS Trust 2016. www.mtw.nhs.uk

RELEVANT STATUTES AND LEGISLATION

- Health and Safety at Work Act 1974
- National Health Service Act 1977
- Inquiries Act 2005
- Fraud Act 2006
- Corporate Manslaughter and Corporate Homicide Act 2007
- Bribery Act 2010
- Health and Social Care Act 2012
- The Human Medicines Regulations 2012
- Defamation Act 2013
- The Medical Profession (Responsible Officers) (Amendment) Regulations 2013

Access: www.legislation.gov.uk

PROFESSIONAL GUIDANCE

- Department of Health (2002). *The NHS as an Innovative Organisation. A Framework and Guidance on the Management of Intellectual Property in the NHS*. www.nic.nhs.uk
- General Medical Council (2009). *Confidentiality: Responding to Criticism in the Press*. www.gmc-uk.org
- General Medical Council (2013). *Doctors' Use of Social Media*. www.gmc-uk.org
- NHS England Clinical Reference Group (CRG) for Chemotherapy. SOP. The Cancer Drugs Fund. *Guidance to Support Operation of the CDF in 2015–16*. www.england.nhs.uk
- NICE (2012). *Methods for the Development of NICE Public Health Guidance*, 3rd edn. www.nice.org.uk

12.1 Introduction

Doctors are familiar with the professional regulation of their practice and behaviour through the General Medical Council (GMC), and for their liabilities under civil law in the event that a patient comes to harm. The public outcry in response to a series of reports into healthcare failings and wrongdoing has led to legislation that criminalizes certain acts and omissions. Increased resort to judicial review has also produced a series of key judgments that have more sharply defined the duties and liabilities of those commissioning and providing healthcare. Medical managers need to be aware of the increased range of professional expectations of them as individuals and the statutory duties of healthcare commissioners and providers.

12.2 Rationing

While it may not be acknowledged, all healthcare systems have to ration the availability of care. Ironically, the limitations of cover are often stated more explicitly by private health insurers and are accepted more readily by their clients than are the constraints of a comprehensive healthcare system delivered free of charge at the clinical interface. The medical manager has to deal frequently with a range of competing priorities and influences in making difficult decisions around the provision of care. These include national and local commissioning policies, provider organization priorities, professional ethics, and the interests of local populations, individual patients, academics, and clinicians. While the attention of the patients and the media may be focused on healthcare providers, it is important that there is clarity around the responsibility for decision-making.

12.2.1 Statutory Duties

The Health and Social Care Act 2012 requires the Secretary of State for Health to 'promote a comprehensive health service' and to have regard to the recommendations of the National Institute for Health and Care Excellence (NICE). The provision of services under this act is the duty of the National Health Service Commissioning Board (NHS England) and of clinical commissioning groups (CCGs). The accountabilities in the 2006 Act were changed by the 2012 Act and now require that local CCGs 'arrange for the provision of the following to such extent as it considers necessary to meet the reasonable requirements of the persons for whom it has responsibility . . .'.

The 2012 Act does not place a duty on the Secretary of State to provide a comprehensive health service, but the duty is rather 'to continue to promote' such a service. The resources available to the Secretary of State (or a local National Health Service [NHS] body) have to be taken into account in determining what a 'reasonable requirement' is. In this context, the judgment in the case of R v Secretary of State for Social Services, West Midlands Regional Health Authority and Birmingham Area Health Authority (Teaching), *ex parte* Hincks and others (1980) 1 BMLR 93 stated:

> 'The point on which this appeal turns is in the end a very short one which is whether, in performing his duty of considering to what extent it is necessary to meet reasonable requirements by the provision of accommodation, facilities and services under s3 of the National Health Service Act 1977, the Secretary of State can in regard to forward planning for the National Health Service, have regard to government economic policy.'

Similarly, in Coughlan v. North and East Devon Health Authority *ex parte* Coughlin [2001] QB 213, the Section 1 duty to promote a comprehensive health service was described as a 'target which the Secretary of State should seek to achieve'.

12.2.2 Cost–benefit Analysis—the Role of NICE

NICE has a role in making recommendations for the improvement of health and social care. Much attention has been given to its technology appraisals, which are evidence-based recommendations on the clinical and cost-effectiveness of a drug or technology. One weakness in this process is that, if there is no submission from the manufacturer, the appraisal is terminated. This results in advice being issued to the NHS that NICE is unable to make a recommendation because the manufacturer has not provided a submission. This allows manufacturers effectively to veto the use of a particular product in the NHS.

The cost–utility analysis conducted by NICE is based on the quality and the length of life that patients may gain as a result of an intervention. The health benefits are expressed as quality-adjusted life years (QALYs). Generally, NICE regards interventions that cost the NHS less than £20,000 per QALY gained as cost-effective. Interventions that cost between £20,000 and £30,000 per QALY gained may also be deemed cost-effective if certain conditions are satisfied.

Once NICE has made an unqualified recommendation, commissioners are required to implement the guidance within the recommended timescale. However, in a recent case (Rose, R (on the application of) v Thanet Clinical Commissioning Group [2014] EWHC 1182 (Admin)) the judge found that the CCG had a duty to have regard to NICE recommendations, which constitute generic guidance, as opposed to technology appraisal recommendations, and that there was a duty to give reasoned explanations of why NICE recommendations, which do not constitute a technology appraisal recommendation, were not being followed.

12.2.3 Individual Funding Requests

It is recognized that commissioning contracts and NICE guidance, no matter how comprehensive, cannot cover all conditions and clinical scenarios. Clinicians, on behalf of their patients, are entitled to make a request (an individual funding request, or IFR) to the CCG or NHS England, whichever is normally responsible for funding treatment for the patient's condition. To be considered by the commissioners, either the treatment must be one that is not normally commissioned in the patient's circumstances or the patient is suffering from a medical condition that falls outside the criteria set out in an existing commissioning policy for funding the requested treatment, including entry to a clinical trial which requires individual explicit funding. There is a real need to establish the 'individual' and exceptional nature of the case, as treatments for cohorts of similar patients are excluded from this source and, in such cases, funding must be sought for a service development. Where IFRs have been conducted in accordance with policy, with a strong evidence trail that demonstrates the rationality of decisions and these decisions are explained, the decisions have been successfully defended at judicial review (e.g. R (ota Condliff) v. North Staffordshire Primary Care Trust [2011] EWHC 872 (Admin) and [2011] EWCA Civ 910, 2011 in R (ota AC) v Berkshire West Primary Care Trust).

There is a strong argument for provider organizations to have a recognized procedure to identify and process these applications, so that there can be constructive dialogue between commissioners and providers, including the management of the repercussions of decisions to refuse treatments.

12.2.4 Cancer Drugs Fund

The Cancer Drugs Fund (CDF) was set up in England in 2011 to provide funding up to £200 million, to meet the costs of drugs that were not approved by NICE or had not yet reached the end of a NICE assessment. With relatively little procedural guidance initially, the processes have evolved to become a single, national list of drugs and indications that the CDF will routinely fund. It uses standard operating procedures for administration of the fund and the guidance of the NHS England Clinical Reference Group (CRG) for Chemotherapy.

The drugs fund was a response to pressure in the media for more open access to cancer drugs. It would be hard to sustain a challenge that cancer patients should have preferential treatment over patients with other life-limiting conditions, or that cancer patients should have drugs funded but not receive other treatments such as new radiotherapy modalities. Criticism of the effectiveness of the Fund has become more vocal and its future remains uncertain.

KEY POINTS—RATIONING

- All healthcare systems have to ration the availability of care.
- The Health and Social Care Act 2012 requires the Secretary of State for Health to promote a comprehensive health service.
- The provision of services under this act is the duty of the National Health Service Commissioning Board (NHS England) and of clinical commissioning groups (CCGs).
- NICE has a role in making recommendations for the improvement of health and social care.
- The cost–utility analysis conducted by NICE is based on the quality and length of life that patients may gain as a result of an intervention.
- Clinicians, on behalf of their patients, can make an individual funding request (IFR) to the CCG or NHS England.
- The Cancer Drugs Fund (CDF) 2011 provides funding to meet the costs of drugs that were not approved by NICE. Its future remains uncertain.

12.3 Corporate Manslaughter

The Health and Safety Executive (HSE) has included healthcare providers in its remit, not just in relation to the safety of staff at work, but has also pursued cases where patients have died as a result of failings in clinical care, e.g. R [Health and Safety Executive] v. Mid Staffordshire NHS Foundation Trust 2014. The law in this regard was strengthened by the Corporate Manslaughter and Corporate Homicide Act 2007 (CMCHA), which came into effect in April 2008. The Act aims to ensure that organizations are held to account when a death has been caused as a result of gross failings by its senior management and is intended to make it easier to prosecute organizations, including NHS bodies, where such gross failures in the management of health and safety lead to a death. While the CMCHA provides some partial exemption for emergency responses, such as triage, the duty of care for the provision of clinical treatment in such situations remains.

The Health and Social Care Act 2008 (Regulated Activities) Regulations 2014 enhanced the scope of the enforcement powers of the Care Quality Commission (CQC) in England and this was reflected in a Memorandum of Understanding (MoU) between the HSE, CQC, and the Local Government Association in 2014. This MoU applies to both health and adult social care in England and replaces the 2012 Liaison Agreement between the CQC and the HSE that applied solely to healthcare. This MoU will result in the CQC taking a lead on the management of instances of severe failings in clinical care that may lead to prosecution. It should be noted that prosecution decisions remain with the Crown Prosecution Service. In the event of a prosecution, the Act sets out factors for the jury to consider when deciding if there has been a gross breach of a relevant duty of care. These factors include: the risk of deaths associated with the activities in question; whether there was compliance with health and safety legislation; whether the culture of the organization tolerated breaches; and any relevant health and safety guidance.

It should be noted that, in the first prosecution of a NHS Trust under this Act (R v Cornish and Maidstone and Tunbridge Wells NHS Trust 2016), the judge defined the required level of the 'gross breach' of care as 'on any view, a very high hurdle for the Crown to meet'. Following the controversial conviction of a senior paediatric trainee for gross negligence manslaughter, a Medical Practitioners Tribunal determined that the doctor should be suspended from practice for 12 months but declined the request of the General Medical Council (GMC) that the doctor's name be erased from the medical register. Uniquely among the UK healthcare regulators, the GMC has the power to appeal Tribunal decisions to the High Court. This is in addition to the Professional Standards Agency's power to appeal the findings of all healthcare regulation tribunals, including those of the Medical Practitioners Tribunal Service. The GMC chose to exercise that right and the High Court found in its favour, stating that the Tribunal had not respected the verdict of the jury as it should have, and the doctor's name was erased from the medical register.

The decision of the GMC to appeal the determination of the Medical Practitioners Tribunal in this case caused even more controversy and led to a clamour of concern among the profession. The Secretary of State for Health and Social Care requested that Sir Norman Williams, a former president of the Royal College of Surgeons, lead a rapid review of medical manslaughter procedures. In June 2018, the Williams report (William N 2018. Gross negligence manslaughter. Department of Health and Social Care, London.) recommended that the duplicate power of the GMC to appeal decisions of the Medical Practitioners Tribunal Service to the High Court should be removed and that a working group should be set up to address the law on gross negligence manslaughter.

KEY POINTS—CORPORATE MANSLAUGHTER

- The Corporate Manslaughter/Homicide Act 2007 ensures that organizations are held to account when a death results from gross failings by senior management.
- The Care Quality Commission (CQC) can take the lead on severe failings in clinical care and bring a prosecution.
- Prosecution decisions remain with the Crown Prosecution Service.
- Factors such as risk of death, compliance with legislation, organization culture, and health and safety guidance are taken into account for gross breach of duty of care.

12.4 Intellectual Property

There has been a drive, supported at the highest political levels, to harness the potential of the NHS to create wealth. This has been institutionalized in the formation of Academic Health Science Networks, which have this as part of their remit. It is important to recognize that intellectual property (IP) can be generated not just by research activity but also by innovative delivery or management of care, including information management. While IP produced by employees in the course of their employment or normal duties generally belongs to the employer, there is a need for local policies that define the employment models and that clearly define the ownership arrangements for IP generated outside of normal working hours.

There are legal channels designed to deal with IP cases—the Intellectual Property Enterprise Court for claims up to £500,000 and the Patents Court for claims in excess of that amount. Clearly, it is far better to have policies in place that prevent such claims and that foster innovation and deal with individual employees' expectations while protecting the rights of the employer. There is Department of Health (DH) guidance that can help with the preparation of such policies ('The NHS as an Innovative Organisation. A Framework and Guidance on the Management of Intellectual Property in the NHS', published in 2002). Where there are academic clinical staff involved in generating IP, there needs to be clear and well-documented understanding of the role of each organization and the arrangements for the promotion of the generation of IP and for the proper allocation of pecuniary and other benefits flowing therefrom. For example, although the researchers may be employed by a university medical school, the provision of research facilities and access to patients by the NHS organization may need to be recognized in an agreement so that both organizations may benefit from any pecuniary gains arising from a discovery. Where clinical trials or other research is funded by a commercial sponsor, it is usual for the IP to reside with the sponsor and for this to be specified in the research contracts. However, the freedom to publish the findings should also be specified in the terms of the research contract. The fundamental message is that IP and its ownership should be defined before the initiation of the research activity.

KEY POINTS—INTELLECTUAL PROPERTY

- Intellectual property (IP) can be generated by research activity, innovative delivery or management of care, including information management.
- IP produced by employees in the course of their employment or normal duties generally belongs to the employer.
- The IP Enterprise Court and the Patents Court are the legal channels designed to deal with IP cases.
- Department of Health guidance exists for the generation of policies relating to IP.

12.5 Dealing with the Media

Until relatively recently, the media referred to the press, radio, and television. The explosive growth in activity on social media forums has added layers of complexity and has increased the potential pitfalls for the unwary (see Chapter 3). Medical managers should be aware that the professional standards of conduct expected of them may often exceed the legal constraints on other staff. The confidentiality that underpins the doctor–patient relationship clearly limits the capacity of a doctor to respond to criticism in the media, if that response involves revealing anything that might have been revealed in circumstances where clinical confidentiality would be expected. This duty of confidentiality endures after the death of a patient. While, in general, it is ill-advised to engage in disputes in the media, in some circumstances it may be necessary to respond. Any such response should not bring any confidential information into the public domain that has not already been published by the patient or their agent.

Organizations sometimes seek to utilize the authority of their senior medical staff in responding to the media. It is particularly important to avoid comments that may be interpreted as being critical of healthcare organization or of fellow professionals. This appearance can arise when selected quotes are taken from pre-recorded interviews or statements. For this reason, some seasoned interviewees favour 'live' interviews, although this can present a challenge for the less experienced. Doctors should always be conscious that their professional regulators have a duty to guard the trust and confidence of the public in the profession. Regulatory proceedings ensue when it is perceived that statements have potentially damaged that public trust. Where there is any doubt about potential breaches of the professional code, it is important to seek advice from a professional indemnity organization or a legal firm with expertise in the area of the professional duty of doctors.

The burgeoning use of social media can cause particular problems. These can arise from a blurring of the boundaries between professional and social personae, comments that may unintentionally impinge on public trust in the profession or the unintended breach of patient confidentiality. The criticism of a colleague in social media may both breach professional standards and lead to a claim of defamation. The culture of immediate commentary often does not allow sufficient time for reflection and judicious editing. Professionals should be aware that comments made on social media may be disseminated further by others and that it may prove impossible to retract the original comments. It should also be noted that the Defamation Act 2013 requires that the statement has resulted in serious harm. The wide dissemination of an ill-advised email by a 'copy to' or 'reply to all' command could cause this threshold to be reached.

The GMC also advises doctors who identify their professional status on social media to identify themselves. While there has been dissent expressed by some about this recommendation, by its very nature it serves to emphasize the need to recognize one's professional responsibilities in public forums, even if the medium is electronic and apparently evanescent.

KEY POINTS—DEALING WITH THE MEDIA

- The explosive growth in activity on social media forums has added much complexity in relation to media issues and has increased the potential pitfalls for the unwary.
- A doctor's duty of confidentiality limits the capacity of the doctor to respond to criticism in the media.
- This duty of confidentiality endures after the death of a patient.
- Confidential information cannot be released into the public domain without the consent of the patient or their agent.
- The criticism of a colleague in social media may breach professional standards and lead to a claim of defamation.
- The GMC advises doctors who identify their professional status on social media to identify themselves.

12.6 Due Diligence

The concept of due diligence has a range of meanings, depending on the circumstances. This often refers to the appropriate investigation of the financial background of an organization with which it is proposed to transact a merger, takeover, or some other contractual arrangement. While medical managers are unlikely to have a remit that includes the financial aspects of due diligence, there are some areas where there is a duty to undertake proper background checks.

These requirements include the duties of responsible officers in England, when organizations are making appointments, to ensure that medical practitioners have qualifications and experience appropriate to the work to be performed, that appropriate references are obtained and checked, and that any steps necessary are taken to verify the identity of medical practitioners (The Medical Profession (Responsible Officers) Regulations 2010, Part 3, Additional Responsibilities of Responsible Officers: England). The 2013 amendments to these regulations add the duty to ensure that medical practitioners have sufficient knowledge of the English language necessary for their work to be performed in a safe and competent manner (The Medical Profession (Responsible Officers) (Amendment) Regulations 2013).

These statutory duties require that the responsible officer ensures that systems and procedures are in place to meet the requirements of the legislation. These duties need to be understood by the Human Resources department, and policies should reflect the accountabilities of the responsible officer for the proper appointment procedures for doctors.

Although less clearly defined in statute, it could be argued that the duty of providers to ensure patient safety and the requirement for commissioners to have regard to patient safety in their duty to secure continuous improvement in the outcomes that are achieved from the provision of the services (Health and Social Care Act 2012 c.7 Part 1 'Further provision about clinical commissioning groups', Section 26) both require due diligence around clinical outcomes and patient safety when new contractual arrangements are made with a healthcare provider. This includes the outsourcing of services or waiting lists and the sharing of aspects of care with other organizations within a clinical pathway or across clinical networks.

KEY POINTS—DUE DILIGENCE

- The concept of due diligence in relation to medicine places a duty on employers to undertake proper background checks.
- Employers must ensure that doctors have appropriate qualifications, experience, suitable references, and English language competence.
- An organization's responsible officer must ensure that systems and procedures are in place to meet the requirements of the legislation.
- Clinical commissioning groups (CCGs) must show due diligence when new contractual arrangements are made with a healthcare provider.

12.7 Corporate Duty of Candour

Candour is best defined as a full disclosure of the truth, with the intent of benefitting the person to whom the information is provided, even if this may disadvantage the person or organization divulging the information. In a seminal judgment on the issue of legal privilege and disclosure, the Appeal Court noted that, having refused to order production of a document, it did so reluctantly because the court thought that there was something seriously wrong with the law if the child's mother could not find out what exactly caused him to suffer brain damage (Lee v South West Thames Regional Health Authority [1985] 2 All ER 385). In 1998 the GMC defined and subsequently reinforced the professional duty to make full and open disclosure to patients when something untoward happens in the course of their care:

> 'You must be open and honest with patients if things go wrong. If a patient under your care has suffered harm or distress, you should; (a) put matters right (if that is possible), (b) offer an apology, (c) explain fully and promptly what has happened and the likely short-term and long-term effects.'
>
> Good medical practice © 2013 General Medical Council.

Thus, there has been a long-standing professional requirement for candour on behalf of doctors.

The Francis Inquiry into the failures of care at the Mid Staffordshire NHS Foundation Trust (The Report of the Mid Staffordshire NHS Foundation Trust Public Inquiry, February 2013) concluded that, although candour is essential to the delivery of high-quality healthcare, it was frequently deficient. The Report included recommendations that the duty of candour become a legally enforced requirement for both registered healthcare professionals and healthcare providers when a patient suffered serious harm or death. The duty was defined as being for the provider organization to inform the patient or relatives and for the healthcare professional to inform the provider organization. It was further proposed that it should be a criminal offence for a registered healthcare professional or director of a provider organization to obstruct this duty or to make misleading statements.

The government response to this was to seek strengthening of the professional duty of candour for healthcare professionals and to introduce a statutory duty of candour for health and social care providers from April 2015 (Health and Social Care Act 2008 (Regulated Activities) Regulations 2014, Section 20). This duty requires that organizations are open and truthful with patients and relatives or carers and provide apologies when things go seriously wrong. A breach of these regulations can lead to the CQC taking regulatory actions, including seeking a prosecution of the organization.

Although the legislation may appear to be clear in its intent, there are subtleties in determining the threshold for notifying patients of adverse events. The delivery of healthcare is complex, and many minor incidents and accidents occur during the course of a patient's treatment. It could be argued that the notification of every minor accident and error could impede the delivery of care and create unnecessary anxiety for patients and their carers. Furthermore, it would be an abuse of the process to use the duty of candour as a mechanism to raise the profile of issues about staffing or resources that should be properly raised through other channels. The proper observation of this duty requires that clinical judgement is exercised, with the rights and wellbeing of patients being held as paramount at all times.

KEY POINTS—CORPORATE DUTY OF CANDOUR

- The GMC requires doctors to make full and open disclosure to patients when something untoward happens in the course of their care.
- Doctors should: (a) put matters right if possible; (b) offer an apology; (c) explain fully and promptly what has happened and the likely short- and long-term effects.
- Organizations have a statutory duty of candour to patients when things go wrong.
- If regulations are breached, the CQC can take regulatory actions, including seeking a prosecution of the organization.
- The notification of every minor accident and error could impede the delivery of care and create unnecessary anxiety for patients and their carers.
- The proper observation of this duty requires that clinical judgement with the rights and wellbeing of patients being held as paramount at all times.

12.8 Hospitality and Commercial Interests

Doctors have important roles in the management of resources, both in terms of individual patient care and in influencing the wider selection and purchasing of drugs, medical devices, and services. This latter role can include participation in research, attendance and presentations at conferences, as well as direct contributions to business cases and the appraisal of procurement options.

The Human Medicines Regulations 2012 Regulation 300 prohibits the promotion of medicinal products to any healthcare professional qualified to prescribe or supply medicine, by any gift, pecuniary advantage, or benefit unless it is inexpensive and relevant to the practice of medicine or pharmacy. The provision of hospitality at a meeting or event held for the purposes of the promotion of a medicinal product must be restricted to hospitality limited to the main purposes of the meeting or event. Hospitality at an event held for purely professional or scientific purposes may be provided only if the hospitality is strictly limited to the main scientific objective of the event. Similarly, no prescriber or pharmacist may solicit or accept any gift, pecuniary advantage, benefit, or hospitality that is prohibited by the regulation, including sponsorship of a person's attendance at a meeting or event and the payment of travelling or accommodation expenses. Convictions under these laws can result in a fine or a jail term of up to 2 years. It should also be noted that acts of bribery or fraud are covered by the Bribery Act 2010 and the Fraud Act 2006, and convictions under the Bribery Act can lead to up to 10 years' imprisonment and an unlimited fine.

Clearly, healthcare organizations should not rely on the statutory offences to ensure the proper conduct of their professional staff in this regard. There should be policies in place that reflect the NHS guidance issued in 1993 (NHS Management Executive HSG 93(5) Standards of business conduct for NHS staff) and the subsequent legislation detailed. Where the healthcare provider is in a partnership with academic institutions, there should be clarity for the partner organizations and for staff about which policies govern specific activities, again with due observance of statutory regulation.

KEY POINTS—HOSPITALITY AND COMMERCIAL INTERESTS

- Doctors have important roles in influencing the selection and purchasing of drugs, medical devices, and services.
- The law prohibits the promotion of medicinal products to any healthcare professional by gift, pecuniary advantage, or benefit unless it is inexpensive.
- Hospitality at an event held for scientific purposes may be provided if it is limited to the main objective of the event.
- Convictions under these laws can result in a fine or a jail term of up to 2 years.
- NHS guidance issued in 1993 is available for healthcare organizations to inform their staff of what is permitted under the law.

12.9 Student and Trainee Liability

Liabilities in relation to students and trainees include the vicarious liability of employers for the adverse effects on patients of negligent acts and the liabilities arising from the organization's duty of care to staff and students with regard to their health, safety, and wellbeing. In this section, we will solely address the former issue of liabilities for injury resulting from the negligence of trainees and students. It is generally accepted that NHS indemnity arrangements for trusts extend to include liability for the actions of those who are not strictly employees whenever the NHS body owes a duty of care to the person harmed. This includes students, locums, academic staff with honorary contracts, clinical trials personnel, charitable volunteers, and people undergoing further professional education, training, and examinations.

However, where a healthcare provider organization does not belong to the NHS Clinical Negligence Scheme for Trusts, the vicarious liability for harm caused by a student or trainee will rest with the organization but may not be included in its insurance arrangements. If the student is placed by a university, it is likely that the university holds indemnity against any liability for a student's action other than in the situation where the university is held legally liable for a student's actions because of a failure to properly inform the provider organization of deficiencies in the student's expected skills or behaviours. For these reasons, provider organizations need to assure themselves that their indemnity arrangements include their vicarious liability for the results of the actions of students or trainees who interact in any way, directly or indirectly, with patients to whom the organization has a duty of care.

KEY POINTS—STUDENT AND TRAINEE LIABILITY

- Employers have responsibility for the adverse effects on patients of negligent acts by students and trainees.
- An organization has a duty of care to staff and students with regard to their health, safety, and wellbeing.
- NHS indemnity arrangements for trusts extend to include liability for the actions of those who are not strictly employees.
- Universities that place students in a healthcare provider organization usually hold indemnity against any liability for a student's action.
- Provider organizations need to assure themselves that their indemnity arrangements include their vicarious liability for the results of the actions of students or trainees.

12.10 Pearls and Pitfalls

12.10.1 Pearls

- Never criticize colleagues on social media.
- Always make a full and open disclosure of mistakes to your patients when they occur.
- All new medical employees at whatever level in a hospital should have their registration and credentials checked prior to patient contact.
- Declare any forms of hospitality from third parties to your responsible officer. Most Trusts will set a monetary limit over which a declaration is mandatory.
- Always inform patients of the involvement of healthcare students during their care and get consent for any procedures they undertake.

12.10.2 Pitfalls

- The rationing of services in any NHS hospital should not get to a level where individual patient care is compromised.
- Bring to the attention of hospital managers issues where you perceive there are failings in clinical care processes.
- Discuss with your employer the terms of agreement on IP matters before contractual arrangements with third parties.
- If documentation of clinical issues is poor or absent, a legal defence, when things go wrong, can be very difficult.
- Unsupervised students or trainees can compromise patient safety and lead to negligence claims.

12.11 Further Reading

- The Mid Staffordshire NHS Foundation Trust—Public Inquiry. Robert Francis QC. Final Report 2013. http://webarchive.nationalarchives.gov.uk
- NHS Business Services Authority. NHS Management Executive HSG 93(5) Standards of Business Conduct for NHS Staff 1993. www.nhsbsa.nhs.uk
- NHS Litigation Authority. NHS Indemnity Arrangements for Clinical Negligence Claims in the NHS. www.nhsla.com

12.12 Multiple Choice Questions

✓ Interactive multiple choice questions to test your knowledge on this chapter can be found in the Online appendix at www.oxfordmedicine.com/essentiallegalmatters.

CHAPTER 13

Legal Basis for Prescribing

David de Monteverde-Robb

CONTENTS

CHAPTER SUMMARY

Licensed Medicines

Use a licensed medicine wherever possible. Medicines licensed in the country of use should be prescribed before the use of imported ones.

Newly Licensed Medicines

Ensure that there are mechanisms to fund new treatments before prescribing or recommending them. Report any new or serious potential side effect or interaction using the relevant national scheme, e.g. yellow cards in the UK.

Off-Licence Medicines

Use only when there is no licensed medicine available and there is authoritative guidance relating to its efficacy.

Unlicensed Medicines—'Specials'

Use a special where a licensed medicine is not available in a convenient formulation, e.g. in a liquid form, rather than adulterating the formulation of a licensed medicine.

Adulterated Licensed Medicines

Where a patient cannot be given the conventional dosage form and no 'specials' product exists, it may be necessary to resort to crushing or other forms of adulteration. Consult with a pharmacist to check for the availability of alternative medicinal products that may not be listed in standard reference sources such as the *British National Formulary*.

Imported Medicines

Only use where the range of licensed and 'specials' products do not meet the need of an individual patient or specialist cohort of patients. Inform the patient how to take the medicine, as the packaging may not be in English.

Medicines Purchased on the Internet

Check the provider is credentialled—with the General Pharmaceutical Council quality logo. If not, then seek an alternative supplier owing to the risks of counterfeiting.

Homeopathy

Respect your patient's belief in such treatments but do not prescribe therapy without a proven or suspected clinical benefit. Herbal medicines in particular have a potential to interact with other allopathic medicines. Where there is little risk, allow patients to self-medicate in accordance with their health beliefs.

Herbal, Chinese, and Ayurvedic Medicines

The composition, potency, and safety of such products cannot be guaranteed. There are toxicity risks which, if known, should be discussed with the patient. Ultimately the choice is that of the patient, but he or she should be made aware that there are unknown risks.

IMPORTANT CASE LAW

- Donoghue v Stevenson [1932] AC 526
- Loveday v Renton and Wellcome Foundation [1990] 1 Med LR 117
- Best v Wellcome Foundation Ltd [1994] 5 Med. L.R. 81
- EC Commission v United Kingdom (Re the Product Liability Directive) [1997] 3 CMLR 923
- Thomson v James and others (1998) 41 BMLR 144
- Richardson v LRC Products Ltd (2000) 59 BMLR 185
- Foster v Biosil (2000) 59 BMLR 178
- Abouzaid v Mothercare (UK) Ltd 2000 WL 1918530
- Worsley v Tambrands [2000] PIQR 95
- A and others v National Blood Authority and another [2001] 3 All ER 289
- Montgomery v Lanarkshire Health Board [2015] UKSC 11

RELEVANT STATUTES AND LEGISLATION

- Human Medicines Regulations 2012
- Medicines Act 1968
- Misuse of Drugs Act 1971
- Consumer Protection Act 1987
- Sale of Goods Act 1979
- European Directive on Product Liability Council Directive No 85/374/EEC
- Vaccine Damage Payments Act 1979

Access via www.legislation.gov.uk

PROFESSIONAL GUIDANCE

- British Medical Association (2015). *Prescribing in General Practice*. www.bma.org.uk
- GMC (2007). *0–18 Guidance for All Doctors: Prescribing Medicines*. www.gmc-uk.org
- GMC (2008). *Consent: Patients and Doctors Making Decisions Together*. www.gmc-uk.org
- GMC (2013). *Good Medical Practice*. www.gmc-uk.org

- GMC (2013). *Good Practice in Prescribing and Managing Medicines and Devices.* www. gmc-uk.org
- GMC (2015). *Prescribing for Friends and Family.* www.gmc-uk.org
- GMC (2015). *Prescribing Unlicensed Medicines.* www.gmc-uk.org
- Medical Defence Union (2013). *Prescribing.* www.themdu.com
- Medical Defence Union (2014). *Self-prescribing.* www.themdu.com
- Medicines & Healthcare Products Regulatory Agency Guidance (2014). *Legal Requirements for Children's Medicines 2014.* www.gov.uk/government
- NICE (2014). *BNF Guidance on Prescribing.* http://www.evidence.nhs.uk/formulary/bnf/ current/guidance-on-prescribing

13.1 Introduction

The science and art of prescribing is multifaceted and technically complex, requiring careful judgement of the competing risks of harm and benefits of treatment. Good prescribing requires intimate knowledge of your patient's illness, comorbidities, and concurrent treatments. When prescribing, a doctor must be aware of a drug's potential for toxicity, its metabolic or excretory pathway, its interactions, its cautions and contraindications, and its legal status. Failure to prescribe medicines safely is associated with 32% of the most serious medication incidents reported in the UK despite the numerous safety mechanisms in place to avert such incidents. A pharmacist or nurse, and often both, will assess a prescription before any administration has taken place. Protocols, guidelines, decision support in electronic prescribing software, electronic medicines data resources, and availability of senior advice are customarily available in various combinations. Nevertheless, the most common types of errors are ambiguous or wrong doses or frequencies and prescribing the wrong medicine. To reduce medication errors and harm, it is recommended to use the 'five rights': the right patient, the right drug, the right dose, the right route, and the right time.

Since the enactment of the Human Medicines Regulations 2012 by the UK parliament, prescribing of medicines in this country may be undertaken by any suitably qualified doctor, dentist, independent or supplementary prescribing nurse, optometrist, or pharmacist. Subsequently, in 2013 additional groups have also been given prescribing privileges, including physiotherapists, radiographers, chiropodists, and podiatrists. Of these groups, only doctors, dentists, nurses, and pharmacists may prescribe controlled drugs. All groups have a duty only to prescribe medicines within their area of competence and scope of practice. Optometrists, for instance, may only prescribe medicines for ocular conditions affecting the eye and/or surrounding tissue. Although a prescription may now stem from a variety of sources, the underpinning legal status of medicines and art of prescribing applies to all and is unchanged.

KEY POINTS—INTRODUCTION

- Good prescribing requires intimate knowledge of a patient's illness, comorbidities, and concurrent treatments.
- A doctor must be aware of a drug's potential for toxicity, its metabolic or excretory pathway, its interactions, its cautions and contraindications, and its legal status.
- The most common types of prescribing errors are wrong doses or frequencies and prescribing the wrong medicine.
- The Human Medicines Regulations 2012 governs the law on prescribing in the UK.
- In the UK, prescribing of medicines may be undertaken by doctors, dentists, trained non-medical prescribers including specialist nurses and pharmacists.

13.2 Understanding the Medicines You Prescribe

13.2.1 Product Licence

Legally, the safest medicine you can prescribe for a patient is one that has a product licence in the country of your practice and where you use that medicine in accordance with its licence. This requires keen attention to the summary of product characteristics (SPC). This will detail the posology, including at-risk populations, cautions and contraindications, and the required monitoring before and during therapy. For the prescriber and the patient, a product licence, which by UK law must be given by the Medicines and Healthcare Products Regulatory Agency (MHRA), is a level of guarantee that the medicine will conform to the following:

1. Act in the way it is claimed.
2. Has been assessed in clinical trials.
3. Side effects are acceptable in relation to its efficacy.
4. The manufacturing process is of a high quality.

In the European Union (EU), medicines licensed in one country can be extended on application to further member states. Usually a medicine licensing application will be made simultaneously throughout the EU via the centralized procedure of the European Medicines Agency (EMA).

13.2.2 Duty of the Pharmaceutical Industry

Pharmaceutical manufacturers have a duty to make only fair and honest claims about the medicines they produce. They have a duty to make publicly available the results of their research. There is an ethical imperative to report the results of all clinical trials, including those of unreported trials conducted in the past.

There is also a duty to warn of the known side effects of a medicine, both those identified in clinical trials and those that are either sufficiently serious or commonplace from post-marketing surveillance. This information is contained in the patient information leaflet supplied in medicine packaging and in the SPC. Known side effects are usually given a described frequency of occurrence, from very common (>1/10) to very rare (<1/10,000). Using a medicine in accordance with the dose in the licence ensures the highest probability of avoiding unnecessary toxicity, while the stated doses are the optimally balanced counterpoises of safety and efficacy.

For legal purposes, although all medicines have a known toxicity profile, some will be classified as 'unavoidably unsafe'. Drugs such as immunosuppressants and chemotherapy have effects that can be very serious or, indeed, life-threatening. Such adverse events would not be acceptable in the treatment of a minor ailment but, in life-extending treatment, this level of risk may be deemed acceptable. Where an unavoidably unsafe therapy is required, that will in all likelihood cause manifest toxicity, a patient must give informed written consent and be advised to read the manufacturer's patient information or other specialist information. In doing so, the patient is appraised of the risks of treatment and the prescriber is given a degree of protection against medical liability.

13.2.3 Newly Licensed Medicines

In the UK, once a new medicine is given a product licence and marketing authorization, it may be prescribed legally on private prescriptions. These medicines will not at this stage be available to prescribe on the National Health Service (NHS) until a funding route is established. New drugs within the same therapeutic class, such as new insulins or new inhalers, will often be permitted on the NHS if the organization, hospital, or clinical commissioning group (CCG) accepts the medicine onto the local prescribing formulary.

13.2.4 Reporting Side Effects

The Commission on Human Medicines (CHM) and the MHRA encourages the reporting of all suspected reactions to newer drugs and vaccines, which are denoted by an inverted black triangle symbol (▼). All medicines that are newly licensed in the UK carry a black triangle warning, as do some medicines with ongoing safety concerns. Clinical trials conducted for licensing are usually short and do not recognize late emerging or rare effects. Similarly, use of medicines in patients with extremes of stature or age, renal or hepatic impairment, or in the presence of multiple comorbidities or polypharmacy will not have been studied in licensing trials.

KEY POINTS—UNDERSTANDING THE MEDICINES YOU PRESCRIBE

- Prescribed medicines must have a product licence.
- In the UK, the Medicines and Healthcare Products Regulatory Agency (MHRA) grants licences.
- A product licence guarantees the medicine will act in the way it is claimed, has been assessed in clinical trials, and that side effects are acceptable in relation to efficacy.
- Drug side effects are usually given a described frequency of occurrence, from very common (>1/10) to very rare (<1/10,000).
- Pharmaceutical manufacturers have a duty to make fair and honest claims about their medicines, make available the results of their research, and to warn of the known side effects of a medicine.
- Where an unavoidably unsafe therapy is required that will in all likelihood cause manifest toxicity, a patient must give informed written consent.
- All medicines that are newly licensed in the UK carry a black triangle warning, as do some medicines with ongoing safety concerns.

13.3 Liability of Prescribers and Suppliers of Medicines

Under strict liability, pharmaceutical manufacturers and any other party involved in the distribution chain of medicines are potentially liable if a product is found to be sold in a defective condition that is unreasonably dangerous to the consumer. Many courts have accepted the concept of the 'unavoidably unsafe', as described by the adverse events list. This applies to most medicines where benefit is expected to outweigh described dangers. Products would not give rise to strict liability if they were found to be 'unavoidably unsafe'. Liability is often restricted to only risks known in the literature or product information at the time of treatment and not the time that a complaint or legal proceeding occurs. Proven liability is rarely upheld under strict liability criteria, although many breaches of warranty are known. Most plaintiffs seeking recovery under warranty do so against the provider (prescriber), seller (usually the pharmacy), or the manufacturer. For prescribers, a breach of warranty could include representations about a medicine that are unfounded, ultimately false, or misleading. Pharmaceutical representatives also need to present information on the efficacy and safety of medicines fairly and honestly. A prescriber is also duty bound to ensure that claims of efficacy for recommended therapies are based in fact.

Cases against prescribers may also arise from negligence. Failure to adhere to a medicine's product licence or SPC at any level, including a failure to make dose adjustments for organ impairment or a failure to monitor (e.g. liver function tests) could imply negligence if such actions were to result in measurable harm. Almost all other pharmaceutical liability centres around product defects, inclusive of manufacturing defects, design defects, and failure to warn. The latter may also apply to inadequately labelled medicines as dispensed by a pharmacy, or to a prescriber who fails to describe the risks associated with a treatment adequately.

After prescribing a medicine, your responsibility for that treatment and that patient continues for as long as you care for the patient and as long as he or she takes that medicine. If you prescribe a medicine as part of a team, you are individually responsible for any monitoring of that treatment for the duration of the time that the team cares for the patient. Where you transfer the care of a patient to another practitioner or team, it is incumbent on you to state what actions and monitoring are outstanding and required for a therapy to ensure the efficacy and safety of the therapy; for instance, periodic liver function tests, chest X-rays, HbA1c, or whatever the appropriate testing is for a therapy.

KEY POINTS—LIABILITY OF PRESCRIBERS AND SUPPLIERS OF MEDICINES

- Under strict liability, pharmaceutical manufacturers and those involved in the distribution of medicines are potentially liable if a product is found to be defective.
- Products do not give rise to strict liability if they are found to be 'unavoidably unsafe'.
- Plaintiffs seeking redress under warranty do so against the manufacturer, prescriber, and seller of a drug or medical product.
- Cases against prescribers of medicines may also arise from negligence claims.
- Your responsibility to your patient after you have prescribed medications continues for as long as the patient takes the medicine under your care.

13.4 Consent and Prescribing

It is required that any person with capacity gives permission before any type of medical treatment or examination may proceed. The prescribing practitioner offering treatment must give the following advice on issues, including:

- An outline of the benefits and most common and significant risks that may result from its undertaking.
- What action to take in the event of such a reaction occurring.
- When, how, and for how long to take the medicine.
- What monitoring, follow-up, or review will be required.

Furthermore, the process of consent must include the risks and benefits of alternative treatments, including no treatment. Consent can be written, verbal, participatory, or passive, and is guided by the level of the potential risks. Non-medical prescribers are obliged to ask patients to consent to treatment by a non-physician. Before writing a patient's prescription, where possible, one must enquire about the use of other concurrent treatments, whether non-prescription, herbal, illicit substances, and medicines purchased online. It is the responsibility of the prescriber to ensure that any medicines offered are compatible with other 'remedies' taken.

Cases in English law where a healthcare provider is subject to civil action following perceived failure to obtain adequate consent before prescribing medications are rare. However, in line with the ruling of the Supreme Court in the case of Montgomery v Lanarkshire Health Board [2015] UKSC 11 it would be prudent to no longer view patients as uninformed and incapable of understanding the consequences of taking prescribed medication.

KEY POINTS—CONSENT

- A prescribing practitioner must inform a patient of the risks, benefits, timing, and monitoring of any drugs he or she proposes to give.

- Non-medical prescribers are obliged to ask patients to consent to treatment by a non-physician.
- It is the responsibility of the prescriber to ensure that any medicines offered are compatible with any other 'remedies' taken.

13.5 Selecting an Appropriate Treatment

Where a licensed medicine is available for a condition, this should be selected over any unlicensed alternatives. Often, multiple licensed therapies will be available. For reasons of efficiency, hospitals and primary care healthcare providers will operate a drug formulary in such circumstances to guide their prescribers. Occasionally, a medicine may be licensed with a highly specific indication for which no alternative licensed medicines exist. In principle, the therapy provided for the indication must be licensed if one exists. New high-cost therapies require approval from the National Institute for Health and Care Excellence (NICE) or the Scottish Medicines Consortium (SMC) before they can be prescribed. However, even those medicines that are already clinically approved need a commissioning agreement from the body who pays for the treatment—usually NHS England or the local CCG.

Tips for good practice in medicines selections include:

- Be familiar with the national and local guidance for the medicines you are prescribing.
- Be familiar with your hospital or area formulary. Prescribe medicines that are available.
- If a new effective medicine becomes available, check its national/local funding status with your pharmacy department (in hospital or local CCG).
- Avoid choices within a therapeutic class that have more potential for interactions or modes of excretion unsuitable for your patient.
- As far as practical, choose agents that are licensed, widely available, and given by the safest route available.
- Prescribe medicines licensed in the country of use before prescribing medicines from another country.

KEY POINTS—SELECTING AN APPROPRIATE TREATMENT

- Medicines licensed in the country of use should be selected over any unlicensed or off-licence alternatives.
- Most hospitals and primary care healthcare providers will operate a drug formulary to guide prescribers in their choice of medicines.
- Formulation and pharmacokinetic or interaction differences may guide selection to a non-formulary choice.
- New high-cost therapies require assessment by NICE and approval by NHS England or local CCGs.

13.6 Non-Standard Prescribing

13.6.1 Imported Medicines

To prescribe safely, we must know our patient's medication history. When a patient tips out his or her mountain of medicines on the table, have you noticed that often one or more packets is written in a foreign language, overlabelled in English? This is a symptom of the parallel trading of medicines in Europe. Applications may be made for parallel importing of a medicine to be marketed in the UK, providing that the imported product has no therapeutic difference from the same UK product. There are many commercial and therapeutic reasons why this may occur, none of which has a bearing on the prescriber who writes the prescription saving that the patient may wonder why they have been prescribed a Greek medicine. Parallel imported medicines must be overlabelled with package instructions in English and must contain a patient information leaflet in the English language. The practice is beyond the prescriber's control, but the prescriber may need to explain this to the patient.

Imported medicines are a different matter. Several companies have specialized in importing medicines to the UK that have no equivalent (available) licensed medicine in the UK market. They facilitate patient access to medicines that would otherwise not be available and are potentially life-saving. Often very safe and efficacious medicines are not marketed in the UK for simple commercial reasons, such as the patent holder having commercial interests solely in the Far East. Alternatively, importation may be required to circumvent temporary national supply issues following manufacturing difficulties.

Legally and practically, there are a number of limitations and caveats with imported medicines.

- Dosing may reflect the pharmacogenomic ethnic prevalence of the target population (e.g. a Japanese medicine), and the toxicity and efficacy profiles may differ in a predominantly Caucasian population.
- Manufacturing standards may differ if manufactured in a country outside the 'WHO [World Health Organization] list of countries with the highest standards'.
- Patient information and packet instructions may not be available in English.

It is imperative that patients consent to and are apprised of the risks of treatment with an imported medicine. If the use of an imported medicine becomes common in an area of practice, such as in specialist hospital services, then the clinical area should create standard leaflets or frequently asked questions for patients to help them understand their treatment and ensure that all patients are given relevant and comprehensive information.

KEY POINTS—IMPORTED MEDICINES

- Parallel imported medicines must be overlabelled with package instructions in English and contain a patient information leaflet in English.
- Imported medicines are occasionally needed to facilitate patient access to medicines that would otherwise not be available and, in some circumstances, are life-saving.
- Imported medicines may have been subject to lower manufacturing standards and may have different toxicity and efficacy profiles.
- Patients should be apprised of the risks of treatment with an imported medicine.

13.6.2 Adulterated Licensed Medicines

Adulteration of licensed medicines is commonplace, but the implications are largely unrecognized by prescribers. Adulteration is any modification of the presentation or form of a medicine before it is taken. This can include halving a tablet, crushing, dissolving, or mixing with food. While this may be within the licence for many scored tablets, it constitutes adulteration for all modified-release preparations and many medicines with enteric coating. Often the available formulation choices are limited and, to treat with a particular medicine, no rational alternative will exist. Prescribing a medicine that can only be administered to a patient via adulteration of the physical structure constitutes use outside of its licence. The manufacturer of the medicine would not be responsible for the consequences of using the medicine. The *British National Formulary* contains brief information of the available formulations of a medicine.

Nearly all young children and all sedated adults in intensive care will be unable to swallow oral tablets and capsules. Occasionally there are alternative liquid formulations, sprinkle capsules, sublingual, or oro-dispersible tablets. More often than not, the only viable option involves dispersing or crushing a tablet in a given volume of water and administering the total volume of liquid in adults or, for children, drawing up a portion of the resultant solution. The application of science here is poor. How hydrophilic is the active compound? What dissolves in the water—the flavouring, the excipients, the drug? Or does the active medicine fall to the bottom of the cup only to be washed out or discarded after the 'drug' has been given? Often a medicine will be formulated to release slowly throughout the day, particularly analgesics and cardiac medicines. Crushing modified-release tablets will lead to a 'dose dump' where the dose designed to release over 12–24 hours will be absorbed rapidly, causing high peak serum concentrations, leading to toxicity. Crushing enteric-coated tablets will expose the active substance to gastric acid and may limit the potency of the dose. Pharmacists are able to give specialist advice on the most appropriate formulation of a medicine. It is incumbent on the prescriber to consider how his or her patient will take a medicine.

In the operating theatre and in critical care, injectable medicines are often given outside of the licensed method of administration. Changes will involve the nature of the diluents used, the volume of diluent used, the rate of administration, mixing of medicines (without appropriate stability data), and also the route of administration. For these unlicensed practices, rigorous data for efficacy are lacking and the safety of such practice is underevaluated. Where such prescribing is unavoidable, the parent organization should provide internally published advice to support such practice by using guidelines, monographs, and similar documents to provide shared corporate responsibility. The golden rules of safety with adulterated medicines are:

- Consider the pharmacokinetic properties of the original product and try to match these.
- Consider the safety of those preparing or giving an adulterated medicine if cytotoxic or immunosuppressant.
- This is a choice driven by necessity not convenience.
- Consult standard reference sources before changing the formulation.

KEY POINTS—ADULTERATED LICENSED MEDICINES

- Adulteration of a medicine is any modification of the presentation before it is taken.
- Prescribing a medicine that can only be given via adulteration of the physical structure constitutes use outside of its licence.
- The manufacturer of a medicine bears no responsibility for the consequences of using adulterated medicines.
- It is the responsibility of the prescriber to consider how his or her patient will take a medicine.
- Avoid changing the licensed route of administration where possible.
- Match the pharmacokinetic properties of the original medicine as closely as possible.
- Consider the safety of those who are giving the medicine.

13.6.3 Off-Licence Use of Medicines

Sometimes a prescriber may use a medicine for an indication beyond that for which it is licensed. Over time, many of these 'off-licence' uses become established practice. Indeed, many progress to become licensed indications in themselves. Classic examples include uses of gabapentin, amitriptyline, aspirin, and erythromycin. Gabapentin and amitriptyline were originally licensed as a treatment for epilepsy and depression, respectively. While gabapentin is now licensed for peripheral neuropathic pain, amitriptyline remains unlicensed for this indication despite both being commonly prescribed staples of therapy as per the NICE clinical guideline for neuropathic pain.

Aspirin was an antipyretic and analgesic before it was used for its antiplatelet aggregation effects. Erythromycin, an antibiotic, is often used in critical care to aid gastric emptying.

Off-licence medicines used at a dose in accordance with the licensed indication carry a guarantee that the toxicity profile is established and should be acceptable. The efficacy of the intervention is, however, not guaranteed by the manufacturer and is often inferred from the findings of a limited number of small-scale clinical trials of varying quality. It is, however, generally preferable to use an 'off-licence' treatment in preference to an unlicensed medicine. It is incumbent on the prescriber to inform a patient where a medicine is being used off-licence.

KEY POINTS—OFF-LICENCE USE OF MEDICINES

- A prescriber may use a medicine for an indication outside its licence.
- Off-license use at licensed dose predicts an acceptable toxicity profile.
- Efficacy is not guaranteed by the manufacturer.
- Off-licence use of a drug is preferable to use of an unlicensed medicine.
- The prescriber has a duty to inform a patient where a medicine is being used off-licence.

13.6.4 Unlicensed Medicines and 'Specials'

An unlicensed medicine is typically one of two different products. The first is a rarely used or historical product with low levels of clinical evidence supporting its use and there are often concerns regarding the clinical safety. These are products that have a small market value, which prohibits investment in the process of licensing.

The other type is medicines made by small manufacturing units to meet a specific demand of practicality. In the pharmaceutical vernacular they are known as 'specials'. 'Specials' are unlicensed medicines made by holders of a 'specials' licence as granted by the licensing authority. In the UK, these small manufacturers must comply with good manufacturing practice (GMP) and are inspected by the MHRA. Often such companies make liquid formulations of medicines or small-scale batches of niche injectables. Many NHS hospitals have licensed manufacturing units to supply the needs of patients that would not be addressed by other commercial manufacturers. Marketing of unlicensed medicines is highly restricted and no therapeutic claims are permitted.

KEY POINTS—UNLICENSED MEDICINES AND 'SPECIALS'

- An unlicensed medicine is a rarely used product with low levels of clinical evidence supporting its use and possible clinical safety issues.
- 'Specials' are unlicensed medicines made by holders of a 'specials' licence granted by a licensing authority. They are used to meet specific demand.
- In the UK, these small manufacturers must comply with GMP and undergo inspection by the MHRA.
- Marketing of unlicensed medicines is highly restricted and no therapeutic claims are permitted.

13.6.5 Orphan Drugs

To achieve designation as an orphan drug the following must apply:

- Novel therapeutic entities must be intended for a condition that is life-threatening or chronically debilitating, at a prevalence in the EU of not more than 5 in 10,000 people.
- It must be proven that the market would not generate sufficient returns to justify investing in the development of the therapy.
- The medicine would be of significant benefit to those affected.

Companies who obtain orphan designation are granted scientific assistance during development, fee reductions, and are granted 10-year market exclusivity. As a consequence of the rarity of the condition to be treated, an orphan drug has only limited clinical trial data available. The toxicity profile of orphan drugs will be primarily based on small-scale clinical trials and post-marketing surveillance. Prescribers of orphan drugs must monitor patients carefully and report any data relating to suspected toxicities or interactions to the licensing authorities.

KEY POINTS—ORPHAN DRUGS

- Orphan drugs are agents used to benefit patients with rare conditions but do not attract sufficient returns for manufacturers to develop the therapy.
- Companies who obtain orphan designation are granted scientific assistance during development, fee reductions, and a 10-year market exclusivity.
- Prescribers of orphan drugs must monitor patients carefully and report any treatment-related toxicities or interactions.

13.7 Herbal Medicines

Herbal medicines are medicinal products whose only active ingredients are made by subjecting herbal substances to processes such as distillation, extraction, fractionation, fermentation, or concentration. Herbal substances can be part of an algae, fungi, lichen, plant, or plant exudate. They are subject to the pharmacovigilance system as used by licensed medicines and they must have a written SPC, i.e. comprehensive product-specific information about clinical efficacy and safety. Herbal medicines may be applied externally, via inhaler, or taken orally. They must only be indicated for the treatment of conditions that do not require a diagnosis or monitoring from a medical practitioner.

Herbal medicines must have a plausible mechanism for pharmacological effect or efficacy. There must also be a basis of traditional use. Herbal medicines must have been used continuously as a medicine for at least 30 years and at least 15 years within the EU. Vitamins and minerals may occasionally also be added to the active herbal substance, where their action is ancillary to the action of the herbal substance. Some are available to buy as part of a general sales list, which is essentially unrestricted, where they are considered reasonably safe to supply without the supervision of a pharmacist. Others, that have a higher degree of potency, a more involved indication for use, or a chance of interaction with traditional medicines, are restricted to sale under pharmacist supervision. Advertisements for herbal products must contain the phrase 'exclusively based on long standing use', although some products such as St John's Wort have been subjected to review by meta-analysis of randomized controlled trials by the Cochrane Review Group.

KEY POINTS—HERBAL MEDICINES

- Herbal medicines usually contain substances that can be part of an algae, fungi, lichen, plant, or plant exudates.
- Herbal medicines must have a plausible mechanism for pharmacological effect or efficacy and have been used as a medicine for 30 years.
- They are subject to the pharmacovigilance system as used by licensed medicines and must have written Summaries of Product Characteristics (SPC).
- They are indicated for the treatment of conditions that do not require a diagnosis or monitoring from a medical practitioner.

- Most are available for purchase 'over the counter' but others need dispensing by a pharmacist.

13.8 Homeopathy

Generally based around the ideas developed in the 1790s by Samuel Hahnemann, a German medical doctor, homeopathy is based on the principle that 'like cures like'—as substances that cause symptoms can also be used to alleviate them and that succussion (dilution and shaking) increases the potency of the substance. In the UK, 'homeopathic medicinal products' (HMP) are products made in accordance with a homeopathic manufacturing procedure as described by the European Pharmacopoeia.

Licensing of homeopathic medicines is a process of ensuring safety and quality of products, but not efficacy. There are subtle differences between HMP and national homeopathic products (NHP). Largely this is summarized as the NHP having certain exemptions, having been established therapies prior to the implementation of the Medicines Act 1968, although their quality and safety must still be assured. HMP must be no more than one part per 10,000 of the mother tincture, and in the case that the 'active' substance is used in allopathic medicine, it must contain no more than 1/100th of the smallest concentration used in allopathy. It may be taken only orally or applied externally. No therapeutic indication may be specified on any associated packaging; indeed, the packaging must state 'homeopathic medicinal product without therapeutic indications'.

A homeopathic medicine must only be used for the treatment of minor symptoms or conditions that would ordinarily and with reasonable safety be treated without the supervision or intervention of a doctor. At the time of writing, NICE and the US Food and Drug Administration (FDA) do not recommend that homeopathy is used in the treatment of any medical condition. No good-quality evidence exists for efficacy of treatment for any homeopathic medicines and some claims are scientifically implausible (such as prevention of infections). When patients admitted under your care have a history of treatment with homeopathic medication, although it would usually be considered safe to permit your patient to continue with their treatment, it cannot be provided on the NHS and it would also not be considered detrimental to care for it to be ceased. Where a patient expresses a desire to continue treatment, providing no supply is required and he or she can safely swallow or apply the medicine without the help of a nurse, it would broadly be considered to be a matter for the patient to decide to continue or not. For hospital inpatients, some may see writing a prescription for a homeopathic medicine on a medication chart as endorsement of the therapy, and an obligation for nursing staff to ensure it is given. Conversely, it could be seen simply as a recognition of the 'treatments' the patient is taking. Whatever stance an individual prescriber takes for inpatient prescribing, it would be unusual to include homeopathic medicines as part of a patient's discharge summary as this could imply responsibility for a primary care practitioner to continue such a treatment although it is not available on the NHS.

KEY POINTS—HOMEOPATHY

- Homeopathic medicinal products (HMP) must be no more than one part per 10,000 of the mother tincture.
- Licensing of homeopathic medicines is a process of ensuring safety and quality of products, but not efficacy.
- They are used for minor conditions not usually needing medical supervision and no therapeutic indication may be specified on any associated packaging.
- No good-quality evidence exists for efficacy of treatment for any homeopathic medicine (HMP or NHP), and NICE do not recommend their use.

- Homeopathic products are not provided on the NHS, but patients can use them if they can supply and apply their own.
- They do not have to be written on a hospital drug chart or discharge summary.

13.9 Medicines Obtained Without Prescription

The internet is often used by the general public to find answers to health questions. Some take this further and use the internet to obtain medicines without a prescription and without medical supervision from unregistered pharmacies and other overseas suppliers. Drugs from such sources may not have an auditable chain of supply. The drugs themselves may be diluted, fake, out of date, or may not be manufactured to the rigorous requirements of medicines regulation agencies such as the MHRA, EMA, and FDA. More dangerous still, medicines obtained in this manner may be adulterated with allopathic medicines other than the labelled content. They can contain no active ingredient, the wrong active ingredient, or the wrong amount of active ingredient. The manufacturing process can be unhygienic, led by unqualified personnel, and, in the most extreme circumstances, has been found to contain fatal doses of wrong ingredients. Medicines purchased over the internet from websites that conceal their true location have been found to be counterfeit in over 50% of cases.

All medicines brought into the hospital from home should be assessed before being given. Any products that could be counterfeit or obtained illegally should be replaced by medicines of reputable derivation. Medicines with printed instructions in a language or script other than that of an EU country should be given a particularly high level of scrutiny.

In 2015, the European Parliament passed the Falsified Medicines Directive, which must be fully enacted before 9 February 2019. Two mandatory safety features will be implemented across the EU to allow medicines to be identified and authenticated. Firstly, each individual package of a licensed medicine will be given a unique identifier, which must be checked at multiple points along the supply chain, including at the final step before the supply to a patient. Secondly, there must be tamper-proof packaging.

KEY POINTS—MEDICINES OBTAINED WITHOUT PRESCRIPTION

- Drugs bought over the internet may be diluted, fake, out of date, or may not be manufactured to rigorous standards.
- All healthcare professionals should discourage their patients from obtaining medicines by such means.
- Suspicious medicines brought into hospital should be replaced by those of reputable derivation.
- Medicines purchased over the internet from websites that conceal their true location have been found to be counterfeit in over 50% of cases.
- A unique identifier and tamper-proof packaging for medicines are part of the measures of the new EU Falsified Medicines Directive 2015.

13.10 Non-Allopathic Medicines

Traditional Chinese medicine (TCM) is one of the oldest and widespread systems of treatment for illness in the world. It includes the use of concoctions of naturally occurring substances as medicines tailored to the individual and the symptomatology, as well as holistic approaches, including acupuncture, massage, exercise (qigong), and diet. TCM has been unable to substantiate its therapeutic claims by the standards of allopathic medicine (mainstream use of agents to treat disease)—the randomized placebo-controlled clinical trial.

Although the industry is worth more than $13 billion a year, it is largely unregulated. There are increasing reports of safety concerns or toxicity relating to the use of TCM. In 2001, the UK Committee for Safety of Medicines issued a warning that people who take TCM could be risking their health and that they 'continue to find... traditional Chinese medicine containing potentially dangerous and often illegal ingredients'. In 2003, the UK set up its own Chinese Medicine Council to self-regulate the industry. Most TCM in the UK continues to be sold as health products or food because of the difficulty in meeting the standards required for classification as a complementary medicine. Until farmers, wholesalers, Chinese medicine practitioners, and the countries in which these products are sold adopt tighter regulation to ensure the quality of the supply chain and the products themselves, the risk of poisoning and contamination remain.

Ayurvedic medicine includes the use of special diets, herbal compounds, and other health practices such as massage. Ayurveda, Siddha, and Unani are all traditional complementary systems of medicine practised in India and each has commonality with the contamination risks from TCM. Contamination with heavy metals remains a concern for Ayurvedic medicine. Patients wishing to consume non-allopathic traditional medicines should be discouraged from taking medicines with unknown provenance. The ingredients and pharmacological and physiological actions are often uncertain, unlisted, and retain the possibility of significant interactions with prescribed allopathic medicines.

KEY POINTS—CHINESE, AYURVEDIC, AND NON-ALLOPATHIC MEDICINES

- Traditional Chinese medicine (TCM) involves the use of concoctions of naturally occurring substances as medicines tailored to the individual and the symptomatology.
- TCM has been unable to substantiate its therapeutic claims by the standards of allopathic medicine.
- There are increasing reports of safety concerns or toxicity relating to the use of TCM.
- Most TCMs in the UK continue to be sold as food products because of the difficulty in meeting regulatory standards.
- Patients should be discouraged from taking medicines with unknown provenance as they risk interactions with prescribed allopathic medicines.

13.11 Pearls and Pitfalls

13.11.1 Pearls

- Only prescribe therapies with proven efficacy.
- Use medicines licensed in the country of use wherever possible.
- Ensure that decisions to use medicines other than licensed medicines are driven by necessity rather than convenience.
- Ensure that your patients are fully informed in the decision to use any treatment and are aware of the implications for safety and efficacy when using imported, off-licence, or unlicensed medicines.
- If prescribing unlicensed medicines, select a medicine with a known, assured, and high-quality manufacturing process and route of supply.

- Advising on the appropriate and safe use of medicines is a core skill of pharmacists. They are a readily available resource of advice.
- Make a concerted effort to match the intended pharmacokinetic profile of a medicine if the original formulation must be altered.

13.11.2 Pitfalls

- Poor prescribing is the leading cause of serious reported medication incidents in the UK.
- Be aware of the mechanism of action, the potential toxicity, the requirements for monitoring, potential interactions, and the cautions and contraindications before prescribing a medicine.
- Know your patients—their presenting illness, comorbidities, and the other treatments they are taking.
- Before prescribing or recommending a medicine, ensure that treatment is funded and that the medicine can be readily obtained.
- Consider the legal status and provenance of any medicines you prescribe.
- Consider the potential health and safety concerns that may arise for those giving a medicine that is adulterated, especially chemotherapy, immunosuppression, and hormonal treatments.
- Never change the intended route of administration of a medicine unless there are supporting organizational or national guidelines.
- Be prepared to report all adverse events and interactions with newly licensed, orphan, or unlicensed medicines. Report all new and significant findings with any medicine.
- Be aware of medicines that carry the black triangle symbol (▼). This can be found in the manufacturer's information, the patient information leaflet, and the electronic medicines compendium beside the drug name at the top of each document. The safety of these medicines is still being evaluated.
- Medicines of unknown provenance may be counterfeit and may either not work or have toxic effects. Adopt prescribing practices that encourage patients to obtain medicines via conventional supply routes.

13.12 Further Reading

- Brown S (2013). *The Medical Law and Ethics that Pertain to Safe Prescribing*. Medical Protection Society 2013. www.medicalprotection.org
- Coghlan ML, Haile J, Houston J, et al. (2012). Deep sequencing of plant and animal DNA contained within traditional Chinese medicines reveals legality issues and health safety concerns. *PLoS Genet*. 8, e1002657.
- European Medicines Agency. (2016). *Guide to Information on Human Medicines Evaluated by EMA*. www.ema.europa.eu
- European Parliament. (2016). *The Falsified Medicines Directive (Directive 2011/62/EU) and the Delegated Act on Safety Features (Commission Delegated Regulation (EU) 2016/161—'the Deregulated Regulation')*. http://ec.europa.eu
- Grissinger M (2010). The Five Rights: A destination without a map. *Pharmacy and Therapeutics*, 35(10), PMC2957754.
- Human Medicines Regulations (2012). No. 1916, 24th August 2012. London: The Stationery Office. http://www.legislation.gov.uk
- Liu S-H, Chuang W-C, Lam W, et al. (2015). Safety surveillance of traditional Chinese medicine. *Drug Saf*, 38(2), 117–28.
- Macaulay C (2013). *GMC Tightens Rules on Self-prescribing*. Medical Defence Union. www.themdu.com

- Medicines and Healthcare Products Regulatory Agency (2014). *The Blue Guide, Advertising and Promotion of Medicines in the UK*, 3rd edn. www.gov.uk
- Saper RB, Kales SN, Paquin J, et al. (2008). Lead, mercury, and arsenic in U.S.- and Indian-manufactured Ayurvedic medicines sold via the Internet. *JAMA*, 300(8), 915–23.
- World Health Organization. (2016). *Substandard, Spurious, Falsely Labelled, Falsified and Counterfeit (SSFFC) Medical Products—Fact Sheet*. www.who.int

13.13 Multiple Choice Questions

✓ Interactive multiple choice questions to test your knowledge on this chapter can be found in the Online appendix at www.oxfordmedicine.com/essentiallegalmatters.

Glossary of Legal Terms

Abuse Defined by the Department of Health in their 'No Secrets' document. 'Abuse may consist of a single act or repeated acts. It may be physical, verbal or psychological. It may be an act of neglect or an omission to act, or it may occur when a vulnerable person is persuaded to enter into a financial or sexual transaction to which he or she has not consented, or cannot consent. Abuse can occur in any relationship and may result in significant harm to, or exploitation of, the person subjected to it'.

Access to Health Records Act 1990** An Act to establish a right of access by individuals to reports relating to themselves provided by medical practitioners for employment or insurance purposes and to make provision for related matters.

Actus reus The guilty act.

Adoption and Children Act 2002** An Act to restate and amend the law relating to adoption; to make further amendments of the law relating to children; to amend Section 93 of the Local Government Act 2000; and for connected purposes.

Adulteration of medicines This is any modification of the presentation or form of a medicine before it is taken.

Adults with Incapacity (Scotland) Act 2000** An Act of the Scottish Parliament to make provision as to the property, financial affairs, and personal welfare of adults who are incapable by reason of mental disorder or inability to communicate; and for connected purposes.

Advance decisions Under Sections 24–26 of the Mental Capacity Act 2005 a person of 18 years or over with mental capacity can make a decision to refuse future treatment if a need for treatment arises when they lack capacity. Practitioners must consider whether an advance decision was validly made and intended to apply in the circumstances that have arisen.

Advisory Conciliation and Arbitration Service ACAS statutory code on disciplinary procedures (introduced in 2009) is a principles-based good practice approach rather than a mandatory procedural requirement. It aims to encourage early and informal resolution of concerns at work to reduce the necessity for formal procedures.

Age discrimination Unfairly treating someone differently because of age.

Age of Legal Capacity (Scotland) Act 1991** An Act to make provision in the law of Scotland as to the legal capacity of persons under the age of 18 years to enter into transactions, as to the setting aside and ratification by the court of transactions entered into by such persons and as to guardians of persons under the age of 16 years; to make provision in the law of Scotland relating to the time and date at which a person shall be taken to attain a particular age; and for connected purposes.

Age of majority In England, Wales, and Northern Ireland until 1969 the age of majority was reached when one became 21 years old and applied to the right to vote, own property, get married, and make a legal will amongst other rights of adulthood. Through the Family Law Reform Act 1969, the age at which one became considered legally an adult was reduced to 18; and explicitly the right to give consent to medical treatment or investigation. The act also directly stated that young people aged 16 and 17 must too be presumed competent to give consent, and permission of a parent to treatment is not necessarily required.

Article 2 Human Rights Convention** This establishes a right to life. This has been interpreted in case law to create an obligation on public bodies to provide care to patients with mental disorders to reduce the risks of suicide.

Article 3 Human Rights Convention** This establishes the right to freedom from torture and has been interpreted to find the unnecessary use of physical force to deliver psychiatric treatment as an infringement of this right.

Article 5 Human Rights Convention** This establishes the right to liberty. It states: 'Everyone has the right to liberty and security of person. No one shall be deprived of his liberty save in the following cases and in accordance with a procedure prescribed by law [including] (e) the lawful detention of persons for the prevention of the spreading of infectious diseases, of persons of unsound mind, alcoholics or drug addicts or vagrants'.

Article 8 Human Rights Convention** This establishes the right to privacy, grants the 'right to respect for private and family life'. However, Article 8(2) permits infringements 'necessary in a democratic society in the interests of national security, public safety or the economic well-being of the country, for the prevention of disorder or crime, for the protection of health or morals, or for the protection of the rights and freedoms of others'.

Assent Assent is the agreement of someone not able to give legal consent to participate in an activity. Work with children or adults not capable of giving consent requires the consent of the parent or legal guardian and the assent of the subject.

Battery* The intentional or reckless application of physical force to someone without his or her consent.

Best interests Any act done for, or any decision made on behalf of, a person who lacks capacity must be done, or made, in that person's best interests. That is the same whether the person making the decision or acting is a family carer, a paid care worker, an attorney, a court-appointed deputy, or a healthcare professional, and whether the decision is a minor or major issue. A person trying to work out the best interests of a person who lacks capacity to make a particular decision should: (1) encourage participation; (2) identify all relevant circumstances; (3) find out the person's views; (4) avoid discrimination; (5) assess whether the person might regain capacity; (6) determine if the decision concerns life-sustaining treatment; (7) consult others; (8) avoid restricting the person's rights; and (9) weigh up all of these factors to work out what is in the person's best interests.

Births and Deaths Registration Act 1953** An Act to consolidate certain enactments relating to the registration of births and deaths in England and Wales with corrections and improvements made under the Consolidation of Enactments (Procedure) Act 1949.

Bolam test A doctor is 'not guilty of negligence if he has acted in accordance with a practice accepted as proper by a responsible body of medical men skilled in that particular art'.*

Bolitho test If it had been demonstrated that the professional opinion defending the doctor's action was incapable of withstanding logical analysis, the action could be regarded as negligent.

Breach of duty* Breach of a duty imposed on some person or body by a statute. The person or body is liable to any penalties imposed by such statute.

Bribery Act 2010** An Act to make provision about offences relating to bribery; and for connected purposes.

Burden of proof The burden of proof identifies who bears the burden of proving the claim. In general, the person making an allegation must prove his or her claim. Thus in criminal cases the burden lies with the prosecution, who must prove the case against the defendant to succeed. This means that there is no burden of proof on the defendant to prove his innocence, but the prosecution must prove every element of the crime. In civil cases, the burden of proof lies with the claimant. In very rare cases, the burden of proof may be reversed in relation to certain elements of a claim.

Caldicott Guardian A Caldicott Guardian is a senior person responsible for protecting the confidentiality of patient and service user information and enabling appropriate information sharing. Each National Health Service (NHS) organization is required to have a Caldicott Guardian; this was mandated for the NHS by Health Service Circular: HSC 1999/012.

Capacity Competence to enter into a legally binding agreement.

Care Act 2014** An Act to make provision to reform the law relating to care and support for adults and the law relating to support for carers; to make provision about safeguarding adults from abuse or neglect; to make provision about care standards; to establish and make provision about Health Education England; to establish and make provision about the Health Research Authority; to make provision about integrating care and support with health services; and for connected purposes.

Causation* The relationship between an act and the consequences it produces. In tort, it must be established that the defendant's tortious conduct caused or contributed to the damage to the claimant before the defendant can be found liable for that damage.

Child Assessment Order This is undertaken by an authorized person under the act, usually the local authority, to allow clinicians to examine a sibling (for example, when parents are uncooperative). It is little used but its duration is a maximum of 7 days.

Child A child is defined by the law as those under 18 years old.

Children Act 1989** The Children Act 1989 allocates duties to local authorities, courts, parents, and other agencies in the UK, to ensure that children are safeguarded and their welfare is promoted. It centres on the idea that children are best cared for within their own families; however, it also makes provisions for instances when parents and families do not cooperate with statutory bodies.

Children and Families Act 2014** An Act to make provision about children, families, and people with special educational needs or disabilities; to make provision about the right to request flexible working; and for connected purposes.

Civil law Involves private individuals suing other legal persons (e.g. other private individuals, a public authority, or a company) in the County or High Court, before a judge, who will decide both liability and the quantum of any damages payable.

Claimant* A person applying for relief against another person in an action, suit, petition, or any other form of court proceeding.

Code of Practice* A body of rules for practical guidance only or that sets out professional standards of behaviours but does not have the force of law. Generally, failure to comply with a Code of Practice does not automatically expose the party in breach to prosecution or any civil remedy. It may, however, be relied on as evidence tending to show that he or she has not fulfilled some relevant statutory requirement.

Common law Common law is law that is created by judges when deciding cases. Decided cases create precedents, which are generally followed in subsequent cases under a doctrine called *stare decisis*. The doctrine refers to the general order within the legal hierarchy where decisions of a higher court are binding on a lower court in the hierarchy. If a precedent was set by a court of equal or higher status to the court deciding the new case, then the judge should follow the rule set in the earlier case.

Competence A person of sound mind and sufficient understanding.

Complaint* The initiating step in civil proceedings consisting of a statement of the complainant's allegations.

Confidentiality The ethical principle or legal right that a physician or other health professional will hold secret all information relating to a patient, unless the patient gives consent permitting disclosure.

Consent* Deliberate or implied affirmation; compliance with a course of proposed action.

Consumer Protection Act 1987** The Consumer Protection Act 1987 gives you the right to claim compensation against the producer of a defective product if it has caused damage, death, or personal injury. The act also contains a strict liability test for defective products in UK law, making the producer of that product automatically liable for any damage caused. Part 1 of the Consumer Protection Act 1987 implemented the European Community Directive on Liability for Defective Products 1985 (85/374/EEC), which introduced the notion of strict liability for defective products into UK law.

Contributory negligence Where a claimant's own negligent actions contribute either to the occurrence of an accident, or to the extent of injuries suffered as a result of an accident for which he or she is not to blame, his or her damages may be reduced to reflect his own culpability.

Coroner A coroner is an independent judicial officer appointed by the local authority and responsible for investigating deaths in certain circumstances.

Coroners Act 1988** This Act relates to legislation governing the appointments of coroners, reporting of deaths, post-mortem examinations, inquests, legal powers of coroners, and offences and penalties.

Coroners and Justice Act 2009** An Act to amend the law relating to coroners, to investigation of deaths, and to certification and registration of deaths; to amend the criminal law; to make provision about criminal justice and about dealing with offenders; to make provision about the Commissioner for Victims and Witnesses; to make provision relating to the security of court and other buildings; to make provision about legal aid and about payments for legal services provided in connection with employment matters; to make provision for payments to be made by offenders in respect of benefits derived from the exploitation of material pertaining to offences; to amend the Data Protection Act 1998; and for connected purposes.

Coroner's Court The duty of a coroner is to investigate certain deaths, mainly where the coroner has reason to suspect that the deceased died a violent or unnatural death, or the cause of death is unknown, or the deceased died while in custody or otherwise in state detention. A coroner may sit alone or, in limited circumstances, with a jury. Doctors may be required to give evidence about a post-mortem examination or any medical conditions that the deceased may have been suffering from prior to his or her death.

Corporate manslaughter The law in this regard was strengthened by the Corporate Manslaughter and Corporate Homicide Act 2007 (CMCHA), which came into effect in April 2008. The Act aims to ensure that organizations are held to account when a death has been caused as a result of gross failings by its senior management and is intended to make it easier to prosecute organizations, including National Health Service bodies, where such gross failures in the management of health and safety lead to a death. While the CMCHA provides some partial exemption for emergency responses, such as triage, the duty of care for the provision of clinical treatment in such situations remains.

Corporate Manslaughter and Corporate Homicide Act 2007** An Act to create a new offence that, in England and Wales or Northern Ireland, is to be called corporate manslaughter and, in Scotland, is to be called corporate homicide; and to make provision in connection with that offence.

County and High Courts Civil cases generally start in the County Court (for low-value cases) or the High Court (for high-value or complex cases). Clinical negligence cases, being civil law cases, are normally decided by the County Court, with only a small proportion being heard by the High Court (where the value and/or complexity of the claim is exceptional). Appeals from final decisions of the County Court or of the High Court generally go to the Court of Appeal (Civil Division).

Court of Justice of the European Union The Court of Justice of the European Union (CJEU) is an institution of the European Union (EU) which decides cases relating to EU law.

Court of Protection The Court of Protection makes decisions on financial or welfare matters for people who cannot make decisions at the time they need to be made. It is responsible for: (1) deciding whether someone has the mental capacity to make a particular decision for themselves; (2) appointing deputies to make ongoing decisions for people who lack mental capacity; (3) giving people permission to make one-off decisions on behalf of someone else who lacks mental capacity; (4) handling urgent or emergency applications where a decision must be made on behalf of someone else without delay; (5) making decisions about a lasting power of attorney or enduring power of attorney and considering any objections to their registration; (6) considering applications to make statutory wills or gifts; and (7) making decisions about when someone can be deprived of their liberty under the Mental Capacity Act. It is based in London and most cases are heard by district judges and a senior judge, but they can sometimes be heard by High Court judges.

Criminal law Criminal law is imposed and enforced by the state by means of: (1) a criminal prosecution (taken by the Criminal Prosecution Service); (2) a criminal trial (if heard in the Crown Court this is likely to involve a jury); and (3) a sentence, which is passed by a judge.

Criminal offence A criminal offence is an act that is forbidden by the criminal law and carries with it a punishment for breaching the law, which may include loss of liberty. It is made up of two distinct elements: (1) the *actus reus*; (2) the *mens rea*.

Criminal Procedures (Insanity and Unfitness to Plead) Act 1991** An Act to amend the law relating to the special verdict and unfitness to plead; to increase the powers of courts in the event of defendants being found to be insane or unfit to plead; and to provide for a trial of the facts in the cases of defendants found to be unfit to plead.

Data Protection Act 1998** An Act to make new provision for the regulation of the processing of information relating to individuals, including the obtaining, holding, use, or disclosure of such information.

Declaratory relief The courts may also provide declaratory relief in the form of a declaration. For example, in a medical treatment case, the Court of Protection may make a declaration that it is lawful to administer particular treatment, for example, a blood transfusion, against someone's wishes.

Defamation Act 2013** The Defamation Act 2013 is an Act of the Parliament of the UK, which reformed English defamation law on issues of the right to freedom of expression and the protection of reputation. The Act changed existing criteria for a successful claim, by requiring claimants to show actual or probable serious harm before suing for defamation in England or Wales, setting limits on geographical relevance, removing the previous presumption in favour of a trial by jury, and curtailing sharply the scope for claims of continuing defamation (in which republication or continued visibility constitutes ongoing renewed defamation).

Deprivation of liberty safeguards 2007** The Mental Capacity Act deprivation of liberty (DoL) safeguards (formerly known as the Bournewood safeguards) were introduced into the Mental Capacity Act 2005 through the Mental Health Act 2007. The MCA DoL safeguards apply to anyone: (1) aged 18 and over; (2) who suffers from a mental disorder or disability of the mind—such as dementia or a profound learning disability; (3) who lacks the capacity to give informed consent to the arrangements made for their care and/or treatment; and (4) for whom DoL (within the meaning of Article 5 of the European Convention on Human Rights) is considered after an independent assessment to be necessary in their best interests to protect them from harm. The Safeguards cover patients in hospitals and people in care homes registered under the Care Standards Act 2000, whether placed under public or private arrangements. The Safeguards are designed to protect the interests of an extremely vulnerable group of service users order to: (1) ensure that people can be given the care they need in the least restrictive regimes; (2) prevent arbitrary decisions that deprive vulnerable people of their liberty; (3) provide safeguards for vulnerable people; (4) provide them with rights of challenge against unlawful detention; and (5) avoid unnecessary bureaucracy.

Directive An official or authoritative instruction. In relation to European Union community legislation, directives are addressed to one or more member states and require them to achieve (by amending national law if necessary) specified results.

Disclosure The release of information about a person or entity. Of a corporation, the filing of documents and statements required by law; in litigation, the release of documents and other information subpoenaed or otherwise sought by the other side.

Double effect Prescribing (or giving) opiates with the intention of alleviating pain, but with the possible 'side effect' of shortening life, is therefore lawful, under the so-called 'doctrine of double effect'.

Due diligence The concept of due diligence has a range of meanings, depending on the circumstances. This often refers to the appropriate investigation of the financial background of an organization with which it is proposed to transact a merger, takeover, or some other contractual arrangement. For medical managers the requirements include the duties of responsible officers when organizations are making appointments to ensure that medical practitioners have qualifications and experience appropriate to the work to be performed, that appropriate references are obtained and checked, and that any steps necessary are taken to verify the identity of medical practitioners. There is a duty to ensure that medical practitioners have sufficient knowledge of the English language necessary for their work to be performed in a safe and competent manner.

Duty of candour Candour is best defined as a full disclosure of the truth, with the intent of benefitting the person to whom the information is provided, even if this may disadvantage the person or organization divulging the information. Doctors should: (1) put matters right if possible; (2) offer an apology; and (3) explain fully and promptly what has happened and the likely short- and long-term effects. Organizations also have a statutory duty of candour to patients when things go wrong.

Emergency Protection Order These are usually used by social services; the duration is a maximum of 8 days but can be extended by 7 days on one occasion only.

Equality Act 2010** An Act to make provision to require Ministers of the Crown and others when making strategic decisions about the exercise of their functions to have regard to the desirability of reducing socioeconomic inequalities; to reform and harmonize equality law and restate the greater part of the enactments relating to discrimination and harassment related to certain personal characteristics; to enable certain employers to be required to publish information about the differences in pay between male and female employees; to prohibit victimization in certain circumstances; to require the exercise of certain functions to be with regard to the need to eliminate discrimination and other prohibited conduct; to enable duties to be imposed in relation to the exercise of public procurement functions; to increase equality of opportunity; to amend the law relating to rights and responsibilities in family relationships; and for connected purposes.

European Convention on Human Rights** A universal declaration of Human Rights was first proclaimed by the General Assembly of the United Nations on 10 December 1948. The Declaration aims at securing the universal and effective recognition and observance of human rights and fundamental freedoms.

European Directive on Product Liability The Directive establishes the principle that the producer of a product is liable for damages caused by a defect in his product. The Directive contains an exculpation clause for the producer (for example, if he or she can prove that he or she did not put the product into circulation, that the product was not defective when put into circulation, that the product was not produced for economic purposes, that the defect is due to compliance of the product with mandatory regulations issued by the public authorities, that the state of scientific and technical knowledge at the time when the product was put into circulation was not such as to enable the existence of the defect to be discovered, etc.).

European Primary Medical Qualifications Regulations 1996** European Union Council Directive 93/16/EEC made under Article 47 EC, was implemented into domestic law by The European Primary Medical Qualifications Regulations 1996 ('the Regulations'), which came into force on 10 July 1996. Articles 2 and 4 are the core provisions of the Directive. Article 2 relates to primary medical qualifications. It obliges the member states to recognize the diplomas, certificates, and other evidence of formal primary medical qualifications awarded to nationals of member states, by giving such qualifications, as far as the right to take up and pursue the activities of a doctor is concerned, the same effect in its territory as those which the member state itself awards.

Euthanasia Translated from the Greek as 'good death'. Passive euthanasia is where death results from the withdrawal of treatments and active euthanasia is where a drug is given with the intention of hastening death. Voluntary euthanasia is where the individual has made the request; non-voluntary euthanasia is where a person is unable to give their consent but has previously expressed a wish to die if they were in that state, and involuntary euthanasia where a person does not want it. Active euthanasia is regarded as either manslaughter or murder and is punishable by law.

Family Law Reform Act 1969** An Act to amend the law relating to the age of majority, to persons who have not attained that age, and to the time when a particular age is attained; to amend the law relating to the property rights of illegitimate children and of other persons whose relationship is traced through an illegitimate link; to make provision for the use of blood tests for the purpose of determining the paternity of any person in civil proceedings; to make provision with respect to the evidence required to rebut a presumption of legitimacy and illegitimacy; to make further provision, in connection with the registration of the birth of an illegitimate child, for entering the name of the father; and for connected purposes.

Female Genital Mutilation Act 2003** Act of the Parliament of the UK applying to England, Wales, and Northern Ireland. It was introduced by Baroness Rendell of Babergh (Ruth Rendell) on 14 July of that year as House of Lords Bill 98[2]. It extended previous legislation by also making it illegal for UK nationals to perform female genital mutilation outside the borders of the UK, and increased the maximum penalty from 5 to 14 years.

Fraser Guidelines Lord Fraser indicated that a doctor will be justified in prescribing contraception without the parents' consent or knowledge provided they are satisfied that: (1) the girl under 16 years of age will understand their advice; (2) the doctor cannot persuade her to inform her parents; (3) she is very likely to having sexual intercourse with or without contraception; (4) unless she receives contraception her physical or mental health are likely to suffer; and (5) her best interests require the doctor to give contraception or advice without parental consent. The guidance about contraception became known as Fraser Guidelines.

Fraud Act 2006** An Act to make provision for, and in connection with, criminal liability for fraud and obtaining services dishonestly.

General and Specialist Medical Practice Order 2010** Abolishes the Postgraduate Medical Education and Training Board (PMETB) and provides for its functions to be performed by the General Medical Council (GMC). This change implements recommendations made by the report of the Tooke inquiry into Modernising Medical Careers that there should be far-reaching reforms to the structure of medical education and training in the UK.

Gillick competence Per Lord Scarman, 'a minor's capacity to make his or her own decision depends upon the minor having sufficient understanding and intelligence to make the decision and is not to be determined by reference to any judicially fixed age limit'.

Gross negligence* A high degree of negligence, manifested in behaviour substantially worse than that of the average reasonable man. Causing someone's death through gross negligence could be regarded as manslaughter if the accused appreciated the risk he or she was taking and intended to avoid it but showed an unacceptable degree of negligence in avoiding it.

Guidance Advice or information aimed at resolving a problem or difficulty, especially as given by someone in authority.

Health and Safety at Work Act 1974** An Act to make further provision for securing the health, safety, and welfare of persons at work, for protecting others against risks to health or safety in connection with the activities of persons at work, for controlling the keeping and use and preventing the unlawful acquisition, possession, and use of dangerous substances, and for controlling certain emissions into the atmosphere; to make further provision with respect to the employment medical advisory service; to amend the law relating to building regulations, and the Building (Scotland) Act 1959; and for connected purposes.

Health and Social Care Act 2012** An Act to establish and make provision about a National Health Service Commissioning Board and clinical commissioning groups and to make other provision about the National Health Service in England; to make provision about public health in the UK; to make provision about regulating health and adult social care services; to make provision about public involvement in health and social care matters, scrutiny of health matters by local authorities, and cooperation between local authorities and commissioners of healthcare services; to make provision about regulating health and social care workers; to establish and make provision about a National Institute for Health and Care Excellence; to establish and make provision about a Health and Social Care Information Centre and to make other provision about information relating to health or social care matters; to abolish certain public bodies involved in health or social care; to make other provision about healthcare; and for connected purposes.

Health Care and Associated Professions (Indemnity Arrangements) Order 2014** The order implements the main recommendations made by the Finlay Scott review, which include the requirement for practising regulated healthcare professionals to have insurance or indemnity as a condition of registration or obtaining a licence to practise.

Health Care and Associated Professions (Miscellaneous Amendments) Order 2008** This statutory instrument was brought into force on 3 November 2008 and relates to changes to the system for the approval of providers of primary UK medical qualifications. These changes included the establishment of a new list of approved providers, which is kept by the General Medical Council (GMC). It also brought into force, on 1 January 2009, the new governance arrangements for the GMC that are set out in that Order. The principal change was the change from a Council that has a mix of elected medical, nominated medical, and appointed lay members to a Council that is fully appointed, the constitution of which is set out in a separate Order of the Privy Council.

Herbal medicines These are medicinal products whose only active ingredients are made by subjecting herbal substances to processes such as distillation, extraction, fractionation, fermentation, or concentration.

Hospitality The provision of hospitality at a meeting or event held for the purposes of the promotion of a medicinal product must be restricted to hospitality limited to the main purposes of the meeting or event. Hospitality at an event held for purely professional or scientific purposes may be provided only if the hospitality is strictly limited to the main scientific objective of the event. Similarly, no prescriber or pharmacist may solicit or accept any gift, pecuniary advantage, benefit, or hospitality that is prohibited by the regulation, including sponsorship of a person's attendance at a meeting or event and the payment of travelling or accommodation expenses.

Human Medicines Regulations 2012** The Secretary of State and the Minister for Health, Social Services and Public Safety make the following Regulations. They do so in exercise of the powers conferred by Section 2(2) and (5) of the European Communities Act 1972(1), having been designated for the purposes of Section 2(2) of that Act in relation to medicinal products (2) and to measures in the veterinary and phytosanitary fields for the protection of public health (3). They do so in exercise also of the powers conferred by Sections 87(1), 88(1) and (2), 91(2), and 129(1), (2) and (5) of the Medicines Act 1968(4), having consulted such organizations as appear to them to be representative of interests likely to be substantially affected by these Regulations in accordance with Section 129(6) of that Act.

Human Rights Act 1998** An Act to give further effect to rights and freedoms guaranteed under the European Convention on Human Rights; to make provision with respect to holders of certain judicial offices who become judges of the European Court of Human Rights; and for connected purposes.

Immigration, Asylum and Nationality Act 2006** An Act to make provision about immigration, asylum, and nationality; and for connected purposes. These provisions came into force on 29 February 2008 and aim to prevent illegal migrants working in the UK. Failure to comply with these regulations can result in a civil penalty of up to £10,000 for every illegal worker.

Implied consent The conduct of the patient, such as proffering an arm for a blood sample to be taken, is sometimes referred to as implied consent.

Incapacity A lack of full legal competence in any respect.

Information disclosure negligence Where patients suffer an injury as a result of medical treatment, they may claim that if they had been properly informed they would not have consented to the treatment, and so would have avoided the injury. This legal action is based on negligence. In other words, it is alleged that the practitioner failed in his or her duty of care to the patient, in this case by not providing sufficient information.

Inquiries Act 2005** An Act to make provision about the holding of inquiries.

Institutional abuse Neglect or poor care practice within an institution or care setting, e.g. hospital or care home.

Intellectual property Intellectual property (IP) can be generated not just by research activity but also by innovative delivery or management of care, including information management. While IP produced by employees in the course of their employment or normal duties generally belongs to the employer, there is a need for local policies that define the employment models and that clearly define the ownership arrangements for IP generated outside of normal working hours.

Interim care order This is undertaken by the local authority usually (or National Society of Prevention of Cruelty to Children). Before 2014 its duration was limited to a maximum of 8 weeks and it gives joint parental responsibility to social services.

Interim Orders Panel The General Medical Council will refer cases to an interim orders panel (IOP) of the Medical Practitioners Tribunal Service where it is deemed that a doctor's ongoing unrestricted practice could undermine public confidence in the profession or cause harm to patients while the allegations are investigated. The IOP must take a proportionate approach to the allegations and evidence, balancing the interests of the practitioner and public protection. The panel has to justify its decisions in light of the history and give reasons, assess ongoing risk, and whether there is a real risk of repetition.

Jurisdiction* The power of a court to hear and decide a case or make a certain order. The territorial limits within which the jurisdiction of a court may be exercised.

Lasting power of attorney A lasting power of attorney (LPA) is a way of giving someone you trust the legal authority to make decisions on your behalf if you lack mental capacity at some time in the future or no longer wish to make decisions for yourself. There are two types of LPA: (1) for financial decisions; and (2) for health and care decisions. The LPA for financial decisions can be used while someone still has mental capacity. An attorney (the person who makes decisions for you) can generally make decisions on things such as: buying and selling property, paying the mortgage, investing money, paying bills, and arranging repairs to property. The LPA for health and care decisions covers decisions about healthcare as well as personal welfare and can only be used once a person has lost mental capacity. An attorney can generally make decisions about things such as where you should live, your medical care, what you should eat, who you should have contact with, and in what kind of social activities you should take part.

Legally valid consent A legally valid consent to treatment requires that the patient has capacity, that the decision is voluntary, and that the patient understands the nature and purpose of the act.

Legislation* The whole or any part of a country's written law. In the UK the term is normally confined to Acts of Parliament.

Liability A legal duty or obligation.

Magistrates' and Crown Courts Criminal cases are normally heard in the Magistrates' Court or Crown Court. Most minor criminal offences are dealt with in the Magistrates' Court but more serious criminal cases are transferred to the Crown Court.

Manslaughter* Homicide that does not amount to the crime of murder but is nevertheless neither lawful nor accidental. Manslaughter can be committed when there is no *mens rea* (criminal intent) for murder if the accused committed an act of gross negligence.

Medical Act 1983 (as amended by the Professional Performance Act 1995)** An Act to amend the Medical Act 1983 to make provision relating to the professional performance of registered medical practitioners and the voluntary removal of names from the register of medical practitioners; to amend Section 42 of that Act; and for connected purposes.

Medical mismanagement A death, although apparently due to natural causes, will not be so if the death was wholly unexpected and may have resulted from a culpable human failure.

Medical Practitioners Tribunal Service The Medical Practitioners Tribunal Service (MPTS) was launched in 2012 and its role is to protect patients by making independent decisions about a doctor's fitness-to-practise, measured against professional standards set by the General Medical Council (GMC). Although the MPTS is part of the GMC it provides a hearings service that is fully independent in its decision-making and separate from the investigatory role of the GMC. It is led by a Chair with senior judicial experience and accountable directly to Parliament.

Medical Profession (Responsible Officers) (Amendment) Regulations 2013** The Responsible Officer Regulations give specified senior doctors (responsible officers) in certain organizations (designated bodies) functions that will ensure that all doctors work within a managed environment, in which their performance, conduct, and behaviour are monitored against agreed national standards. Where there are concerns about a doctor's fitness to practise, the Regulations empower responsible officers to instigate investigation of the doctor's performance and to ensure that the appropriate action is taken.

Medicines Act 1968** An Act to make new provision with respect to medicinal products and related matters, and for purposes connected therewith. It governs the control of medicines for human use and for veterinary use, which includes the manufacture and supply of medicines. The Act defines three categories of medicine: prescription-only medicines (POM), which are available only from a pharmacist if prescribed by an appropriate practitioner; pharmacy medicines (P), available only from a pharmacist but without a prescription; and general sales list (GSL) medicines, which may be bought from any shop without a prescription.

Mens rea The guilty mind.

Mental Capacity Act 2005** Legislation relating to the decision-making process for people unable to make decisions for themselves. The Act governs decision-making on behalf of adults, both where they lose mental capacity at some point in their lives (for example, as a result of dementia or brain injury) and where the incapacitating condition has been present since birth. It covers a wide range of decisions, on personal welfare as well as financial matters and substitute decision-making by attorneys or court-appointed 'deputies', and clarifies the position where no such formal process has been adopted. The Act includes new rules to govern research involving people who lack capacity and provides for new independent mental capacity advocates to represent and provide support to such people in relation to certain decisions. The Act provides recourse, where necessary, and at the appropriate level, to a court with power to deal with all personal welfare (including healthcare) and financial decisions on behalf of adults lacking capacity.

Mental Health Act 1983** The provisions of this Act shall have effect with respect to the reception, care, and treatment of mentally disordered patients, the management of their property, and other related matters. It is the main piece of legislation that covers the assessment, treatment, and rights of people with a mental health disorder.

Mental Health Act 2007** An Act to amend the Mental Health Act 1983, the Domestic Violence, Crime and Victims Act 2004, and the Mental Capacity Act 2005 in relation to mentally disordered persons; to amend Section 40 of the Mental Capacity Act 2005; and for connected purposes.

Minimally conscious state A minimally conscious state (MCS) is a disorder of consciousness distinct from persistent vegetative state and locked-in syndrome. Unlike persistent vegetative state, patients with MCS have partial preservation of conscious awareness. The natural history and longer term outcome of MCS have not yet been thoroughly studied.

Misuse of Drugs Act 1971** An Act to make new provision with respect to dangerous or otherwise harmful drugs and related matters, and for purposes connected therewith. Offences under the Act include: possession of a controlled drug unlawfully, possession of a controlled drug with intent to supply it, supplying or offering to supply a controlled drug (even where no charge is made for the drug), and allowing premises you occupy or manage to be used unlawfully for the purpose of producing or supplying controlled drugs.

National Clinical Assessment Service The National Clinical Assessment Service (NCAS) was established to improve arrangements for dealing with poor clinical performance of doctors. NCAS provides 24-hour telephone advice, supports local case management and performance assessment, with implementation of recommendations arising from assessment.

National Health Service Act 1977** An Act to consolidate certain provisions relating to the health service for England and Wales; and to repeal certain enactments relating to the health service which have ceased to have any effect.

National Health Service Act 2006 ** An Act of the Parliament of the UK. It sets out the structure of the National Health Service in England. It was significantly altered by the Health and Social Care Act 2012.

National Health Service (Primary Care) Act 1997** An Act to provide for new arrangements in relation to the provision within the National Health Service of medical, dental, pharmaceutical, and other services; to make provision about medical lists and vacancies and the sale of medical practices; to make provision about the expenditure of Health Authorities and Health Boards; to make provision about ophthalmic services; and for connected purposes.

National Health Service Reform and Health Care Professionals Act 2002** An Act to amend the law about the National Health Service (NHS); to establish and make provision in connection with a Commission for Patient and Public Involvement in Health; to make provision in relation to arrangements for joint working between NHS bodies and the prison service, and between NHS bodies and local authorities in Wales; to make provision in connection with the regulation of healthcare professions; and for connected purposes.

National Institute for Health and Care Excellence The National Institute for Health and Care Excellence (NICE) has a role in making recommendations for the improvement of health and social care. Its technology appraisals are evidence-based recommendations on the clinical and cost-effectiveness of a drug or technology. The cost–utility analysis conducted by NICE is based on the quality and the length of life patients may gain as a result of an intervention.

National Minimum Wage (Amendment) Regulations 2015** The national minimum wage (NMW) offers protection to workers whilst incentivizing work. To increase the clarity of NMW rules, new regulations, the National Minimum Wage Regulations 2015, came into force on 6 April 2015. These regulations have merged a number of amendments into one single set of regulations as part of the Red Tape Challenge, to make it simpler for businesses to understand their obligations. Since they were first introduced, the National Minimum Wage Regulations 1999 have been amended over 20 times. As well as the annual changes to the minimum wage rates, there have been a number of substantial changes to the rules. For example, changes have been made in relation to exemptions to the NMW and also to what counts as hours worked. It is important that employers understand their obligations and workers understand their rights. The regulations contain detailed rules that underpin the minimum wage regime. The regulations now group topics together so that, for example, all exclusions to the NMW sit together—whereas previously rules were scattered across a number of disparate regulations.

Neglect This requires a gross failure to provide the very basics of life, such as nourishment, liquid, warmth, or medicine to someone in a dependent position.

Negligence* Carelessness amounting to the culpable breach of a duty; failure to do something that a reasonable man (i.e. an average responsible citizen) would do, or doing something that a reasonable man would not do. In cases of professional negligence, involving someone with a special skill, that person is expected to show the skill of an average member of his profession.

Negligence claim A negligence claim requires the patient to establish on the balance of probabilities that he or she was owed a duty of care; that the duty was breached (the doctor fell below the appropriate standard of care and was negligent); and that the breach of duty caused harm to the patient.

Neonatal death Infants who are born with signs of life but who do not survive up to 28 days.

Orphan drugs These are drugs used to benefit patients with rare conditions but do not attract sufficient returns for manufacturers to develop the therapy.

Parens patriae In the legal concept known as *parens patriae* the state has a duty to protect dependent persons from harm.

Police protection order A police protection order can be placed by the police in case of an emergency. The maximum duration is 72 hours, and the child is removed to suitable accommodation or there is prevention of removal from safety (e.g. hospital ward).

Post-mortem report* This is a medicolegal document produced for the coroner but which is disclosed to the family.

Public Health (Control of Disease) Act 1984** An Act to consolidate certain enactments relating to the control of disease and to the establishment and functions of port health authorities, including enactments relating to burial and cremation and to the regulation of common lodging houses and canal boats, with amendments to give effect to recommendations of the Law Commission.

Public Interest Disclosures Act 1998** An Act to protect individuals who make certain disclosures of information in the public interest; to allow such individuals to bring action in respect of victimization; and for connected purposes.

Rationing The medical manager has to deal frequently with a range of competing priorities and influences in making difficult decisions around the provision of care. These include national and local commissioning policies, provider organization priorities, professional ethics, and the interests of local populations, individual patients, academics, and clinicians.

Regulation In relation to European Union community legislation, regulations are generally binding in their entirety and directly applicable in all member states without the need for individual member states to enact these domestically.

Rehabilitation of Offenders Act 1974** An Act to rehabilitate offenders who have not been reconvicted of any serious offence for periods of years, to penalize the unauthorized disclosure of their previous convictions, to amend the law of defamation, and for purposes connected therewith.

Remedy* Any of the methods available at law for the enforcement, protection, or recovery of rights or for obtaining redress for their infringement.

Resolution* A decision reached by the majority of the members of an assembly.

Revalidation The purpose of medical revalidation is to improve the safety, quality, and effective delivery of care for patients by bringing all licensed doctors into a governed system that prioritizes professional development and strengthens personal accountability.

Safeguarding Vulnerable Groups Act 2006** An Act to make provision in connection with the protection of children and vulnerable adults. The Act provides the legislative framework for a new vetting and barring scheme for people working with children and vulnerable adults. The Act establishes a central database of offenders and any person named on the list will be barred from working with children and/or vulnerable adults, or subject to monitoring.

Sale of Goods Act 1979** An Act to consolidate the law relating to the sale of goods.

Special medicine Medicines made by small manufacturing units to meet a specific demand of practicality.

Standard of proof* This means that the prosecution must prove their case 'beyond all reasonable doubt'. The standard of proof in criminal cases is a high one but the phrase 'beyond all reasonable doubt' does not mean 'beyond a shadow of a doubt' or as a matter of absolute certainty. It has been described as being the same as being 'satisfied so that you are sure'. In contrast, the standard of proof in civil cases is the lower standard of 'the balance of probabilities'. This means that the facts to be proved must be shown to have been more likely than not to have occurred; in other words, more than 50% likely.

Statutes There are two primary sources of law in our domestic legal system: statutes and common law. Statutes are contained in written Acts of Parliament (also referred to as 'primary legislation'). There is a parliamentary process that needs to be followed before a Bill becomes an Act of Parliament. It involves five distinct stages in each House of Parliament: first reading; second reading; committee stage; report stage; and third reading. There may then be a stage of consideration of amendments. A Bill becomes an Act of Parliament when it is given Royal Assent.

Stillbirth A child which has issued forth from its mother after the 24th week of pregnancy and which did not at any time breathe or show any other signs of life.

Stillbirth Act 1992** An Act to amend the law in respect of the definition of stillbirth; to make certain consequential amendments of the law; and for connected purposes.

Substituted judgment A substituted judgment allows a surrogate to make a decision that a person would have made if they had capacity.

Suicide Act 1961** An Act of the Parliament of the UK. It decriminalized the act of suicide in England and Wales so that those who failed in the attempt to kill themselves would no longer be prosecuted.

Summary of product characteristics This details the posology of the medicine in question—including at-risk populations, cautions and contraindications, and the required monitoring before and during therapy.

Supervision Orders These are undertaken by social services or the National Society for Prevention of Cruelty to Children. They last 12 months in the first instance and are usually reviewed annually. The courts have powers to authorize or prohibit medical examination of a child.

Supreme Court Appeals from the Court of Appeal, in civil and criminal cases, go to the Supreme Court, which is the court of final appeal in domestic law. It only hears cases of general public importance. Appeals to the Supreme Court require permission either from the Court of Appeal or (more usually) from the Supreme Court itself to proceed.

Test of materiality* The test of materiality is whether, in the circumstances of the particular case, a reasonable person in the patient's position would be likely to attach significance to the risk, or the doctor is or should reasonably be aware that the particular patient would be likely to attach significance to it.

The European Court of Human Rights The European Court of Human Rights (ECtHR) is an international court which rules on cases alleging violations of the European Convention on Human Rights (ECHR).

The Prohibition of Female Circumcision Act 1985** This is an Act of the Parliament of the UK. It made female genital mutilation a crime throughout the UK. It was introduced to the House of Lords by Wayland Young, 2nd Baron Kennet and passed on 16 July 1985. The Act was replaced by the Female Genital Mutilation Act 2003 and the Prohibition of Female Genital Mutilation (Scotland) Act 2005, respectively, both of which extend the legislation to cover acts committed by UK nationals outside of the UK's borders to a court with power to deal with all personal welfare (including healthcare) and financial decisions on behalf of adults lacking capacity.

Therapeutic privilege A therapeutic privilege refers to an uncommon situation whereby a physician may be excused from revealing information to a patient when disclosing it would pose a serious psychological threat, so serious a threat as to be medically contraindicated. The exception of therapeutic privilege does not apply when disclosure will merely lead to refusal of care that the physician thinks beneficial.

Tort* A wrongful act or omission for which damages can be obtained in a civil court by the person wronged, other than a wrong that is only a breach of contract. The law of tort is mainly concerned with providing compensation for personal injury and property damage caused by negligence.

Vaccine Damage Payments Act 1979** An Act to provide for payments to be made out of public funds in cases where severe disablement occurs as a result of vaccination against certain diseases or of contact with a person who has been vaccinated against any of those diseases; to make provision in connection with similar payments made before the passing of this Act; and for purposes connected therewith.

Voluntariness The patient must have a free choice whether to accept or decline treatment.

*   Reproduced from *A Dictionary of Law*, 6th edition, Elizabeth A. Martin, copyright (2003) with permission from Oxford University Press

** Contains public sector information licensed under the Open Government Licence v3.0 (http://www.nationalarchives.gov.uk/doc/open-government-licence/version/3/)

Index

Tables, figures and boxes are indicated by an italic *t*, *f*, and *b* following the page number.